A Cup of Buddha

A Blueprint to Truth

Thomas D. Craig

BOOKS

Winchester, UK
Washington, USA

First published by O-Books, 2011
O-Books is an imprint of John Hunt Publishing Ltd., Laurel House, Station Approach,
Alresford, Hants, SO24 9JH, UK
office1@o-books.net
www.o-books.com

For distributor details and how to order please visit the 'Ordering' section on our website.

Text copyright: Thomas D. Craig 2010

ISBN: 978 1 84694 359 1

A CIP catalogue record for this book is available from the British Library.

Design: Tom Davies

Printed in the UK by CPI Antony Rowe
Printed in the USA by Offset Paperback Mfrs, Inc

We operate a distinctive and ethical publishing philosophy in all
areas of our business, from our global network of authors to
production and worldwide distribution.

CONTENTS

This book
is to you.

You are
beautiful
and
I love you.

Preface

'Beware of the Ides of March,' Shakespeare's words from his play *Julius Caesar* rang out to me as I left South Florida at five in the morning on March 15th in the year 2008. I was broke, alone and now at the age of forty was driving with every material possession I had stuffed into the back of my SUV. From the outside looking in my world had completely crashed. I could hear it in my friend's voices; I could sense it from my father as I borrowed money from him to survive. I could feel the pity and hear the echo of silent voices wondering what happened to me.

I smiled in this thought. I had never felt better. I felt light as if the pressure of the world had released itself off my shoulders. I felt the doorway to all doorways was opening. I drove north for many hours until finally in concert with the sun I jumped on Interstate 10 and headed west across the bayou.

As my mind locked into the monotonous routine of driving, I began to reflect on when I really was at my rock bottom. It was seven years earlier, in June of 2001; I was at my material and superficial apex yet I was dead spiritually. At the time, I was the perceived rock star on a fast track to 'success'. I had a cute family, plenty of money and a great job as a senior executive for a well known technology company. My life was a Christmas card that parents post on the fridge to talk about during Bridge club.

It was here at the age of thirty-three I had spent the last ten years of my life running like a hamster toward the worldly success metrics-wife, check; children, check; executive, check; house, check; money, check. I spent all of my energy in trying to get 'ahead', sixty plus hour weeks falling asleep with my crackberry phone, graduate school, training toward my black belt, technology certifications, and endless travel. I was a good soldier. Horrible husband and completely lost as an individual, but materially I looked successful.

I had just moved to south Florida from Seattle, Washington having been part of the management team that sold a company for close to 200 million dollars to a technology company in Fort Lauderdale. I was professionally alone having been the only person on the management team making the move to the new corporate headquarters 3000 miles away from my home, but I was excited; I wanted to make a difference.

Then, my world changed.

Unknown to me, a conversation had been taking place in the new company. Change is inevitable and I was the outsider coming in to a stable, routine environment. Worse than this, I was young, given a contract as Vice President making more money than I thought I would ever make in my lifetime, and the choice assignment and team within the department. As you can imagine this didn't sit well with the incumbent management staff.

As day one in the new company was unfolding and I was still unpacking my boxes in the humidity of summer in south Florida I was called into my Senior Vice President's office. There had been pushback within the executive team. I was asked to relinquish the Vice President title and the position that I was assigned and had moved across the country to work. This left me without a role outside of a general 'strategy' position, a lame duck. I agreed to the change even though I had a signed contract stating otherwise. In truth, I never cared about the title, or the money, I was attached to generating success, to 'winning'. I wanted to do this by working hard and making a difference just as I had been taught by the hardest worker I have ever seen, my father.

Distraught, I went home that evening and looked at myself in the mirror. I really stopped and looked at myself. My first thought was where did I go? I thought I was looking at a stranger. I weighed close to 200 lbs., over 30 lbs. where I should be on my 5 ft 10 inch frame. I was pale with dark circles under my eyes. I looked old and without life. I looked asleep. I sat in the closet and cried. What happened? It seemed as though I just graduated from college yet here I was at the time almost 34 years old and adrift. All those years spent 'getting ahead', chasing and I was completely lost.

I woke the next morning, put on my jogging shoes, ran to the beach and meditated. As Lao Tzu says, 'every journey begins beneath one's feet,' my feet were planted in the sand, warm, and connected to the earth. Immediately I felt like I was home. It was the first time I had meditated in many years. I can still hear and feel the pounding of the waves and the wind blowing the salty air into my face. The wind lifted me. The sun rose and radiated security and comfort. I could feel the energy vibrate inside of me. It was as if the Universe was welcoming me home. Even though my eyes were closed I was beginning to awaken.

My mind flashed back to the present as I struggled to stay awake and avoid the deer on the dark, winding road in central Texas. I had been driving close to twenty hours and my head was pounding. My emotions were raw and had been pouring out of me all day.

This day, where two thousand and fifty two years earlier in 44 B.C. Julius Caesar had called out to his friend Brutus, 'Et Tu Brete?'-*even you Brutus*, as Brutus and the Roman Senate vanquished his life. On my own Ides of March in 2008 I was confronting my own Brutus, my own demons. Everything material was now gone. I was attached to nothing. I had gone through a divorce, and after the divorce fell in love and had a deep, meaningful connection with another women for many years only to now on this day have it come to an end. We were on different paths. The company from the acquisition had been shut down, and I was eventually fired. After this I had started my own real estate investment company in Las Vegas a year before the big crash in the worst market in the country. I lost a half million dollars and every penny I had while the business went bankrupt.

Now, everything was gone and I was driving with no destination. This was my journey and I was embracing it. I was on a journey toward peace, a journey to quiet the mind, a journey toward truth.

I drove this day and night, for 22 hours straight. I drove without any intentions or plan. I felt alive and light as if transcended above my car. I was in a trance listening to the same album over and over again and I cried, all of my emotions poured out of me. I called lost relationships, asked for forgiveness and expressed gratitude. I completely let go.

During the drive I couldn't get my mind off the topic of truth. It wouldn't leave. I had vivid images of writing; three to four distinct topics came into my mind and wouldn't leave including the concept for *A Cup of Buddha* right down to the titles of the individual chapters. This vision of truth pounded in my head until finally at three in the morning I pulled into a truck stop somewhere in west Texas and parked next to a row of eighteen wheelers. I tried to sleep in the back of my SUV amongst what was left of my belongings, pulling plastic bags over my body for blankets.

Unable to sleep I rose three hours later and drove. In fact the car practically drove itself with one destination in mind, Sedona, Arizona. Sedona was calling me. I had been to Sedona a few times before and felt the energy, the power of this majestic place. I woke with a purpose; I had to fulfill this vision. It was now not an option. I was driving to Sedona and I was going to write. I hadn't written anything outside of my journal since college. Sure, I took a fiction writing class in my twenties only to quit as I was afraid to show my work. I wasn't afraid now, I was going to Sedona and I was going to write this book, I was certain of it.

Just as the day before, the concepts of truth in my head were so strong I seriously thought about pulling over in El Paso to write them down in case I forgot. I took a quick side trip into White Sands New Mexico; I sat alone and in the middle of a wind and sand storm, and in the midst of this beautiful chaos I began verbally exploring the concepts of truth and the details of this book. I shouted to myself over the howling wind, happy to be so alive. As the sand whipped into my face, and crawled under my clothes and into every crevice I felt connected to everything. I felt warmth in my heart, and a calming peace throughout my body and mind. I drove the rest of the day and night with a smile on my face, excited for what was in store for me.

I woke early the next morning with a clear vision of trying to locate a young, blond woman who had served me at a restaurant in Sedona about six months earlier. This was not an attraction and suddenly single moment, it was simply a manifestation in my mind to find this person with the clear idea she would be able to help me find a place to stay in town.

I pulled into Sedona with plans to stop at one of two places to find her, a vegetarian restaurant called D'lish and a raw food place along the main highway 89. She was working at the raw food restaurant, I said 'hello' and ordered. I began a conversation with the owner and some other customers and just threw out my manifestation, 'Do you any of you know of a place I could stay in town for a month, month and a half?' After a few minutes the owner came over and said she would see what she could do. In my mind I thought, oh well, the vision of the young blond girl helping me was off, however this owner will take care of me. However, five minutes later the young girl came over and said, 'My name is Kirsten and I am staying in a house my parents own, there is a room if you want to rent it out.' I smiled and said empathetically 'yes!!!'

I left the restaurant, hiked around one of the famous Vortex sites where I came upon a herd of 8-10 deer. They froze and we stared at each other for 5-10 minutes, engrossed in each other's spirit, speaking without words. Invigorated I found my new favorite hangout, RavenHeart Coffee shop and began to write. Here I was forty years old, no material possessions beyond a few items in my car, no writing experience and I finally felt at home.

Not just writing, at home within myself. I had found my way and was not turning back.

A few months later while I was back in Las Vegas finalizing the shutting down of my business and editing this book I survived by staying in one of my foreclosed properties with no electricity, water or air conditioning. I slept in the upstairs closet in case someone broke in at night, stuck a broom handle in the garage door so my car wouldn't get repossessed and tried to survive amongst the cockroaches and black widows in the house. Without air conditioning the temperature in the house never dipped below 100 degrees, and I would wake dripping in sweat, grab water from the neighbors faucet and make rice and beans in the backyard on my camping stove having fit this into my five dollar a week budget. I would travel to the nearest Starbucks to cool off, where I would take a Marine shower in the bathroom splashing some water on my body and then work on my computer. I had electricity, a cool place to sit and cold water. It was here, broke, alone and hungry that I smiled, a smile from the depths of my soul that has never left. I have never been happier or more awake.

Blessings,

Thomas D. Craig

Prologue

Many consider Eastern philosophy obscure, mystical, even confusing. Explanations are often paradoxical, and vague. Books on this topic often dive deep into the discussion matter leaving little room for those new to the topic. In addition, discussions on actually taking the journey toward truth, toward love are at times ambiguous and incomplete.

You often hear of Buddha holding the flower up to a group of followers and it was here that one monk had the sudden realization that all things are connected in this universe; however, you rarely find in depth guidance in how to follow a path of self realization. To bring this up a level, you rarely find a description of how to live a life that will create internal *what is that to you?* fulfillment and happiness. In addition, the bridge from a Judeo/Christian mindset to an Eastern mindset is a drastic one. The root of thinking or non-thinking is extremely different from the Western and Eastern mind. These were the challenges I wanted to address in writing this book. I wanted to take an in depth Eastern philosophical discussion to the 30,000 foot summary level using pop culture, musical references, and quotations.

The result is a series of conversations between two people trying to understand why one of the individuals is peaceful and happy all the time. The discussion turns into how to take this journey toward truth and the challenges one will face. It describes the differences in thought from a Western mind (typically from Judaism or Christian background) to an Eastern mind with heavy emphasis on Taoism, Zen, Buddhism, and various Indian philosophies. At the root of all these Eastern philosophies is a common theme and path through meditation.

Coming from a Christian background, I wanted to express my challenges in understanding the paradoxes behind the black and white messages I was raised with in church in contrast to the intuitive, Eastern approach. Having struggled with this for so long, I wanted to provide insight that crosses the Western to Eastern mindset. The goal of this project is to deliver a book that is high level and easy to read with modern, pop culture references to explain Eastern philosophy.

The Eastern path is beautiful, full of love and harmony. I wanted to gain more interest and exposure to these concepts in a non-threatening way. In addition, I wanted to challenge commonly held beliefs with the static concept of 'GOD'. This is not to state absolutes, or that these perceptions are wrong but to understand that the Divine is LOVE, not fear, or judgment. If one is not coming from a place of love for anything and everything then one is disconnected from the source. It truly is this simple.

These words are not new; these concepts have been around for thousands upon thousands of years. I am simply trying to express them in a different approach that will gain excitement in finding love, finding truth within oneself. From here, the reader can explore these topics in great depth with a variety of explicit documentation. I give this to you with all of my heart, filled with love.

Namaste, journey well...

Thomas D. Craig

Believe nothing
No matter where you read it
Or who said it
No matter if I have said it
Unless it agrees with your own reason
and your own common sense.

Siddhārtha Gautama
Buddha the Awakened One

Chapter 1

Elements of Truth

A master once said we cannot control our circumstances only learn to accept them. All events and relationships come into our lives for a reason, exactly the way they should, and exactly at the right time.

This was the thought that came into my mind on this Thursday afternoon when you peered through the window in my office and knocked on my door.

I remembered you from a month ago when you first joined the company and all of the new recruits were marched into the main office like a detail from Shawshank prison. I remembered you because as you obediently trudged into your new work arena, and realized your home would be a four by four Dilbert cubicle your body sank with sadness.

Looking at you now a month later gazing into my office you still looked sad. Not with your body language or in your face, as usual you dressed impeccable, and professional. It was more than this. It was deeper. It was your eyes. I could feel and see the sadness in your eyes. You looked lifeless, as if sleep walking and in a trance.

Your second knock shook me out of my daze and I opened the door. 'Hello,' I beamed.

'Hello,' you said looking down, weakly extending your hand, 'I was wondering if I could talk to you for a minute.'

I reached out and embraced your hand with both of mine in a mini embrace, 'Of course I have a minute, what's on your mind?'

'Well...' you hastily pulled your hand away, 'I'm not really sure why I am here.'

I wanted to ask you where 'here' really was, or discuss the

concept of why we are anywhere but I thought this was too esoteric in a first meeting. Instead I stayed with your comment, 'well then, why are you here?'

'I don't know. I really don't. I felt drawn to you, to your office, drawn to come and talk to you, to understand this radiance I see coming from you. You are always smiling, warm, happy, I guess.'

I smiled and breathed in these comments. My guess was something much deeper moved you to my office, something deeper than even you consciously knew. I defused these thoughts not wanting to open this Pandora's Box just yet. 'You are too kind, thank you for your words and thank you for just being with me. Please sit down and get comfortable.'

You sat down with a sigh, 'you see, this is what I mean. You are thankful for being with me and I am the one who is asking you for advice. How is it that you are thankful for me?'

'I am thankful for just being present with you right now. You are full of positive energy and I am blessed to be near you.'

'How is it that you are so positive and completely happy all the time? I always see you smiling; this can't be natural, right?'

In concert with your comment, I smiled and took a seat. I was beginning to understand this conversation was not going to take just a minute. 'This is my choice in life. We either do or we do not. It is simply a choice driven by will. I simply choose to be happy.'

'It cannot be this simple.' You laughed shifting in your chair.

I knew it took a lot of courage for you to talk to a relative stranger on such a deep topic, and by the expression on your face you looked as though you wanted to run back out the door.

Trying not to lose the thought I continued, 'It really is. Life is simply a choice. It is a choice driven by truth from the inner 'you'. My intent in life is to fill myself with happiness, fulfillment, and selfless love. Life is beautiful.'

'The 'inner me'? Truth? I thought I would talk to you and maybe get some advice, comments, or perhaps a book or two recommended?' You stood in frustration and perused the books on my shelf.

'I can recommend more than a couple of books,' I calmly said, pointing toward my book shelf; 'however, do you really believe a few books can get you to a place of complete peace, and love? Inner happiness comes from more than reading a book. I wish it were as simple as asking you to choose a red or blue pill.'

'Ah yes, Morpheus, please take me out of the Matrix.'

I laughed enjoying the fact that you understood my obscure movie reference, glanced at my watch, stood and grabbed my coat. 'Come on, follow me, let's get out of the office and take a walk.'

Scurrying to catch up you still had a look of shock in having approached me on such a deep topic and our sudden departure from the office. Prairie dog heads popped up as we made our way past cubicle street and out the front door. I veered left and onto a path next to the waterway outside of the office.

'I don't think I have ever gone this way.' You said raising your voice still trying to match my pace.

'Ahh......two roads converge in a wood, and I, I took the one less traveled by,' I said in my best Robert Frost tone.

You turned her head and queerly looked at me still trying to figure me out, and now out of the safe confines of the office, you looked even more disheveled stumbling to keep up on the uneven path.

The day was gray with dark clouds threatening to rain. The air felt cold still trying to embrace the newly arrived spring. A few daffodils had bravely popped through the ground next to the trail showcasing a row of trees, a long walkway and a wide canal extending east toward Lake Union and west to the Ballard locks that separated the salt and fresh bodies of water. This trail was notable as it was the beginning phase of a bike route that hugged the waterway eventually circling nearby Lake Washington and into the hills of Redmond some thirty miles to the east.

I breathed in the wet, cold air deeply, and satisfied in cleansing my lungs, I made an offering. 'Come on, there is a great coffee shop up around the corner, cup of tea on me.'

You nodded in agreement and upon entering the coffee shop corralled a booth near the window unbundling your coat as I brought out the steaming tea.

'Much better, now we can talk without the cloak of the office surrounding us.'

I stared at the pot of tea and the two empty cups as my mind wandered to the Zen story about the necessity in emptying your cup in order to learn. The story tells of the master continuing to pour tea into an overflowing cup stressing how one cannot learn until their cup is empty of judgment, prejudice, or preconceived ideas. Your eyes were bright and anxious. Your cup was empty both figuratively and literally as I poured you a cup of tea. I smiled to myself at this thought.

'A few minutes ago you referenced me as Morpheus and taking you out of the Matrix. Well, your comments are not far off. I mean, of course, I am not Morpheus, but the world exists in a veil very similar to the Matrix, and just like the character Neo, people become restless that something is just not right. They feel suffering. They feel the world beat them more and more as time goes on. They cling to desires and attachments only to explicitly or implicitly understand that these 'things' do not deliver peace, happiness, harmony, love... *truth*.

Some of these people become curious and find themselves unsettled. They begin to look deeper at things and realize everything is not as first perceived. They begin to understand that life is an illusion that most people grasp onto, and just like Alice in Wonderland, the journey becomes a question in how far the rabbit hole will actually go.' I blatantly quoted from the movie trying to simplify the discussion.

'If you really look around and watch people and listen to them, you will see and hear anger, bitterness, selfishness, elements very far from truth. You will rarely find someone who is just happy from the inside; not from their job, their family, their house, their car, just happy. Perhaps this is what you noticed from me.'

'Yes, exactly, I noticed something different about your presence. You are calm. You are happy,' you said. 'Getting to your point about the Matrix, then this journey really starts with being curious, is that what you are saying? Curious about what?'

'Intellectually curious, curious about people, about cultures, about all living things, being curious about life really, it is a scary moment when you realize that things typically are not as they have been presented or perceived by you. As I mentioned, the status quo view of the world is an illusion. Our reality exists simply inside of our minds. Until we have the courage to explore concepts outside of the norm we cannot move forward on this journey. Once we understand our connection with everything in this universe and our ability to choose our state of being, we have then chosen our path.'

You sat in reflection at my words as the front door of the coffee shop burst open with three college boys bantering loudly back and forth. I sipped my tea slowly as one of the boys punched his friend in the shoulder, and scurried off to the restroom just out of reach from an immediate counter punch. The remaining two looked us up and down, grabbed their coffee and sat on the sofa across the room. You scooted closer and began to whisper, suddenly self conscious of your surroundings.

'Wait a second. Are you telling me the world as I know it is a scam?' Your whisper escalated and ended in a perfect crescendo on pace with your aggravation.

'Whoa... hold on, I told you this is a scary moment. You have to be prepared to go down this rabbit hole. It is NOT an easy trip.' I sat upright and smiled trying to defuse your animosity.

'Look, you will be going against the conventional wisdom of nearly everyone. You will be ostracized and judged for your beliefs or even your questions. You will be the black sheep, the proverbial fish swimming against the stream. It will not be easy once you start this journey. You alone have to make this choice. As I already said, most choose the status quo to just follow and not question. From the outside looking in, life is easier in this way as one does not have to think, or in the end 'feel' what is true or not.'

I stopped and glanced over at the boys on the coach across the room. 'Some people will spend their life content in punching each other in the arm, and talking about sports, the opposite sex and the weather. In essence, this type of life is perceived as easy as one believes this is the only path, a life of superficial routine. So, I guess, in a sense, this is a red pill or blue pill moment.'

'I am not sure what to say. This seems like a lot of information to absorb, to take in. It is a little hard to understand,' you said again in a whisper avoiding my eye contact.

'I completely understand. I really do. I struggled with this for years, through divorce, through family troubles, through emotional difficulties. Unfortunately, I have to tell you something; once you are curious the faucet is turned on and cannot be turned off. It just flows and flows and flows. In knocking on my door today you have shown that you are already curious. You can go home tonight, pretend we didn't talk, turn on the TV, listen to the latest story of where the hotel heiress is partying, or the reality show about how fat or how much of a loser you are, or perhaps the latest 'biggest storm of the century story, but the itch inside of you will not change. The itch inside to find happiness and truth will grow until your entire body is a rash waiting for ointment.'

'I understand your point about the celebrity watch; however, I guess I am still not getting the depth of the point you are trying to make. Is this an infomercial about turning my TV off and I will have sudden clarity and find peace, or truth as you state?'

'No... this is not an infomercial at all. First off, these are only my opinions from my journey in seeking truth. I believe once you are a 'seeker' then you are always seeking; this does not change. In other words, if you ask me the end point on when you will receive sudden 'awareness', this point does not exist; it is simply relative. I am merely stating that in order to begin your journey you must first understand this paradox that the world is different than first or common perception.'

As I made these comments I realized the full paradox of this statement coming from the neighborhood we were sitting in. Known as Fremont, the locals liked to say it was the center of the Universe. This was a stretch, but it was the center of the counter culture in Seattle complete with a rocket ship, statue of Lenin and concrete Troll under a bridge. The neighborhood prided itself on a summer solstice parade filled with free spirits, naked bike riders, and lots of body paint. Its official motto was 'Delibertus Quirkus'.

Missing the paradox, you paused before jumping back into the conversation. 'OK, I guess I can buy that the world is different than first perception,' you said without conviction.

'OK, let me give you a few examples of this paradox beyond the hotel heiress. This one was just an obvious one for me as it gets more attention than real issues, serious issues such as young men and women dying or becoming handicapped in war. We don't even cover the stories of the war, let alone admit that young lives, so full of energy and life, are dying or getting maimed. I digress; I don't want this to be a political discussion, however, let me ask you a question: Do you know who Smedley Butler is?'

'No, I have never heard of him. Why do you ask?'

'Smedley Butler was a Major General for 34 years in the United States Marine Corp. At the time of his death he was the most decorated marine in the history of the Marine Corp, including being awarded the Medal of Honor twice. Twice! This is impressive in itself; however, Smedley Butler wrote a compelling essay after his service titled *War is a Racket*. Butler stated this about war: 'It is conducted for the benefit of the very few, at the expense of the very many. Out of war a few people make huge fortunes.' (Butler, 1935) What a moment of truth that he exhibited. Can you imagine how difficult this was for him?' I rhetorically asked. 'Talk about a fish swimming against the current. Today there would be a calculated smear campaign, millions upon millions of dollars spent to discredit this man to keep the status quo perception.'

'OK, interesting story, but this guy could be off the wall. I mean, are you an anarchist or a non-conformist? Do you have a conspiracy theory about every event in life such as 9-11, or believe we shouldn't have a government at all?'

Your whisper turned into a rising tone and your eyes dilated and pulsed on beat with your rapidly beating heart; clearly I had struck a chord. On pace with your discord was the amplified parroting of the word 'DUDE' coming from the college kids across the room. I patiently waited for this noise to die down. I couldn't take in their full conversation across the room, nor was I interested, however, I did want to provide as much presence as possible for you. This was your moment and I wanted to make the most of it.

I continued my pause until I felt the energy was at least neutral again. 'Well, I was afraid to start with a political example. Politics and religion, right? In the words from *The Dude* in the movie *The Big Lebowski*, 'it's like my opinion, man'.' I said. 'In full disclosure, in order to be curious you have to be curious about everything, including what I say. So, thank you for questioning. I appreciate your courage.'

'There you go again,' you said staring out the window.

I was worried I was losing you. It was clear you had different expectations of our meeting. I decided to proceed anyways. 'OK, away from politics. Let's have a go at history. History is almost always written from the words of the victor. In other words, our perception of these events has typically been given by those who have benefited the most from the actual event. If the victor typically controls the voice of the event, then how can we be sure to actually have the true events or at least the full spectrum of contrasting views? Right?'

'This makes sense.' You gazed back in my direction.

'Matt Damon's character in the movie *Good Will Hunting*, talks to Robin William's character about the appropriate books he should be reading, he states 'Read Howard Zinn's *People's History of the United States*, that book will blow your socks off.' This statement is true; this book will give you a whole new perspective on American history told from the side of the oppressed, such as the supposed founder of the continent Christopher Columbus. Zinn tells us that Columbus is not the absolute hero we were led to believe. He basically wiped out an entire culture; they ceased to exist shortly after his arrival. His men would kill them for sport; in addition, they were decimated by the newly introduced diseases. Columbus personally took back hundreds upon hundreds, if not thousands, as slaves to Spain. As it has been stated, one man's terrorist is another man's freedom fighter,' I said. 'It is right to question. This should be our duty, our requirement as individuals. Question, be curious, listen, understand and ultimately 'feel'.'

I glanced down and pointed to the front page of the newspaper that had been left on the table, 'I wish our media was curious. I guess curiosity is not good business. This is unfortunate. However, let me ease your mind a little, at least for now anyway, as we will need to really disrupt your mind later for you to get to a place of truth. To ease your mind, understand you can question what you want to question; believe what you want to believe. It is and always will be your choice. Give thanks for your curiosity, bless it, and embrace it. When you get to the core 'you', your intuitive self will bring truth and love, and you, and only you, will decide what 'feels' right. Does this sound OK?'

'OK, I am sorry if I jumped on you.' you said leaning back in your seat. 'It's just that I had a very different perception of how our conversation would be today. Not that it is a bad thing; it is just different.'

'You may not understand this but when you suggest you want happiness and ultimately what I have been calling truth, you are asking the fundamental questions: Who am I and why do I exist? Or more appropriately, who is the 'real' me? And, what is my purpose in life?

We have struggled with these questions for at least as long as we began drawing pictures on rocks some 25,000+ years ago. I certainly wasn't there but I can visualize our ancient relatives pondering everything like a three year old. What are those tiny, white dots in space? The sun? Death? Archeologists were amazed to find burial rituals going back 60,000 years. We already had a concept of death and some meaning to it. It seems fairly obvious we would ultimately question why we are here, who we really are, and what happens after death. Everyone is aware of the famous tombs in Egypt filled with items for them in the afterlife. This alone is 3000 years ago. Right?'

'I am on board with this; I grew up with a Protestant background, so I am familiar with understanding something bigger than just ourselves. I am struggling with how this relates to my fundamental question in wanting to talk to you. I almost forgot, ah, yes, how does this relate to why you are so happy all the time?'

The sofa across the room screeched as if to intensify the question as the college boys abruptly jumped up and almost ran out of the coffee shop creating a deafening silence as the rain continued to drip down the panes of the window.

'Yes, great question,' I said laughing, 'how does all of this relate to why I am so happy? It reminds me of a Zen kōan that states 'The beginning is the end, we start, we finish'.'

'OK, please speak English. Zen kōan? Riddles? I am getting more confused.'

'My point is this conversation begins with a decision from you about whether you want to begin your journey toward 'truth'. In this journey, we start and we finish. It is about the journey not the destination. We are always exactly where we are supposed to be,' I paused looking intently in your eyes. 'Taking this journey is not an easy decision. It has created such conflict in some minds they have gone mad, or at the very least mentally unstable wrestling with the questions you are ultimately asking. We can discuss this later if this is your choice. I have wrestled with these questions for so long, my mind turns into knots at times, and it feels like my head will blow.' I stare out the window taking in a deep breath. 'Does this make sense?'

'It makes sense, but I am very confused as you certainly do not sound at peace.' You shrugged.

'There is a quote from India that states 'we die every day'. Now, before you think I am asking you to join a cult in Jonestown, let me explain. Our fundamental conflict with reaching this place of truth is the conflict between our mind (rational) and our true self (intuition). It has been stated that the longest journey is the 18 inches between our head to our heart. The quote, 'we die every day', is essentially stating that every day we must wrestle control from our mind to our intuitive self. This quote is a reflection of the process of meditation with respect to the body, as it will begin to grow quiet, numbing from the limbs to the inner core functions, to ultimately one, centrally focused, place between the eyes. This is the Chakra called Ajna, the brow Chakra, often referred to as the third eye, or the gateway to the higher self. Whether you have heard of Chakras or not is not important, however; understanding the importance of this one spot of concentration will be a later discussion. Most Eastern philosophies believe that when we die our body follows the exact pattern mentioned above – the numbing of the limbs to the core organs, to the final release point at the point in the mind between the eyes. The belief is that this is the relief point toward upper consciousness, awareness, enlightenment…whatever word you wish to use.

Wow… I did it again, didn't I? I have gone on a long discussion and basically avoided your question.' I said in a big sigh. 'Yes, I am happy and at peace. I look for moments in truth at all times every day. I believe you can find beauty everywhere. My point is that it is a daily struggle, again, 'we die every day' to find this peace.'

'Is it worth it? I mean my head is swimming already.'

'Only you can answer this question, I can only speak for myself as every journey is different. I can give you guidance and a rough blueprint to follow but ultimately you are alone on this journey. I wish I had a set of plans and could say 'here you go, good luck. It will be great.' I can tell you about my journey and tell you how you can begin and perhaps help you along the way. But, ultimately, this is a personal journey. A journey where you will need to find the root of your soul; the root of 'you'; this is a very difficult and at times emotional and even scary journey. And, to answer your question, for me this has been the most rewarding journey of my life. My journey toward truth has been the fundamental statement of my existence. Does this appropriately answer your question?'

'Wow… I will take that as a 'yes'.' You perked up in your seat. 'So, you have me intrigued. I am curious to understand how to get to a point of self realization, to a point of understanding the real me. How do we begin?'

'Well, in the immortal words of Lao Tzu, *'A journey of a thousand miles starts from beneath your feet.'* (Mitchell, 1988) If we are going to take a journey toward truth, we should probably understand where we are trying to get to, right?'

'You mean what you have been defining as truth?'

'Exactly, although I feel as though I am like Cuba Gooding Jr. in the movie *Jerry Maguire* trying to become the ambassador of 'Qwan', or in this case the ambassador of 'truth'. The concept of 'truth' has been around for a long time. It is not the marketing campaign for George Washington in that he couldn't tell a lie after chopping down a cherry tree. In this case, to avoid confusion, think of a lower case 't' in the word 'truth' indifferent to the traditional Truth, in which Merriam-Webster's dictionary defines as 'honesty, and integrity' or 'the true or actual state of the matter'. Certainly lower case 'truth' contains these components but it is much more than this. Let's walk outside as I try to explain.' I slipped back on my coat, nodded to the barista behind the counter and headed out the door with you immediately behind.

'We are going to get wet aren't we?'

'Yes, what a beautiful thought, isn't it?' I smiled.

You glanced in my direction not believing the pure sincerity in my comment. We treaded west on the sidewalk indifferent to the slight drizzle.

'OK, let me try to explain the concept of truth. As you will find out, once we move away from the rational state of mind to the intuitive being, black and white definitions or judgments become impossible. So, I will do the best that I can, but again, in the end this is a personal journey that you alone must define. Does this make sense?' I asked.

'OK, go on.'

'At its core, truth is love. Just as in truth; uncompromised, selfless love is very difficult to define. We have been programmed to throw this word out there at almost anything. 'I love pizza, I love ice cream.' I am certainly not referring to ice cream when I am discussing truth or love. The love I am referring to comes from the depths of your soul. Let me try something. Do you have children?'

'Yes, I have two boys, one is five and the other is three years old.' You said beaming.

'Great! Let me ask you to remember a moment, certainly a moment in truth, or love. Do you remember the birth of your children, the moment they handed you your child for the first time?'

'Of course, it is as vivid as if it happened yesterday. I have goose bumps on my arms just thinking about this moment. I cried. This beautiful, helpless being with huge eyes looked up at me as if to say 'here I am like me or not'.'

You glowed in this moment hugging your own body as if cradling your baby boy. In this moment you were a completely different person than the sad, lifeless being I saw at my door this afternoon. The love inside of you radiated through your eyes, through your entire being. You felt calm, and centered as we continued to walk toward a park bench next to the waterway. I embraced this moment with you, not wanting it to end.

'Yes, exactly' I said. 'This is most certainly a moment in truth. It didn't matter what your child looked like, or even if he wasn't 'perfect' in the worldly superficial sense. You loved that being, that living, wonderful entity with your entire soul, unconditionally, selfless. You knew that you would love that child with your entire being no matter what he did in his life. Right?'

'Yes, how did you know?'

'I have children myself. I know that my love for my children will never change. There is such beauty in knowing this inside. The love is pure, unselfish, and magnificent. Unless you have children it is very hard to understand these feelings.

I have similar feelings or moments in truth in other places as I am sure you do. Nature is a big one for me. Standing at the edge of a canyon, or in the middle of an alder grove, or staring at a tree does it for me. It is said that Buddha once held an entire sermon by holding up a flower. There was one monk who began to smile as he realized this truth, or awareness inside; this ultimate feeling of knowing you are connected to everything.'

We sat on the park bench unconcerned by the dampness and looked out onto the water as two kayakers silently paddled below us. They dipped their paddles into the water simultaneously, synchronized with both each other and with their breath, two boats, one movement.

'Sitting here right now with you is a moment in truth. I have no other thought other than your presence, the breath in my lungs and the beauty in every moment.' I stopped and pointed out a squirrel upside down on the branch of a nearby tree. Nodding toward the squirrel, I continued, 'animals are another for me. Animals, like young children, are always in a state of truth. They do not know any better. Have you ever seen an animal in a bad mood?'

'Come to think of it, no, I haven't.'

'You can yell and scream at an animal, in particular a dog, and the next moment it is sitting next to you full of presence, and love. It might be curious as to what could possibly be wrong with you to ruin a perfect moment of truth. No, I take this last one back, they wouldn't be curious as they would never judge you. This is love. Let me ask you something; have you ever heard of a 'childlike' state or Buddha nature?'

'No, what is this?'

I scanned my surroundings looking for an example, stood and turned around with my eyes fixated on a small playground next to an elementary school. 'Come with me I say, let's walk over by this school so we can observe children, unreserved in their own environment.'

We walked over to the school and observed the children playing.

'This childlike state is a state some eastern philosophies try to attain. Look at these children, their true state of being is uninhibited. If they want to splash in a puddle they splash, if they want to swim they swim, who needs trunks. This reminds me of Tom Hanks in Forrest Gump – 'I just kept running and running. When I was hungry, I ate. When I was tired, I slept, and when I needed to go to the bathroom, well, you know, I went to the bathroom'. I said laughing in my best Forrest Gump impersonation.

'There was a Zen monk by the name of Po-chang, who like Forrest Gump reiterates this point very well in trying to define Zen Buddhism: 'When hungry eat, when tired sleep.' It really is an uncluttered mind, uncluttered by the junk in our heads, or minds. It is recognizing the beauty and spontaneity while living completely in the present not concerned about the past or what will happen in the future. Young children and animals live in this state of truth or presence.' I paused here inspired by action.

I looked at you and yelled 'watch this' on my way into the school yard. I joined the kids on the diamond playing kickball. Without missing a beat, a small, dark haired boy around seven rolled the ball toward me at home plate. I struck the ball past a mob of kids and began running around the bases. In true kick ball fashion I kept running around all of the bases without stopping while one of the boys grabbed the ball and chased after me with the remaining mob of players in tow. I circled third base confident I could reach home but I was cut down a few steps short of home plate. The mob erupted in a cheer having defeated the adult. The entire playground bounced with energy. I gave a cheer and nearly out of breath jogged back over to you standing next to the field, your mouth ajar.

'I can't believe I just watched an executive in my company play kick ball with some first graders. How old are you anyways?' You said laughing.

I joined your laugh and then stated in full seriousness. 'It doesn't matter how old I am, or if I am an executive or a bag boy. Life is worth embracing. It is there right in front of all of us.' I smiled still trying to catch my breath.

'Animals in particular embrace the present moment. They are extremely intuitive. They feel versus think. They feel fear, happiness, sadness, they even feel disease in a human being or that a natural disaster is coming.' I rebuffed the offers of the children to join in the game again and waved goodbye as we walked away beginning to circle back toward the office.

25

'This 'childlike' state we have been discussing is an empty mind.' I continued. 'The Chinese call this wu-hsin, or 'no mind'. Bruce Lee used to train this way. He would start his training of a particular exercise or movement extremely slow. Over and over again eventually speeding up, practicing in a mechanical sort of way over and over again until in his mind he could reach a state of 'no mind'. His body would just react, not think. To him this was the perfect state of being for Martial Arts. His infamous quote from the movie *Enter the Dragon,* when he slaps his student on the forehead and screams, 'Don't think... *FEEL*', invokes this mentality. I think this applies to life itself. Don't you?'

'I am trying to grasp the concept. Let me think or, I guess in this case 'FEEL',' you said smiling. 'Oh, I have an example. I was taking tennis lessons for some time and I would over-think when I was striking the ball. I was even dreaming about tennis technique. In the middle of a stroke I would catch myself 'thinking' of the proper grip, stroke, wind direction, placement of the ball, whatever, I could go on. In the end, the balls were flying all over the place, miss hits. I was actually regressing in my tennis skills for some time.'

'How did you pull out of it? Or, did you?'

'My instructor tried a technique with the ball machine where he turned the speed almost all the way up. The balls were coming at me like never before. I had to just react. I had no time to think. I hit the ball like no other time before – a solid 'whack', right in the middle of the strings every time. I didn't even feel the strokes. When the machine was turned off, I didn't even know what had happened. It felt like an out of body experience,' you said slowly as your eyes glazed over.

'YES!!! Grasshopper, you have it. This is it. You were completely transfixed in the present 'moment'. Athletes like to call this being in the *zone*. This 'out of body' experience you mentioned was the true 'you'. We will get to this true 'you' at some point in our conversations. You had a tremendous moment of truth. You=truth. We have already discussed that truth=love, so if we use the transitive property of equality then you=love. You, at the inner core, are love, a bursting core of energy that emits love. This is it. This is the journey to find and live in these moments at all times. Not just striking tennis balls, or monumental moments like meeting your child for the first time, but real, tangible moments every day. This is why I am smiling. Life is beautiful. Life is a blessing.'

'How is this possible? I get the big moments. But, everyday, I mean look, it took me a while to just come up with one example.' You stopped walking clearly annoyed with this concept.

'Why? Do you think there is a limited amount of these 'moments in truth', like a quota?' I stopped to square off to you.

'I don't know. I am challenged with this one. I mean, look at a typical day, rushing the kids to school, rushing to work, chaos everywhere. How am I supposed to 'feel' these moments when I 'feel' so out of control?'

'Precisely,' I stated, beginning to walk again.

'Precisely!? Am I supposed to feel out of control?' You responded ecstatically trying to catch up.

'Therein lies the exercise. You have chosen to feel out of control. This is not right or wrong, simply a choice. Life ultimately becomes a choice. We are either bringing our self up or bringing our self down. We can choose to feel overwhelmed. We can choose to blame others. We can choose to blame our circumstances. In the end, however, we are the product of our own choice, our own realization to our environment, our own intent, our own manifestation. Our reality is simply the product of our thought, our intent, our action and ultimately our choice. As I mentioned, there is beauty everywhere at all times. Without the clutter and with positive intent, we can find truth every-where. Does this make sense?'

'It seems a lot easier said than done.'

'Like I stated before, we either do, or we do not; it is simply a choice. Let us not try to solve the dilemma just yet. Let's just understand. I understand your frustration. Trust me, beyond my mind turning in knots; I have held doubt, anger, bitterness, depression and other bottled up emotions throughout my journey. In fact, in full disclosure again, some of these still come up. I can still remember just sitting, crying, and crying. As you strip away layers, and finally get to this inner 'you', the emotions pour out of you. We have tarnished our inner self, our true self. We wrap ourselves in labels and words and superficial items. We wrap ourselves in a flag and call this patriotism; we wrap ourselves in symbolic armor to shield our emotional self. We do not let anyone inside; we talk about sports and the weather and all the while we are sad.'

'I have to say it again; you always look and 'feel' happy. I have trouble visualizing you moping around the house in your pajamas not showering for days in a state of depression.'

'We die every day. This is all I can say. We all have our moments. If you came to me looking for the perfect human being you came to the wrong place. In fact, there is no place. It would be a lonely journey trying to find this being as they do not exist. All we can do is be the best we can possibly be at any given moment. In a state of truth or love, we will give honesty from ourselves. It is OK to feel vulnerable. It is OK to feel frustrated, to feel defeated. As I mentioned to you, when you get on this journey emotions will flow out of you. You will cry; you will find things inside of you that have been bottled up for some time. Embrace these emotions. You are alive and a real being. Feel blessed for these moments,' I clamored. 'In the end, we will live from our heart, full of truth, full of love, no judgments, only forgiveness and gratitude.'

You looked at me for a long time clearly surprised at the turn of events in the day. Having not spoken to me before outside of a few 'hello's, my guess is this was a lot to take in. I let these last statements breathe, and paused on the path to look at the water, watching each drop of rain paint a new landscape across the stillness.

You sighed, digging deeper, 'I want to get back to your comment that there is beauty in everything. Every time you say this I cannot help but think of the most horrible moments in history like the Holocaust. How can you possibly find beauty or truth in these moments?'

'Great question, some moments are certainly more challenging than others to find beauty. My personal challenging thought is of a slaughterhouse. I have trouble visualizing the positive in such a negative, life extinguishing place. However, you brought up a really good example. How can one possibly see beauty in an event that killed millions of people? Well, you certainly have to look much harder; you have to have incredible patience and will to understand this concept. Great men and women in history have been defined by such grace. To have this awareness is truly grace, truth; it takes an amazing person to be at this point spiritually to comprehend this. Think of Gandhi, and Martin Luther King, Jr. They embraced the concept of ahimsa or non-violence. Some believe Gandhi modeled this after the Russian peasant turned author, purposely turned peasant again, Leo Tolstoy. Tolstoy was a strong advocate of this practice, a philosopher and sage later in his life who was familiar with many of the concepts of Eastern philosophies.

With respect to the Holocaust, the words of Viktor E. Frankl's book, *Man's Search of Meaning,* reflect the concept of finding beauty in everything much better than I can try and communicate. Frankl was part of the Holocaust, and he witnessed atrocities no human being should ever see in their lifetime. Frankl believed that the meaning of life is found in every moment and that life never ceases to have meaning even in suffering and death. Frankl states, 'We who lived in concentration camps can remember the men who walked through the huts comforting others, giving away their last piece of bread.

They may have been few in number, but they offer sufficient proof that everything can be taken from a man but one thing: the last of the human freedoms – to choose one's attitude in any given set of circumstances, to choose one's own way.' (Frankl, 1959) Frankl also quotes the philosopher Nietzsche: 'He who has a why to live can bear with almost any how.' (Frankl, 1959) Compelling, isn't it?'

'Wow...It makes one ashamed to complain about their troubles. Doesn't it?'

'I know, right? I remember watching the movie *The Lost Boys of Sudan* and saying to myself I will never complain again. These boys went through the worst of human conditions. Parents murdered or lost, most if not all other family members missing, amputated limbs, and some were forced to murder and become drug addicts. They hiked hundreds of miles to refugee camps with little to no amenities for months and years at a time with most dying along the way. Finally some of them had the opportunity to move to America for a fresh start. Here they were stereotyped, disregarded, completely out of place and left to fend for themselves in jobs typical Americans did not want. Yet, through all of this, they smile, deep smiles from within their souls. They see beauty, they see truth. I am inspired by their spirit.'

'It really puts perspective on things doesn't it?'

'This is why I believe we should all travel, visit other cultures to shock our every day perceptions; take curiosity on the road if you will. Read, listen to music, let that inner child out, spend time in nature, listen, hug a stranger, and find these 'moments in truth' each and every day. These moments are beautiful. Whenever I am in a bad mood, or feel sorry for myself, I see the face of one of these boys, with his smile, flipping burgers and just happy with life. What a blessing this young man has given me and I don't even know him.'

'I think I am getting the concept of truth. It is much deeper than I had anticipated.' You said in a deep sigh.

I smiled at your understanding the vastness in the concept of truth. 'Think of it as your naked soul exposed to the world. Everyone and everything can see through you; they can see all truths. You are at your most vulnerable, yet most powerful self. Everything has been stripped, no masks, no roles, nothing material, just the inner 'you', connected to the universe, full of vibrant energy, full of love, full of truth. Understand?'

'I think this is a concept to be viewed in action to fully grasp. However, I do have a strong appreciation of where you are coming from.'

I looked at my watch and laughed. 'Wow, that was some break, huh?'

'Yeah....you are providing quite the example for us under-lings in the company.' You said laughing. 'I am really glad I knocked on your door today. I have thoroughly enjoyed the conversation. What's next for me to understand? I want to embrace this journey.'

I smiled, proud for this moment in your life, knowing you were about to take the most difficult yet rewarding journey of your life.

'I will do anything to help you.' I said. 'Moving forward we have a lot of topics to discuss, from understanding 'truth' we need to explore more about who you really are outside of roles and labels. We need to explore the destructive forces within the mind and the fear that overwhelms us. We need to look closer at the tools of positive intent, words and action to help us on this journey and we need to look at how our bodies are a foundation for the vibrancy of our energy. Finally, we need to look at how to clear our mind, strip away those destructive layers through meditation to get to the real 'you' and live in this true, intuitive state of being or state of truth. So, shall we continue the journey and explore who you really are?'

'I would love to. I am fully embracing this. Wait, what time is it?'

'Five o'clock.'

'Oh no, I have to pick up my children. I cannot believe how the time just flew by. Promise me this. I have to hear more. I need to hear more. When can we talk again?'

'Tomorrow, lunch, does this work?'

'Perfect, thank you so much, please let me know if I am imposing on your time.'

'Not in the very least. We can start back up at lunch tomorrow.'

'Agreed,' you said vanishing into the car garage.

Chapter 2

Who are you?

Friday came with a flurry of activity at work. I pushed through a morning meeting, popped into my office for a quick moment to check my messages and noticed an e-mail from you.

'I can't wait to talk to you. I had an amazing night, I look forward to sharing!!!' You signed with three exclamation points.

'I look forward to it.' I replied. 'Let's meet for Thai food at Chillies Paste, six blocks west on 36th. Twelve-thirty, I will meet you there.'

I purposely chose to meet at the restaurant and a place out of the immediate circle of the office knowing how deep perceptions and judgment, particularly in a work environment, can influence another individual. I thought this was best, not for me, as I could care less what others thought about my circumstances, however, I didn't feel you were ready for external pressure at this point in your journey.

The rest of the morning sped by into the afternoon. I blocked off a few hours on my calendar to give ample presence to our conversation and headed out alone to the restaurant.

Upon arriving, I noticed you already seated in the corner of the room. Overhead, on a brightly painted orange wall was a large photo of Buddha sitting with his eyes closed in meditation. 'Perfect,' I thought. The aroma of coconut and lime drifted out of the kitchen and into my nostrils watering my mouth in anticipation.

'How are you doing?' You called out, standing to shake my hand.

I shook your hand while pulling you closer in a cordial business or *man* hug while answering in my best Brooklyn

33

accent, 'How *YOU* doing?'

'Huh?'

'Nothing, so, tell me, how did it go last night?'

'Well, that is why I couldn't wait to talk to you. I really enjoyed yesterday's conversation, really enjoyed it. I guess I was in a state of awareness last night, noticing things I hadn't in the past.'

'For example?' I pushed for more details.

'Ok, I will give you a few things I noticed last night. It was chaotic as usual, rushing through dinner, trying to get the boys ready for bed and I felt my patience shorten, and I distinctively noticed a moment I would have raised my voice and assumed dictatorship in the past. It jumped out at me. The boys were not doing anything big, you know, pushing each other mentally back and forth just to bother each other. It happens every day. I think at the root of it is to get more attention from me. It was at this moment when I usually do my best Stalin imitation that I caught myself. I immediately took a deep breath and chose a different path. I called both boys to me; I hugged them deeply and said I love both of them more than anything in the world, even when they are not nice to each other or disrespectful to me. They looked at each other, and then looked at me like I was from another planet.'

'Yes, go on, what happened?' I asked excited.

'My oldest, still not grasping the concept, asked me, 'Really, you will love me no matter what? No matter what I do you will love me?' he asked me. 'Yes', I told him. 'No matter what you do the rest of your life, no matter what; I will always love you with all of my heart'. I told them we were joined by our blood and nothing will ever change this. They hugged me, apologized, and told me how much they loved me and then went to bed as calm and unassuming as I have ever seen. I was so in awe I almost called you.'

'Love is a beautiful thing, isn't it?'

'I had no idea of the power that love or truth can bring.'

The waiter interrupted our moment, poured two cups of water and asked if we needed more time. We both smiled just then opening the menus and asked for a few more moments.

I briefly scanned the menu, found my usual item and continued the momentum of the power of love. 'Love is the supreme law of the universe. It binds everything. Every time I think of the power of truth, the power of love, I think of the monk smiling as he looked at the flower in Buddha's hand. Once you have this realization, this truth that we are connected to everything in this universe, life really becomes much easier, much simpler. You start to question anything that does not fit into this bucket, the bucket of truth. Thank you for sharing; this was a beautiful moment you had with your family last night.'

The waiter returned again clearly wanting to optimize the restaurants table space.

We both ordered, and then you looked at me inquisitively, 'Are you a vegetarian?'

'Yes.'

'Really....I would never have guessed this.'

'Oh, we will get to this topic at some point; however, we have a lot of other things to cover first. Are you ready to get started?'

'Sure, let's do it!'

'OK, let's do it. Now that we are curious and willing to move forward in the journey, we need to understand a few more things. I want to start by asking some fundamental questions concerning who you really are. Are you ready?'

'I guess, I don't know about this one. Is this going to be a Dr. Phil moment?' You said with a soured look.

'Dr. Phil? No! Come on, this will be simple. Basically, I want to understand how you perceive yourself. If I was to ask you, who are you? How would you define yourself? Be honest; don't give me the answer you think I perceive or that I am looking for.'

'This is a tough question, isn't it? I guess I would have to say things like I am a parent, a spouse, 33 years old, average weight, a sibling, a marketing representative.....wow!, what else? I could say things such as I like music, hiking, and cooking. Does this help?'

'It is a good start for us.' I said with a smile. 'Now, with all of these descriptions, how would you rate how you feel about your identity from 1-10 with 10 being the highest?'

'My identity? What do you mean?'

'Basically, with everything you defined about yourself, how do you feel about yourself from 1-10? Got it?'

'Oh, that is simple enough. I feel pretty good about myself most of the time. I mean we all have our moments, right? I would probably rate myself an 8 or even a 9 on certain days.'

'Good, very good, now let me give you a hypothetical situation; let's say you've been stranded on a deserted island. You have nothing but the clothes on your back. Hypothetically for a few moments you have been relieved of all of those roles you defined earlier. You are sitting in sand with some tattered clothes and have no roles what so ever, just you. Got it?'

'Roles? What do you mean? Like being a marketing rep?'

'Yes, like being a marketing rep, or a spouse, or parent, or child, or anything else that is in essence a role or label that you may describe yourself. Now tell me, how do you rate or feel about yourself?'

'I would like to think nothing changes .....' you paused with a sigh, 'but I am struggling a little bit. I feel a little lost. I guess, maybe a 5 or 6 in all honesty.'

'OK, I appreciate your honesty. How do you feel about this? Are you surprised by the exercise? Are you surprised at listing yourself a 5 or 6?'

'Yes... I am. I am still struggling with how lost I feel without the roles. It shouldn't feel this way, should it?'

'This is a question that you must come to grips with yourself. Obviously, you are feeling uneasy about it. It is a little scary to think you might be something outside of your roles. Isn't it?'

'Yes. I have been defining myself based on roles for years. I am suddenly struck with the concept that I may be something different than external perceptions.'

'RIGHT! It is difficult, isn't it? Like you said, one feels lost without these labels. If you are not these labels then who are you really? This is a deep question to ponder and one we need to explore further.'

The waiter brought our food and asked if we were OK, I nodded yes as your eyes screamed 'no' still transfixed in deep thought. The restaurant was buzzing now, each table filled with the boisterous lunch crowd. We took in some food before I continued.

'This exercise is called the I/R or Identity/Role theory. Psychologists use it sometimes. When I first heard of it, the teacher was telling a story about how he had been stuck by his father's perceptions of success. His father had always told him 'not to be like a Rockefeller' as if having money was a bad thing. His father had told him that if he could ever make $50,000 a year he would be extremely successful. The teacher told us that when he took the exercise he basically broke down because he looked at his income over the past years and he was right there – $49K, $51K, $50K. He was dumbstruck. The thought that he was defining himself from external sources was liberating for him. Good story, huh?'

'Yes, very much so, but I don't understand. How should we be defining ourselves?'

'A 10!!!... You are and always will be a 10. This is how you should perceive yourself. You are truth, you are love, and you are a bundle of wonderful energy vibrating in the universe. You are everything. All of us, not because of the color of our skin, or our status in life, or where we were born. We are all beautiful. 'I look for the day when people will judge me by the content of my character versus the color of my skin' – Martin Luther King Jr. I listen to his I have a dream speech at least once a month. There is such beauty inside.'

'I need to tape this so I can carry your voice around with me whenever I need a pep talk.'

'Once you get on with your journey you will not need me; you will understand all of this yourself.' I paused while we both ate thinking of how I could better explain this concept. Inspired I jump back in with a thought. 'Let me try something, close your eyes.'

'Here?'

'Yes, here, no one is concerned with you, don't worry about them.'

You surveyed the room looking for known associates. Not finding any you slowly closed your eyes.

'OK, let's say your partner chooses to take the kids tomorrow for an all day play day. You sleep in, take a long shower and then you are alone in your house. What is your existence?'

'My existence?' Your eyes opened quickly.

'Eyes closed, come on, *wax* on, *wax* off,' I said in my best accent mocking the movie *The Karate Kid*. 'Yes, your existence. Tell me what you feel, what is your existence in your mind at this very moment you finally feel that you are alone.'

You shifted uneasily both at the question and feeling self conscious in having your eyes closed. You thought deeply in the question until finally blurting out, 'my existence is that I need to clean the house, and do some laundry.'

'What is your existence?' I calmly repeated.

You paused again with a sigh. 'My existence is that I am alone. My existence is that my spouse and kids are gone.'

'What is your existence?' I said louder.

'I don't know.' You said softly beginning to get emotional.

'What is your existence?' I said in a loud, direct tone that reached deep inside of you as well as a few of the diners sitting near us.

Your eyes began to well up and your lips quivered. You

breathed in deeply, completely focused in the moment, now unaware of the noise and sets of eyes across the room staring at the two of us. 'I am calm, and rested. I am happy that I have my life, this moment. I am blessed for my health, my beautiful kids and my partner. I step outside and feel the air and the sun. I close my eyes and smile embracing this moment in my life.' You are crying now. Tears dripped down your check as if racing to share this moment with another. 'I smell the air; it smells new, and wet with a hint of honeysuckle. I feel as though anything is possible for this day, for my life.' You stopped here, satisfied.

I smiled and gave you this moment in silence.

You drifted off on these thoughts for several minutes before slowly opening your tear filled eyes. 'I don't ever remember feeling this way in my life,' you said quivering.

'This moment which you just embraced is available every moment of every day; it is with us at all times.' I said smiling, and now shedding my own tears moved empathetically by this moment in truth.

You sat in silence, still and completely calm as the waiter brought the bill. Neither of us moved completely unaware of our surroundings. Finally I grabbed the bill and insisted on paying.

You snapped out of your daze and tried to grab the ticket out of my hand without success. 'Let me pay, I am the student here.'

I paused looking intently at you. 'It is my pleasure; I am gracious for this moment. At every moment in our lives we are each a student and a teacher. Understanding this concept is a vehicle to set you free. I am just as much a student to you as you are to me.'

'How are you a student to me?' You said laughing.

'I have learned more from you the past two days than you will ever know. Yesterday I was reminded of how deep one human being can love another. Today I am reminded of the transcendence in staying present in one's existence. Thank you for this; I am blessed for these moments.'

You sat reflecting on my thoughts, beginning to understand the power inside of you. We put on our coats and headed for the door. I veered left planning to take a long circle back to the office.

'Awhile ago I commented that you are everything. Do you remember?' I asked.

'Yes.'

'Before we talk further about this comment, I want you to reflect on these thoughts:

You are nothing. You are me. I am you. You are truth. You are love. You are everything.

Thoughts?'

'My first thought is to call you Yoda, as this is a bit obscure, a bit poetic, don't you think?'

'Yes, it is both, isn't it? Beautiful though, right?' I asked. 'Before I break out in a very bad Yoda accent; let me try to explain this a bit further. However, as I warned you yesterday, once we begin down this rabbit hole or open Pandora's Box things are not black or white. Fair?'

'Ok, this is fair. I will try to keep an open, unassuming mind.'

'Let's start with the physical self. When you look in the mirror what do you see?'

'Hmmm….someone that looks tired and is aging MUCH too fast.' You said looking for me to join in your laughter. 'I could lose a few pounds, I am starting to get crow's feet next to my eyes; I even found a gray hair a few months back. I have noticed things are even beginning to sag…..I don't know. What else do you want?'

I shrugged taking in your comments stopping at a coffee shop. 'Come on, let's get a cup of tea and sit outside so I can address these thoughts.'

We sipped our tea taking a seat on a bench outside of the coffee shop. The day was warmer than yesterday, gray but without the threat of an immediate rain. Cars and people sped by all on the way 'somewhere'.

I took in a few more sips of tea before I continued on our previous thread. 'Things beginning to sag?' I looked at you with one eyebrow up. 'Geez let me bring a person in their 60s or 70s and have them hear this. Either way, it is all an external perception. When we talk later about positive intent and words, remember these comments about yourself. Ultimately, we are our thoughts; the energy we put out is the energy we get back. This superficial perception is everywhere.'

I looked around for reference points, and not finding anything immediate, I asked you to join. 'Look around, tell me what do you see.'

We both spent some time looking around the busy street. Two doors down from the coffee shop a hair and nail salon bustled with customers. A woman pranced out of the salon dressed in high heels, a fashionable tight suit wrapped in a fur coat and draped by a Chanel purse. She wore huge sunglasses that overpowered her face creating a resemblance to a movie star from the 1960's. The woman paused to look over her shoulder ensuring she was noticed then continued her waddle down the street. You spotted the woman, looked at me, and nodded. Words were not needed.

During this exchange, two women left the coffee shop pushing a stroller with a little boy and took a seat next to us. As they sat down the boy, about two years old, looked the two of us up and down with his bright blue eyes completely curious in his every moment. Just then a man tied up his golden retriever next to a post on the sidewalk. The dog was initially concerned that his master was leaving, then quickly focused on his surroundings and made a bee line for the little boy. He sniffed the boy up and down then quickly tasted him with his tongue as the boy giggled in delight. The two of them stared at each other for many minutes in some kind of a Jedi Knight Mind trance, both speaking without words completely present and engaged with each other. I began to get emotional watching such a moment when I overheard his mother talking to her friend completely unaware of the events.

'If my husband would stop being so *lazy* then we could get that new car that I want. I have been telling him for years to get a new job. I mean he doesn't make anything. I have been driving this car around for five years.' The women angrily pointed with her hand at an invisible car stressing her point.

Her friend nodded in affirmation.

I looked at you hoping that you took in this same moment while you focused on the boy clearly identifying with your own children nodding back to me, 'I am beginning to see your point.'

'It is everywhere.' I said softly. 'Turn on the television; talk to people, just open your eyes and it is all about the same thing – appealing to the ego. Women lose weight, get plastic surgery, look like broom poles without having a soul. People buy this, and buy that to appeal to this superficial desire, this powerful ego. Advertisers understand that most people do not rate themselves a 10, that people feel inadequate in some way. If I get another penis enlargement email, I mean really! They must do great business sending out all of these emails. These emails are appealing to the ego of men and telling them that they are somehow inadequate. Look at Viagra. I could go on.'

I reached into my pocket and pulled out my iPod and a mini speaker. 'Here, listen to this, India Arie states this very well in her song *I am not my hair.*'

You looked me up and down as I turned on the song.

We both grew silent and listened to the words-

'I am not my hair, I am not this skin, I am not your expectations no no, I am not my hair, I am not this skin, I am a soul that lives within.'

I shut off the song and nodded. 'Pretty much sums it up. She has a great take on who she really is.'

I jumped back into my DJ mode and pulled up another one of her songs. 'Here, listen to her words in this song called *Video-*

'Sometimes I shave my legs and sometimes I don't, sometimes I comb my hair and sometimes I won't, depends on how the wind blows I might even paint my toes, It really just depends on whatever feels good in my soul, I'm not the average girl from your video, and I ain't built like a supermodel, but, I learned to love myself unconditionally, because I am a queen, I'm not the average girl from your video, my worth is not determined by the price of my clothes, no matter what I'm wearing I will always be India Arie.'

I paused letting these words sink in and watched the little boy continue to bounce and dance even after the song was over. 'Music and movies are huge muses in my life. These songs really sum up the whole identity/role, physical feature perception, don't they?'

'I love her music; I guess I really never paid attention to the lyrics before, really substantial, very conscious. I will put her music on now whenever I want to set my mind straight about my physical self.'

I placed my iPod back into my coat, reached into my back pocket and pulled out a small version of the *Tao Te Ching* and browsed to one of my marked passages. 'Another great quote from a favorite book of mine, the *Tao Te Ching* which is attributed to Lao Tzu, states:

'When I let go of what I am, I become what I might be.'

Beautiful, right?'

You looked me up and down wondering what else I was going to pull out of my pockets. 'Yes, I have heard of this book. I

43

would like to hear more.'

'Sure, the root of our discussion about understanding our inner self is really summed up in this passage in the Tao Te Ching:

'*Knowing others is intelligence*
Knowing yourself is true wisdom
Mastering others is strength
Mastering yourself is true power.' (Mitchell, 1988)

The Greeks felt the same way; they put the phrase 'Gnothe Seauton' (Know Thyself) above their doors as a reminder of the importance of this exercise. The full quote is:

'*Worship the Gods if you must; but your first duty is to find out who and what you are yourself.*' (Johnson, 1939)

Buddha held similar thoughts:

'*It is better to conquer yourself than to win a thousand battles. Then the victory is yours. It cannot be taken from you, not by angels or by demons, heaven or hell.*'

The two women next to us were finished with their conversation and once again diverted their attention to the little boy. The mother grabbed the stroller and began to walk down the sidewalk. The boy strained his head trying to watch us as we waved goodbye.

I sipped my tea and continued, 'going back to the Tao Te Ching, I will continue to bring up this book in our discussion as it is so beautifully written and so elegant in its message. I would certainly put this book on the must-read list. It is one of those books you continuously read over time. Your perceptions will change based on the conditions in your life, and each time it seems like the message from the book is perfect for that moment.'

'It must be important; I have never seen anyone tote a book around like that before.'

'Well it is a *pocket* version,' I said laughing. 'Let's change up a little and take this a step further. Let's dive into the actual physical self, the 'what are you actually made of?' question. This is an interesting exercise. When we break our physical self up under a microscope we are made up of billions upon billions of atoms. In essence, if we could pull ourselves apart with very small tweezers we would leave a pile (albeit a very small pile) of mostly hydrogen atoms (roughly 63%), oxygen (25.5%), carbon (9.5%), along with small amounts of nitrogen, calcium, phosphorus, and very small contributions from chlorine, potassium, sulfur, sodium, and magnesium. Bill Bryson breaks this down in great depth in a book called *The History of Nearly Everything*.

Now, looking at this concept further and below these atoms, at the subatomic level, we are made up of elementary particles. Quantum Mechanics and Quantum Theory study these particles among other things and scientists are finding that the basic scientific laws developed by Newton and others have little to no meaning in this quantum world. This world makes no rational, scientific sense, at least in the traditional model. It is the ultimate 'rational' versus 'intuitive' battle going on in the universe, very similar to the earlier discussion of our rational 'mind' and our 'intuitive' self. Fritjof Capra covers this paradox in a book called *The Tao of Physics*. If we look at this deeper and take a look at each elementary particle, scientists are finding that rather than looking at each particle as a point, the particles are actually points joined together into an incredibly small *'string'* that vibrates. You might hear this called The String Theory. So, basically an elementary particle should be thought of as a tiny vibrating object – *ENERGY*. This is you, and basically any matter in the Universe – a bunch of vibrating energy.

Look at these rays of sun streaming down to our skin, or listen to the vibration of the music I have been playing. You and I are this same vibration of energy. We are connected with everything. Wow, my mind is turning in knots. Are you still with me?' I panted.

'Sort of, I am getting a little lost. I am also bewildered about how you know all of this.'

'Well, you are not the only one who is confused. I can barely pronounce Quantum Physics or String Theory. I am certainly not the one to be explaining these theories as I was just expressing the concept to look deeper into 'you',' I said. 'How do I know all of this? I am just curious. I am constantly reading. I told you that once Pandora's Box is open you get blown all over the place. All of this scientific stuff is confusing, but extremely interesting, isn't it?'

'Yes, terribly so, I do not remember science books or classes describing science relative to ourselves. I want to learn more.'

'Great, you can go right now to the Internet and someone with too much time on their hands has calculated how many atoms from Jesus or William Shakespeare that we breathe in and out of our bodies during our lifetime. Fascinating, isn't it?'

'Ok, you lost me. Please explain,' you sighed.

'It is what I have been saying; we are all made of the same particles. These particles or atoms are just reused over and over again. The energy inside of us that ignites these particles never dies. In essence, we are a bunch of energy beneath a bag of bones and flesh. Listen to the basic law of energy: First Law of Thermodynamics – *Energy cannot be created or destroyed*. It can only be transformed from one form to another. The total energy is constant within any system. Interesting, isn't it?'

'Interesting, but what does this mean?'

'It is really simple at its core. Basically, at some point your physical body or vessel will cease to exist. It will deteriorate and the basic building blocks of your body will be reused or trans-formed into something else. Think of the big pile of atoms with the tweezers. The 'you' is not the flesh and bones (or atoms) it is the energy that brings it to life. At this point, when your vessel has had enough, 'you', this energy, will simply transform into something different. You have atoms from ants, trees, birds, fish, and other humans in you right now. Remember, you are every-thing, but yet, you are nothing as you are not these atoms. You are this vibrating energy that cannot be destroyed.'

'Wow, I guess I should reconsider swatting this fly that won't leave me alone.' You said brushing away an invisible object.

'Exactly, with respect to the law of karma and reincarnation, that living creature could be your brother or sister,' I stated.

'Law of karma?'

'Karma, you have heard of karma, right?'

'Yes, I hear people throw it out now and again with respect that things are just the way they are, but this is much deeper.'

'The concepts of karma and reincarnation have been around for thousands upon thousands of years. There are slightly different interpretations across philosophies but in essence karma is whatever energy is put out will come back. Or, put in slightly different words, every doer will receive the exact result or reward of his or her actions and we will all be held accountable for all of our actions in life. We are predestined by what happens in our lives based on numerous things, such as the karma given for this life, and the karma carried forward from previous lives. In other words, this karma is carried forward with us like an accounting book. We will be held accountable at some point for all of our actions, and in turn, through reincar-nation, or the rebirth of our energy we will return in another life form. The Buddhist and Hindis call this the wheel of 84, the 84 Lakhs, or 8,400,000 possible life forms that your energy may exist across all living things such as plants, trees, insects, animals, and humans. So, as I mentioned, these insects might be your brother or sister. You look perplexed.'

You shifted in your seat not sure how to begin, 'I am worried where this is going. Remember, I come from a Protestant background. This is very different to my original experiences or discussions on life after death if you will.'

'Understood, I come from the same background as you. The karma and reincarnation discussion is really not important right now. We can explore this more later if you wish. Let's stay focused on 'who you are'. Agreed?'

'Fair enough....' You said.

'OK, so what are your thoughts about being a boundless source of energy, a source of love?'

'Well, as I mentioned this is a big departure from my background so I will need some time to assimilate, some time to understand or ponder the idea. At the root of this discussion, I am on board with the thought that I am more than my physical body. I guess I have always had this belief at a deep level. I am still struggling with how I define myself outside of roles. I have never looked at myself at this deep level before. I have not explored this concept or the fact that this may be related to my inner uneasiness, or lack of peace. So, although I am still trying to understand the concepts discussed I am open to exploring this deeper.'

I stood and stretched beginning to traverse down the sidewalk ready to walk off my lunch. You closely followed waiting for my response.

'This is all I can ask from you.' I said softly. 'Understanding who you really are inside is a monumental step. This is the great unknown that you must explore at a deep level. You must strip away all of those layers and get to the core 'you'. This core 'you' is absent of gender, absent of race, absent of roles, absent of labels; it is a pure state of being, a pure state of love; it is ultimately truth. If you can get to this point, you will live in a state full of presence, a state of selfless love connected to everything. You will fill this world with positive intent and energy. You will surround yourself with positive beings and you will exude love. People and all living things will be drawn to you. Like a magnet, you will attract this energy in your life and you will vibrate happiness. Again, this is not an easy journey. I have had many discussions with centered, present people that still hold anger and bitterness in their lives. It is obvious to them, as well as me, that they are not at a state of peace, a state of love. They are aware of the journey yet they refuse to take it. They are afraid. They understand the pain they must go through from an emotional standpoint to get to this core being and they refuse to take the journey. We all have skeletons. We hide these emotional scars inside of us, bury them. Especially from an Anglo-Saxon standpoint, we bury these emotions; these are not to talk about or to be dealt with. This is our standard reaction. However, it is important to understand these emotional scars are still with us. These pains do not go away until you face them, one by one, within yourself. I know some people with deep emotional issues from abuse. In all fairness to them, they are hiding from this pain as they do not want to experience it again. It is too painful. However, I see unhappiness, and people masking this pain through alternative means such as drugs or alcohol. This journey is the ultimate discovery for an individual. We shouldn't be afraid; we should face it; embellish this journey. The end result is a state of pure love. How magnificent is this?' I asked.

'This sounds great; however, I totally understand why people have shied away from this journey. We hide these emotions for a reason, don't we?'

'Of course, on the surface it is easier to bury them. We don't find others who empathize with our pain, or we don't want to trouble anyone, or we just cannot handle facing the issue. The failure is typically in not understanding that this is a personal journey and no one or no thing can help along the journey. As I mentioned there is not a book that 'cures' your internal troubles.

You cannot read a book and your ego or your internal emotional layers magically disappear and sudden clarity or happiness appears. At some point, there must be a realization that only you can face these within yourself. I know people who are embarrassed to eat alone, so how can these people possibly take this journey toward their inner self and find their true identity?'

We walked to the end of the block and onto the trail next to the waterway. A row of newly blossomed cherry trees lined the opposite side of the street officially announcing spring and welcoming our arrival. I walked on to the edge of the waterway and peered into the mindless abyss below.

'When I think of the power of being alone and embracing stillness I think of a passage in the Tao Te Ching:

'Ordinary men hate solitude
But the Master makes use of it
Embracing his aloneness
Realizing he is one with the whole universe.' (Mitchell, 1988)

I guess the driver behind this inaction is fear, or understanding how to take the journey. Basically you are asking yourself to take the most difficult journey of your life and not truly understanding the payoff in the end. I completely understand why people have shied away from this journey.' My words drifted off softly as I continued to stare at the reflections in the water.

'So how do you take this journey? Isn't this the fundamental question?' You said.

'Right,' I smiled. 'I guess the purpose of our entire discussion is to answer this very question. In order to get to truth we need to take this journey. Let me give you some thoughts on the journey and the necessary steps along the path. I will explore this in much greater depth after we discuss some of the obstacles along this path to truth. As I mentioned, in order to strip away these layers and get to this point of truth, we need to do some

Who are you?

things. First, I want you to recall my comments that you are this vibrant, beacon of energy full of selfless love. Do you remember this?'

'Of course, this is our ultimate goal, right?'

'Yes! We are all beacons of energy that exude love. Some philosophies in India describe the Divine Source, God, as an ocean of love. We are each a drop of this ocean. In other words, we all have the potential to connect to this ocean, to God. However, for a variety of reasons, primarily driven from a mind out of control, we are disconnected, like a tarnished drop of water. Think of a raindrop in the mud. We are covered in this muck, this dirt, but underneath we are this perfect, beautiful drop of water that belongs in this greater pool of energy, this ocean of love. The musician Jack Johnson has a great song titled Monsoon, where he states this implicitly:

'All of life is in one drop of the ocean waiting to go home, just waiting to go home.'

So at the root of our being we are energy. We are love. We are truth. At this point of realization, we understand that we are connected to everything. We love everything. Look around, life is beautiful. In order to get this point we must clear all of our negative energy.

We will cover this in great depth later, but in essence we need to get clarity and CONTROL of our mind by eliminating any negative energy, or thought. In addition, we need to exude positive energy from our body as this is our platform or vessel to connect to the source, to the Divine. Finally, and most importantly, we need to fill up the empty space left after removing our negative energy with love. We do this by 'tuning in' to this energy from the Divine Source through meditation. This is ultimately where we will strip away these layers, gain control over our mind and ego and connect at a deep level to truth.

51

Thoughts?'

'Wow... This is a journey, isn't it?' You sighed. 'I am getting your point that this journey is more than reading a book. It sounds very complicated, very different from where I have come from in my upbringing. For example, I only know of meditation. I have never experienced it firsthand. I guess my first thought is that I am overwhelmed.'

'Understood, remember I have been wrestling with these issues for a long time. I am still wrestling with these issues. Take your time, embrace and absorb your curiosity and this information and then explore for yourself. Think of this entire conversation as a blueprint to follow – a path to point toward – and you will make your own pace along the journey. Feel what is right for you in your exploration. We will cover a lot of information so look at this blueprint as a plan. Initially, take on parts of the journey that you feel most comfortable with. For example, we will discuss meditation in depth later, but let me give you some thoughts in starting the exploration of the real 'you'. Understand this exploration is to be done alone. This is the only way.

Ultimately it will be you in a dark room coming face to face with the inner 'you' while meditating. You will find your true self over time. In the beginning, start this journey by walking before you run. I recommend setting dates for yourself to be alone; alone to explore your inner curiosity. Get a baby sitter, set a date once a week on your calendar to be alone. Find an activity that stirs your creative self, be it a museum, music, a movie, whatever inspires you. Go do this activity, without friends and with as little talking as possible. You are exploring your inner being.

Another important first step is writing in a journal. Talk to yourself, just write, and do not judge. We will talk about judgment later. Understand that the concept of right or wrong does not exist. Fall in love with yourself. As you move forward, you will spend a considerable amount of time in meditation to still the mind. This is necessary to strip away all of these layers.

This is where the connection to everything will happen. This is where the boundless love will come out. How does this sound?'

'I love the idea of setting a date for myself. I cannot tell you how wonderful this sounds. I love it,' you beamed.

'You cannot love another until you truly love yourself. This includes your children. This is not a selfish act; this is an important exercise to love.' I look at my watch and shrug. 'Looks like we did it again,' I said smiling. 'I better let you get back to work. I am going to stay here a few more minutes and breathe in this moment.'

You nodded in agreement, started to turn on the trail back to the office before asking, 'so, what's next? I want to hear more.'

'We need to explore the battle to gain control of the mind, as this is the major obstacle in getting to truth.'

'I feel as though I will want to talk about this over the weekend. Is this a possibility?' You asked.

'Of course, I would do anything for you. How about a walk around Green Lake tomorrow morning? Meet at the small craft center at 9 am?'

'Perfect.'

You walked back to the office as I stared at the waves of my reflection in the water rippling in and out of permanence, beams of light transcending my immediate existence. The air mixed with salt from the water and pine from the trees lifting my energy with an intoxicating smell yet instilling calmness. I shut out all noises and cleared the chatter in my mind, perfectly still and at peace on the edge of the waterfront.

Chapter 3

The Mind out of Control

Saturday morning was crisp and clear. The ground was damp from the chilled evening as I made my way across the parking lot to the small craft center that sat adjacent to Green Lake. Even though it was before nine on a Saturday morning, the lake was already buzzing with activity. I wasn't surprised as the lake was a Mecca for outdoor enthusiasts. The center was the launch spot for both amateur and competitive crew teams who practiced across the lake all week long. It was also the gathering place for the annual Milk Carton Derby in August where contestants built boats made entirely out of milk cartons and raced other competitors on the lake. Most often these sank leaving the hopeful wet and confused.

Green Lake was also a place to walk and run. At just over three miles around it was perfect for the casual stroll or for the competitive runner who continued to run around until they reached their fill. Ball fields and parks surrounded the area generating a cross of athletes, casual walkers, dogs and children. The water was murky and held its namesake 'green' for the plentitude of algae that filled the lake. This didn't stop the throngs of bathers that flocked to the lake to cool from the rare sweltering day in the summertime.

I sat near the edge of the water watching a crew boat begin their practice session. The coxswain in the front set the tempo and the boat slowly pulled out of the sheltered cove onto the broader lake. The boat glided away as if on glass as all eight oars dipped and rose in perfect cadence. The sun was white and almost blinding as I looked across the park to the east. It was here I noticed you making your way across the far parking lot and onto the trail next to the small craft center. You looked different in your casual clothes, as if letting go of a false persona. You looked ready for a walk, and I was beginning to rethink my jeans, t-shirt and boots look.

'Good morning,' I called out as you came into frame.

You looked surprised squinting briefly with your eyes. 'Oh...I didn't see you sitting over there. Good morning how was your night?'

'Mine was really good; I relaxed, listened to music and read a book. You?'

'I had a great night. We stayed home with the boys, ate dinner, watched a movie and read books together.' You said.

'Sounds like a great night. Thanks for coming out for a walk, I thought we could get some exercise while exploring a few topics in greater depth.' I rose and began walking down the trail counter clockwise around the lake.

You followed and the two of us sauntered down the path without urgency.

'Yesterday I mentioned the mind out of control as the major obstacle in finding happiness, peace and truth. What is your reaction to this thought? I asked.

'My first reaction is not understanding the message. I have spent years upon years of my life building my intellect, looking at the mind as a tool to build, leverage, use. I see it as a powerful instrument. So, I am confused as to how this powerful instrument could be a cause of my problem.'

'OK, fair points; my first response is to ask a question back to you: Does intellect in itself create happiness, love and truth?'

'I guess I would have to answer *NO*... However, how does it prevent happiness?'

'Great question, and as I mentioned previously, as we move from black and white to intuitive understanding, you will ultimately need to understand and define within yourself, but I will try to convey different concepts in why the mind is out of control, and why in this state it is an obstacle to truth. I will cover various Eastern philosophies and try to use a few metaphors to express the message as I fully understand the difficulty in understanding this paradox. I felt the same way as you, and in the end I realized this was my mind trying to hold onto its vice grip of control. Does this sound *OK*?' I asked.

'OK, just remember I am new to these concepts, so continue to simplify the message to the best of your ability.'

We followed the path nearest to the water and stayed to the right hand side away from the bikers and rollerbladers. I paused thinking about the best way to explain the concept of the mind before jumping back into the conversation.

'I will do my best, and I promise you I will get back to the points you made, but first I feel I need to provide a little context in why the Western mind comes from such a different place. Without this context, I believe it is very hard to understand the message. Or, in the very least, it will provide a starting place for the mind to rationalize the message before we understand to let go of the mind and move toward our intuitive self. Does this sound OK?'

'Yes, go on.'

'The Western mind is typically traced back to the Greeks and specifically to Aristotle. Prior to Aristotle, the Greeks had a very similar message to the Eastern mind in that all living things in the Universe were connected by a cosmic breath called Pneuma. This directly corresponds to universal energy mentioned across various philosophies such as the Tao in Taoism, Brahman in Hinduism, Audible Life Stream or Shabd in Sant Mat and Dharmakaya in Buddhism.

Heraclitus used a term called LOGOS to define the source and order of the cosmos. Over time, the Greeks split this unity into the Divine Principle which stood above all Gods and Men. The Greeks moved from the original single unity in the universe to an intelligent and personal God who stands above and directs it. With this the Western mind developed, and was separated by, two main principles – matter and spirit. The Greeks developed the concept of the atom, which they believed to be static matter, unchanging, separate from the spirit. Aristotle built his scheme of the universe around this concept that lasted over 2000 years. This scheme was virtually untouched as it was supported by the Christian Church and was in essence not challenged. The church was, and in a way still is, very powerful in creating fear and insisting on status quo thought to benefit a certain agenda.

Remember, throughout this time was the dark ages where creativity and imagination were suppressed; cleansing yourself was considered heresy. The Spanish Inquisition, Witch burnings – basically those who opposed the church were eliminated. Just look at science; Copernicus had the audacity to suggest the earth revolved around the sun versus the universe around the earth. Galileo took the brunt of the punishment from the church as he was imprisoned within his house for supporting this idea. Uh... I have a feeling I am losing you... Talk to me.'

You had slowed your pace and looked distant, clearly not engaged in this topic. 'In full honesty, I do not feel comfortable discussing ideas that question my religious background,' you said.

'Completely fair, I would never ask you to change your belief system. I would always accept and love you for how you are no matter your beliefs. I apologize if I put out different energy to you. Let me continue moving away from religious context. OK?'

'Thank you. Perhaps I will be ready at some point for this discussion; however, right now I am feeling overwhelmed with the depth of content.'

'Sure, this sounds great. This entire context leads to the background of why you and I, in a Judeo/Christian background, have developed a certain train of thought in difference to other parts of the world. This type of thinking led to the famous Rene

Descartes quote, 'I think, therefore I am'. An Eastern mind might say, 'I don't think, therefore I am everything'. Do you see the paradox?'

'Very much so, I see the paradox but not the obstacle. I still do not understand the mind as an impediment to love, to truth.'

'OK, OK… I am moving toward this point.' I said smiling taking in the myriad of colors running and walking past us. 'I still want to provide context to build on for this discussion. This scheme of the universe and train of thought is the basis behind everything in Western thinking. I will not go into details, but in religion this thought is the basis behind a monarchical God who rules above and imposes his divine laws upon the universe as *He* sees fit. This God is often angry, filled with ego; 'Do this to me and I will destroy or punish you'. You have probably heard of the thought 'a healthy fear of God'. To the Eastern mind, God, or the Divine is pure love. Why would you fear pure love? This monarchical view bled into many other areas of life such as science. The laws of science were seen as the laws of God to which the world was subjected. The very basis of this thinking is to separate the individual and isolated ego; envision Descartes, 'I think therefore I am', from the rest of the universe.

Now, listen to a passage from the Tao Te Ching indifferent to this thinking,

'The ordinary man seeks to make himself the center of his universe; the universe of the sage is at his center.'[1]

This isolated ego creates the individual perceptions such as *I am entitled*, *I am better*, and *I want more*. These are all part of desire driven by the senses. We become attached to the world, whereas all things in this world are impermanent. Hindu and Buddhists call this attachment to static thinking avidyā, or ignorance. The belief is that the mind is disturbed and an individual must overcome this for peace, for love, for truth. Buddha basically states that all life is suffering when the mind is in this state attached to desire and permanence. Buddha mentions that all wrong doing arises because of mind. He stated it is man's own mind, not his enemy or foe, that lures him to evil ways. Thus, he asked the question, 'if mind is transformed can wrong doing remain?'

I gave these words air trying to think of a way to explain. 'The most vivid metaphor I can use is that of the movie we discussed the other day, *The Matrix*. The Matrix is not real, it is an illusion driven by the desire of the mind. Whatever the mind dwells upon becomes part of the individual whether this is for good or bad. Underneath all of this is suffering, which in the movie is represented by those trapped in the 'energy pods', trapped due to their minds clinging to worldly thoughts, permanence inside the Matrix versus the reality of the existence that a few 'enlightened' souls had the insight and courage to free themselves. Money, looks, status, power, sex, drugs... none of this will make you happy, really happy. These are simply masks, roles, labels, not the real 'you' as we already discussed. In the end we all die and nothing from this material world comes with us – not material things, not power, not looks, not family, nothing, just the inner you. This is why people are scared to die, scared to find out the real person inside; they mask this with money and titles and superficial 'things', or they fill their time with minutia, meaningless pursuits to fill time such as TV, drinking, 'chasing'. Yet in the end, we are all the same; we all die, our physical bodies pass, and our energy moves forward. We either come to the realization that we have wasted our life in meaningless pursuits and were never 'fulfilled', or happy chasing after these pursuits or destructive passions, or we don't ever come to this realization. In this, according to Eastern philosophy we start over, we come back again in a new life form and if this is in a human form we have the ability to connect to the divine with hope that we have learned the lesson from our previous lives.

So, to finally answer your questions, the mind *IS* a beautiful instrument. Driven by the inner 'you', by your energy, the mind is the most powerful and beautiful instrument available to you. The challenge is that the mind is and has been out of control for thousands if not millions of years. It is a product of the senses, easily distracted and occupied, taking you away from love, from truth, from your purpose in life. The senses overwhelm the mind and the mind enslaves the soul. This is why the mind is an obstacle. Thoughts?'

I stopped at this statement and pulled off the walking path intent on focusing on your words and giving you my full presence. You followed me and we stood looking out over the water a few feet away. Just beyond our spot was a father teaching his son about 10 years old how to fish. The father baited a hook with a wiggling worm, adjusted a red and white bobber and cast the bait far out into the lake. He then gently handed the pole over to his eager son as they both took a seat in anticipation in what might come next.

After a few moments in reflection, you jumped back into my point about the mind, 'I have a lot of thoughts about the mind; I am just not sure what to say at this point. I am trying to absorb all of these thoughts as these are quite different from my background. Would you say that the desires of the senses are related to the 10 Commandments or other ethical doctrines?'

'Great question, as from the outside without more depth, it sounds in a way as an ethical discussion. In turn, it is not. Look at it; ethics and the 'thou shalt not' messages do not work. The commandments or the ethical doctrines of Confucius have been around for thousands upon thousands of years. These doctrines are put out and are a reflection of a society or culture, and then typically driven by fear in close association with guilt. They do not work. The relationship with the divine, with love, is a personal one first. The root of a person is good; once connected to the divine you are filled with love and this flows outward to your environment. These 'thou shalt not' messages at a smaller, personal level do not work either. As a parent, I can certainly attest to this. The 'do not do this' message is like fuel to a child to actually 'do this' activity. I remember in school, one of the rowdiest kids in school was the preacher's kid. Ethical doctrines and commandments do not curb the mind. Ethics are a product of culture. For example, in one culture it is acceptable to have multiple wives and the mind has been programmed to discriminate to accept this versus another culture who believes this is 'wrong' or 'sinful'. I think of our treatment of Native Americans and our claim that they were 'Godless' and 'savages' because they held different ethical views or intellect than our traditional Judeo/Christian mind. In reality, these people were very connected to everything in the universe and to what they called the 'Great Spirit'.'

I walked slowly next to the water embracing the stillness and connection with nature off the chaotic exercise path. I could feel the wind here closer to the water and the sun, rising toward its apex radiated warmth on my skin.

'Native Americans words convey their connection to nature and all living things very clearly.' I said. 'One of my favorite books is from a Lakota Sioux medicine man by the name of Black Elk, called appropriately *Black Elk Speaks*. We discussed earlier the voice of the oppressed is typically not heard. This book gives the oppressed Native American point of view at major events such as Wounded Knee and the battle with General Custer at Little Big Horn. Black Elk was there. Listen to these beautiful very connected words from Black Elk called True Peace:

'The first peace, which is the most important, is that which comes within the souls of people when they realize their relationship, their oneness, with the universe and all its powers, and when they realize that at the center of the universe dwells Wakan-Taka (the Great

Spirit), and that this center is really everywhere, it is within each of us. This is the real peace, and the others are but reflections of this. The second peace is that which is made between two individuals and the third is that which is made between two nations. But above all you should understand that there can never be peace between nations until there is known that true peace, which, as I have often said, is within the souls of men.'

So, you see, ethics are a product of the culture, a product of ritual, not the essence of love, of truth. At the root of your soul, the inner you, at the state of truth, is complete goodness. The inner 'you' does not need ethical doctrines or commandments. At your truth, intuitive self you are positive, vibrant energy exuding love. However, unless you get to this state of clarity, this state of intuitive self, the mind will continue to hold control and be a slave to the senses, or routine, until it finds a replacement that is more powerful than the existing desire. You cannot rationalize yourself to stop something that is driving your mind; it has to be replaced by something more gratifying. One has to take control back from the mind, and quiet it. It is then that our inner self will take back the reins and have the ability to direct this wonderful instrument as we see fit, toward love, toward truth. Our purpose is to connect to the Divine Source and live in a state of selfless love. At the root of all living beings is love. We are all good, full of the potential to exude love at all times. However, as I mentioned, it is a difficult journey in which we must die every day to attain. Until we understand that life is impermanent and that it is NOT static or black and white, we will continue suffering, we will continue on the same karmic path. We cannot free ourselves and find truth until we reach this point.

Nearly all Eastern philosophies discuss this process of transcending the isolated self or ego and understanding the unity and interrelation with all things. Listen to some of these statements across Eastern philosophies: In Japan, the word Satori means enlightenment, one who draws nearer to God, and is a level of consciousness above the ego, closer to the creator; the Guru Nanak mentions 'conquer the mind and you conquer the world'.

Again from the Tao Te Ching, this is discussed in many passages, listen to these words:

'If you close your mind in judgments and traffic with desires, your heart will be troubled. If you keep your mind from judging and are not led by the senses, your heart will find peace.' (Mitchell, 1988)

Here are a few more from the Tao Te Ching:

'When there is no desire, all things are at peace.' (Mitchell, 1988)

'If you want to be given everything, give everything up.' (Mitchell, 1988)

'If you realize that all things change, there is nothing you will try to hold on to. If you aren't afraid of dying, there is nothing you can't achieve.' (Mitchell, 1988)

'These are great, no book today?' You asked laughing.

'I know these by heart.' I smiled. 'These come to mind often for me. This last saying about losing the fear of dying reminds me of the book and TV series by James Clavell called *Shogun*, Have you heard or seen this show?'

'No. Why does it remind you of this?'

'This book is another great metaphor of the paradox between the Western Judeo/Christian mind and the Eastern mind. A ship from the west, I believe England, is stranded in Japan. These Protestant shipmates, who at the time in the 1600s were unwashed, foul mouthed, sex driven, meat eaters, in difference to the Zen Buddhist, primarily vegetarian, very clean, Samurai culture of Japan. The leader of the ship, the pilot, lives in concert with the Japanese culture and begins to transform his inner being. At the critical moment of the book, he tries to take his life but is stopped at the last moment. He had lost all fear of dying and thus after this point he sees the world drastically different.

He is free. He begins to live in the present and sees beauty in everything. This is a beautiful metaphor that is loosely based on the true story of a sailor from England by the name of William Adams who never returned home after he adopted the Japanese culture. Once we lose these attachments, these desires, these fears, we can get to the clear mind, the 'childlike' mind that we discussed and be free, be connected to the present moment, and be connected to the beauty of life. We silence the disruptive mind through meditation. We move toward our intuitive self by filling ourselves with love and we are connected to everything. However, our mind does not want to give up control. It is driven by routine and the senses and the senses always drive it toward the five destructive passions of the mind.' I paused for reflection.

'Well, of course this leads to the obvious question: What are the five destructive passions?'

'Yes, I thought you would never ask,' I said smiling. 'Let's sit down by the playground so we can discuss this further.'

You followed me along the path until we reached a row of blossoming cherry trees next to a ball field and children's playground. We took a seat in the sunlight and watched the children playing in the sand.

'So....back to your question,' I said with a deep inhale, 'the five destructive passions manifest from the mind out of control, the mind in an abnormal or perverted state. Remember the mind driven by the soul is magnificent. All intelligence, light, beauty, imagination, music, wisdom, love come from the soul. When the mind is not in a state of love driven by the soul then these passions manifest: Lust, Anger, Greed, Attachment and Vanity' (Johnson, 1939).

I paused trying to think of a metaphor to describe these destructive passions, 'have you seen the Fremont Troll?'

'Of course, the Troll is a Seattle landmark.'

The Freemont Troll had been a Seattle fixture and tourist attraction since its inception in 1990 sitting under the Aurora Bridge near the main street of the downtown Freemont neighborhood. The neighborhood commissioned the work of a giant concrete troll crushing a Volkswagen bug as a means of beautifying a trash dump that had developed under the bridge.

'OK, think of the troll as your mind out of control and the VW Bug he is crushing is the love inside of you.'

You looked at me like I had lost it. Undeterred, I looked around searching for something else. I noticed a little boy in the sandbox wearing an Incredible Hulk t-shirt and huge green HULK hands.

I looked at you and nodded toward the little boy, 'OK, see that little boy with the HULK Hands destroying every sand castle in his path.'

'Yes....reminds me of a few boys I know.' You said laughing deeply.

'OK, stay with me here, but an appropriate metaphor for the mind out of control is *The Incredible Hulk*. This boy destroying everything in sight is a great reflection of the mind out of control.'

You shook your head with the direction of our conversation.

'OK, I may be reaching here, but the story of the Incredible Hulk has to be taken directly out of the concepts of Eastern philosophy. Look at it. We have an individual trying to suppress this 'thing' within himself that comes out and controls the individual. This is simply a person wrestling with control over the mind and the senses. In this particular case, he is wrestling with a mind consumed with anger. In the movie he even meditates to try and control this 'thing'. You cannot find a more direct metaphor to visualize the challenges we face to overcome this obstacle with our mind. Now, to add to this metaphor, think of this green, Incredible Hulk as a three year old that has never had parents, guidance, or any imposed control over it. Thousands of times worse than this terminator here,' I said nodding to the little boy on the playground. 'You have children; can you imagine a little Incredible Hulk in your household?'

'Wow, I would have never guessed we would be using the *Incredible Hulk* and *The Dude* from The Big Lebowski in our philosophical discussions,' you said in laughter, 'and, no, I cannot imagine a three year old Incredible Hulk. I am trying to forget my oldest at this age and unfortunately I am still dealing with my youngest in his terrible three's. What a challenge!'

'Exactly, what a challenge, this is the basis in why we must die every day. We must have patience, incredible patience, and understanding that it will take considerable time to gain control back from this little green monster. And, remember this little Hulk will always be lurking, throwing tantrums, and demanding to get its way. Once you understand this, the mind becomes comical. I just visualize this little Hulk in my head throwing a tantrum and I have to laugh. I do not give in. I close my eyes and I breathe. I see this little Hulk in other people all the time; one thing I can say – this little Hulk is persistent. However, staying on the super hero theme, this Hulk does have its own kryptonite. Of course, the real kryptonite is the actual journey, the path, cleansing our mind and body and connecting to the source through meditation. Within this journey, you also have a tool to use against the little Hulk – positive intent, positive words and positive action. We will cover this more later, but I want to paint this picture before we jump into details around the five deadly passions. Think of this little Hulk again, running all over the house needing something to occupy itself at all times. It loves routine, things that please it; it is always searching for pleasure, following desire. And, of course, like a bottomless pit, it is never fulfilled, never satisfied; it always wants more.'

I paused here embracing the warmth of the sun and the wind on my face. I wanted to let these words find root before continuing. I pulled a small blue, sponge like ball out of my pocket and held it up for you to see.

'You are like a clown with all of the things in your pockets.' You laughed shaking your head.

'A happy clown...,' I said. 'OK, so I want you to think of yourself as a magician, and you have this magic blue ball that will completely occupy this little Hulk. Whatever thought is put into this magic blue ball will appear, and thus the little Hulk is quieted, occupied, busy with the ball and ultimately disappears.' I pointed at the ball in the palm of my hand, closed it and reopened to an empty hand.

'Hey.......how did you do that?'

I continued without an answer, 'You, as the magician have the ability to put whatever thought you wish to occupy the mind, or in this case, the little Hulk. This magic blue ball becomes your vehicle toward truth. You will use it in a meditative state to center the mind on one thought away from a scattered, 'monkey mind', until you do not need this ball anymore and you are at this state at all times, this clear 'wu-hsin' no mind. It is here that you will be at your intuitive center, in harmony with the universe and filled with love.

Outside of your sitting meditation, this magic blue ball is your tool throughout the day, your walking meditation. You will use it to stay in this state of love and truth throughout the day. You will use it to suppress the little Hulk. Use it as your focus to live in the present moment indifferent to the five destructive passions. This is your tool to stop the 10,000 thoughts coming at you at all times. Pull out your magic ball and fill it with positive intent, positive manifestations, selfless love, and truth. Remember, whatever the mind dwells upon becomes part of the individual. So, in essence, we choose our reality. Does this make sense?'

'Yes. Please go on. I want to understand these destructive passions,' you said in frustration trying to get me back on point.

'Of course, I have danced around another topic haven't I? Well, the mind, or the little Hulk, is very persistent, and again until we find something greater to entertain the senses, then these senses will ultimately overwhelm the individual – the little Hulk gone wild if you will. I already told you the antidote, which is connecting to the source and love through meditation. If we do not gain control then the mind is drawn toward these destructive passions.

Let's break these down to understand better. The first passion is lust or self indulgence. This contains the obvious one – sexual passion – but it is more than this. It includes all lustful passions that control an individual such as drugs, alcohol, tobacco, and even food. I think we all know someone who is or has been controlled by a substance. This passion controls an individual 24/7; it truly is consuming and has the ability to create great perversions and awful acts. This passion pulls the individual to the level of an animal and binds one to these senses. This passion reminds me of the book *Think and Grow Rich* by Napoleon Hill. This book was a strong basis behind the book and movie *The Secret*. Hill talks about a common trait among successful men in that they have a supporting wife behind them. They are NOT wasting their excess energy in 'chasing skirts'. Sexual passion is a huge binder in life. It consumes so much time and energy. I know men whose entire day is consumed by this one passion. I know, because at one point in my life I was one of these men… food, sports, sex, right?' I said with a shrug.

You glanced at me with a surprised look. 'I had no idea I would be talking to you at this level when I went to knock on your door a few days ago.'

'No reason to shy away from reality. These points in my life are not good or bad, they just are. I do not judge them, however, I am aware of the state of my mind and whether I acted in a state of love or not. I have nothing to hide or be ashamed of. This is life.'

'OK, so if we are going to put everything out on the table. I have to say I hope you are not going to ask me to be celibate, are you? Because, I will tell you right up front, I cannot go there. I love intimacy.'

'First off, I am not going to ask you to do anything. I am simply discussing a blueprint that I have followed. You will have to follow your own path. To answer the thought that I believe is in your head, I am not celibate. Intimacy is a beautiful thing with someone you are spiritually connected to and love. The Taoists believed the intimate union between a man and a woman was divine, the perfect harmony, in essence their heaven. Can you imagine?'

'No, I cannot imagine. My next question is where I can find this?' You said laughing.

'Well... to state the obvious, this one really is your journey, and you will have to find this one yourself,' I said joining in your laughter. 'On the other end of the spectrum is an individual who has evolved spiritually to the point that sex is a meaningless pursuit. They have found something of greater importance and value to them. I think of Gandhi with this action. He went to his wife in the latter part of their lives and told her he wished to pursue celibacy and focus on his spiritual union with the Divine. So, I am not judging or trying to impose some ethical rule; as I mentioned, this does not work. I am simply stating the mind in perversion will be consumed and controlled by destructive forces and LUST in particular is a very powerful one.

In a full state of love, one does not need physical intimacy to connect to another individual. When you view another in their pure state outside of the superficial, you are connected to their true essence. Anything beyond this is additive to this connection. Viewing an individual as an object to satisfy a lustful passion does not come from a place of love. I have seen a man have a lustful urge toward a woman five minutes after intimate relations with another. This is a destructive passion that will consume your life. Again, it is more than just sexual passion, if you are consumed, or lust after anything in life to feel fulfilled, be it cigarettes, beer, drugs, food, whatever, then your energy is constantly trying to fill a void inside with this destructive passion. The only way to fill this void is with love, with a connection to the divine. Without this perception, one keeps searching; one keeps following the senses, not understanding why they are suffering. All the while the mind is in the driver's seat controlling the individual through these desires, through this grasping to permanence. In this, the second destructive passion, ANGER, is very similar. Have you seen this one in action?'

'Of course, anger is present all the time. It just becomes part of your life; you learn to live with it,' you said matter of fact.

'I guess we can learn to understand when it is present, but it certainly doesn't have to be part of your life. Anger, by nature, is the opposite of love, the opposite of where we want to be at all times. Therefore, removing this from within yourself and your environment is imperative. It is impossible for an individual consumed by anger to make any spiritual progress.

One cannot concentrate the mind; concentrate on the magic blue ball while under the spell of anger. Anger destroys peace, builds hatred, stirs up strife, causes confusion, and scatters the mind. Anger is more than yelling and screaming or violence. These are the obvious symptoms. There are minor components of anger as well. These include slander, gossip, profanity, jealousy, destructive criticism, malice, thinking ill of others, nagging, scolding, blaming others, and fighting to name some. I think an easy rule in opposition to this destructive passion is to think about selfless love. No motive, nothing to gain, just love. If your environment or mind does not fit into this 'love bucket' then remove or change it.

The mind really is an interesting thing to study, to understand. Like I said, it is comical to see in action. The other day, I saw a guy in a car cut off another guy, and this escalated into profanity, fist pumping, flipping another individual off, and then, one individual pulls out a handgun and starts waving it at the other. So, one individual loses a second of their time in having to slow down and is now at the point of getting shot. I stare in amazement at the power of the senses, the power of anger, the power of the mind. Wait, you have a look on your face. What is it?'

'I was cut off just two days ago and I was furious, I was shouting at no one in particular, 'How dare you do that to me? You jerk!' Yeah, I was pretty angry,' you looked at me trying to gain acceptance for these feelings.

'You are funny. I appreciate your honesty. Listen to those words: 'How dare you do this to me?' The ego thinks pretty highly of itself. I have to tell you just listening to your story gives me such negative vibes; look at that energy that you put into the universe. Pretty compelling, isn't it?'

'I guess after a while, these type of things just become the norm and you don't really think about them anymore. You convince yourself, so what, so I called the guy a jerk. I mean he was a jerk. Do you know what I am saying?' You again look for affirmation.

'I understand your point, but let's look at this; a person who you do not know pulled in front of you where you had to slow down. You know nothing about this person, their intent, or in the end it 'really' doesn't matter does it?'

'I guess....you are right.'

'What if this person was rushing to the hospital? What if this person didn't see you? What if this person made a mistake? Again, it really doesn't matter. It is a point of judgment, and in this case the ego feeding you with the 'How dare this person do this to ME?'

This example is actually very compelling to me. In addition to the almost shooting I witnessed, my daughter called me on the phone the other night in tears. Although only nine, she has developed enough trust in being able to share on the phone with me her feelings. She was very hurt. You know why? Her mother had been pulled over and given a speeding ticket. Her mother cursed, and filled the air with anger. The emotions bled over into how the children felt, and they, or at least my nine year old was very distraught. She is a very sensitive girl and she was hurt by this. Look at what this simple action put into the universe and the energy that it put forth. Remember we are either bringing our self up or pulling our self down, and thus we either bring others up or we pull others down. This is your choice. You could choose not to let the guy drive in front of you and speed up and make sure that NO ONE bump you from your spot. I almost feel like holding a moment of silence so we can give you back your five seconds. What do you think?' I said laughing.

'Come on, we all have our moments. I just feel that people will start walking all over me. Don't you get this feeling?'

'Great question, I used to think this as well. However, every time you use the word 'me' like this then you are talking about the ego. Sure, there will be those that are not on a spiritual path toward truth that run all over you and everybody else. I cannot help them. No, I don't feel run over as they have taken NOTHING from me. I have had issues with previous relationships in a couple of areas around this topic. One time, we were having dinner and the waiter was not exactly giving the best service; he was slow, forgot a few things, and basically just wasn't on his game. When the check came and 'I' was paying, the woman I was with went ballistic that I was giving a 15% tip. Now, I normally give at least a 20% tip, so I felt this justified the service level. But she went on and on about how this person disrespected her, her mother, and the entire table. 'How dare this person treat 'us' or 'me' this way?' I couldn't grasp this at the time. I actually got very upset as I was the one paying and this ended in a fight as I didn't see this from the outside or have peace within myself to deal appropriately with this situation. The mind just drives these fits of anger and the ego fuels the desire. The energy put forth to get angry has now joined in the inept energy from the waiter. We are now both being brought down into a negative spiral. We can choose a different path.

In this same relationship, I would have issues because I wouldn't get upset about things. You know, a guy dinged the car, losing something, the weather, anything. She felt I was not human, that I was *Ice Man* and she was real in showing her emotions. Emotions are fine coming from a place of truth; however, emotions to feed the little green Hulk pull from any love that we have inside. Again, remember anger is the opposite of love; anytime we put this out there we pull away from peace. So a guy dinged my car, I can either fix it or I don't; this is really the only decision to make, right? I mean what can I do? Will jumping up and down or physically hurting this person change the situation, or most importantly make me feel better? The mind is intense, isn't it?' I asked in amazement.

'I see your point. Typically, once I release this anger out I feel remorse as it does not help the situation. This one will be very hard to control. I feel it just comes out.'

'I understand. It takes time and, as said before, this is a daily event to overcome. We die every day. From the outside it appears anger is directed or harmful toward the person or thing it is directed at; however, ultimately, it destroys you. Buddha's words speak directly to this point:

'Holding on to anger is like grasping a hot coal with the intent of throwing it at someone else; you are the one who gets burned.'

Buddha continued on the topic of anger:

'In a controversy the instant we feel anger we have already ceased striving for the truth, and have begun striving for ourselves.'

How about the next destructive passion – greed?'

'Sure, I guess there is a little King Midas in all of us. How much harm is in this?'

'Again, not to deflect, but this is for you to decide. If wealth becomes master then I will tell you that your life will never be fulfilled. You will always want more. It is certainly OK to have a nice car, clothes, and house. If in the end, you define yourself through these things, then they are in essence controlling you. They are using you and you are consumed and defined by greed. Greed binds us to material things, to the material world. This bleeds into status, rank, classes, and castes. It creates falsehoods, hypocrisy, misrepresentation, bribery, robbery, and perjury. Greed tries to create a perception of this material 'you', which, as we already discussed, is not you at all. We will all die and this power and greed will be meaningless. Greed is more than 'things'. Greed can be associated to power, status, social rank, advancement, salary, 'keeping up with the Jones', all of these things that bind us to wanting more, to believing we deserve more, that we are above other living things. How we treat the environment could be considered greed in not living in balance with nature. I am sure you can see this beyond the King Midas example in both individual and corporate action. The division of people by classes and race has been a staple of our human inter-relation with each other – the whole thought of slaves, and that one class or society is better than another and 'deserves' to have servants, and freedoms indifferent to another.

This type of thinking is again a direct reflection of the Western, monarchical mind. If God can direct who deserves certain 'things' or wealth in life, then if I have these 'things' I must be closer to a God and thus better than those who do not have these 'things'. I will label them as savages and treat them as such. This attitude is still present in certain people and directed toward other living beings.

For example, the majority of people believe animals are the bounty of the human race, that these creatures do not have a spirit, and were created by God for the benefit of man, and thus the destruction or ill treatment of animals is our given right. We can talk more about this later; however, I am certain animals are living, soulful beings that feel, and love. In the middle ages the church actually voted as to whether women and animals had souls (Robbins, 1987). Turns out women barely passed and animals did not. Unfortunately, status in life has not changed much for either. It is interesting seeing this mentality flow from a political and business standpoint. Both serve to gain, and in particular business has only one gain which is greed. There is no accountability other than greed, or shareholder profit. Nothing else matters to achieve this goal. There certainly are some socially responsible companies trying to make a difference like Google and the Bill and Melinda Gates Foundation. The bulk are simply greed in action. The earth is hurting and will eventually have to heal itself, with or without the human race. Our greed toward resources and our attitude that we are 'above' the earth and other living beings is the direct cause of this destruction. Listen to these words from the Tao Te Ching written close to 2600 years ago:

'In harmony with the Tao
the sky is clear and spacious
the earth is solid and full
all creatures flourish together
content with the way things are
endlessly repeating themselves
endlessly renewed.
When man interferes with the Tao
the sky becomes filthy

the earth becomes depleted
the equilibrium crumbles
creatures become extinct.' (Mitchell, 1988)

When our mind is out of balance we are out of balance with the source, with the Tao in this case. With respect to politics you see greed all the time. I think of President Clinton who I had such great respect for as a politician, hung onto his greed for power. He thought he was above the system and had the ability to do whatever he pleased and tried to lie to hold onto his power. This is a direct reflection of the destructive passion of greed. Many people in power will do whatever it takes to hold onto it. I can think of many political examples here. In the end, these 'things', this 'power', is an illusion. However, for some this destructive passion is very consuming, and defines them as an individual.

The little Hulk is quite attached to greed. It likes power. The Tao Te Ching talks directly to this point as well:

'If you look to others for fulfillment
you will never truly be fulfilled.
If your happiness depends on money
you will never be happy with yourself.
Be content with what you have;
rejoice in the way things are.
When you realize there is nothing lacking
the whole world belongs to you.'' (Mitchell, 1988)

Although the temperature was only in the low sixties, the bright sun felt hotter bearing down on the two of us. Having just come out of our dreary winter, I imagined we had to slowly adapt to this foreign object in the sky. I stood stretching my now tight legs, feeling the breeze on my face. The playground was full and bouncing with energy and noise. My little Incredible Hulk friend had left having alienated half the playground in his destructive power. You stood with me, silent, deep in thought I imagined.

I nodded over to the lake and offered a suggestion, 'let's keep walking if you don't mind, I need to stretch out my legs.'

'Sure.'

We made our way back toward the lake and onto the walking trail continuing our counter clockwise circle back to the small craft center. We were about half way around the lake still taking our time in no rush, or determined agenda.

As we walked slowly along the path I began to smell spring in the air. The smell of fresh cut grass filled my nostrils immediately making me think of baseball. As a kid, this was the smell that told me it was spring, that it was baseball season. I smiled in this thought before getting back to the conversation. 'How about attachment? What do you think of this one?'

'Attachment to what? I guess I don't understand this one,' you shrugged.

'The destructive passion of attachment is to bind an individual to people and things until you have no time for anything else, no time for self or spiritual advancement. This passion is the king of procrastination that keeps you from your purpose in connecting to the divine, to truth. Attachment keeps you a slave to work, to family duties, to animals, to anything binding until your death. You look at life on your deathbed and say 'Where did all that time go? I accomplished nothing worth true meaning'.'

'Wait a second... Are you telling me my connection to my family, to my children, is a bad thing? I hope I am hearing you wrong,' you slowed your pace while raising your voice.

'I would never suggest anything you do or feel is right or wrong, bad or good. I will accept you for whatever you believe as long as you are not harming another living being, and even then I will understand this is simply your mind out of control and not the true essence of the inner 'you'. I am not suggesting that having a family, loving them and being present with them is a bad thing at all. I am suggesting that building all of your time and energy around only people and things will keep you busy but with no spiritual advancement, no growth, no chance to find truth. I am suggesting finding a balance for both. This is a hard one for discussion as in the end all things and people are impermanent.

All will cease to exist. Your energy will move forward and this opportunity for love, for truth will pass. Being here, right now in this human form is a gift. We all have this gift in this human form to connect back to the Divine. The deeper you connect into the Divine Source the more your love will shine for your family, and loved ones. There is a saying from Eastern philosophy that states 'When I am attached to nothing, I love everything'.

Attachment consumes your time. You only have so many hours in your life. Bill Bryson in the previously mentioned book, *The History of Nearly Everything*, discusses that the average human lifetime consumes 650,000 hours in this vessel, this form. This makes me think of the TV show, *Seinfeld*, where Elaine had a limited supply of birth control sponges. She would constantly question whether a boyfriend was 'sponge worthy'. I am constantly exploring my activities to understand if they meet my 'sponge worthy' criteria with respect to my time. When I am around family, or loved ones, I ensure that I have set aside this time and I am fully present with them without distractions. I prioritize my spiritual activities every day at a time when it is least likely to interfere with others. My personal choice is to sacrifice sleep. This is how I balance, and have my personal time and my relationships. In the end, if these attachments control you they will take you away from truth, from love. The little green Hulk will say things like 'stay in bed today, it is warm here...sleep'; or, 'just do it tomorrow, you have plenty of time.'

Going back to the Samurai example and the Japanese culture in general, they have great appreciation for living in the present moment, not 'waiting for tomorrow'. Life is precious, who knows what will happen tomorrow, or even an hour from now. If you are a Samurai and you understand your life could end any moment, you begin to appreciate life *RIGHT NOW*. You see the beauty in all things. The code of the Samurai called Budo, which means in essence the way of halting the thrusting blade, reflects the desire for a peaceful society, or saving life. Bu in a way is love (Saotome, 1986). Martial Artists in general are usually the last people to fight as, by training, they have respect for living beings and life in general. The Samurai were not just warriors; they held great pride in bettering themselves and searching for perfection in oneself everyday through poetry, through archery, through calligraphy, anything to better themselves toward a complete being. This belief has an undertone in Zen Buddhist thinking and the Japanese culture as a whole. Think of the Japanese gardens, tea ceremonies, and flower arrangements. The art of finding perfection in the present moment is so beautiful to me. There is nothing binding, no attachment, no procrastination, the outflow of creativity, harmony and love is very evident to me.'

The path headed west along the shore of the lake. Next to the path was another row of cherry trees in full blossom. The pink and white petals burst with colors filling me with happiness. I was calmed by this thought of renewal, and growth. I smiled in this thought. Inspired, I thought of another metaphor to share with you. 'Have you seen *The Last Samurai* movie with Tom Cruise?'

'No, I haven't.'

'Well, in this movie the lead Samurai warrior, played by Ken Wantanabe, is constantly searching for the perfect cherry blossom.' I nodded to the adjacent trees. 'You see, it is not the end result in finding the 'perfect' cherry blossom, it is the journey of searching for the perfect cherry blossom and finding truth at all times. He is constantly in a state of presence seeing beauty in life. The Japanese call this 'Kannagara No Michi'. Kannagara means the stream of God, and this is an intuitive way of life that strives for truth and reality which is God (Saotome, 1986). Do you understand the reference now of being present and not having attachments pull you away from finding truth?'

'Sure, I guess there has to be a balance. I appreciate the examples around presence; this is beautiful. Bu is love, what a wonderful thought. I guess one can work on being present in all moments, with family, at work, right?'

'Yes, exactly, clearing your mind and being present is truth. Your intuitive self will lead you and your expression will be love.

I love the thought of Bu. I named my dog *Bu*. Everyone else thought he was a ghost, but I was reminded of this message of love all day long. People are often confused by the concept of a peaceful, or Zen warrior. This is where this comes from. A Zen warrior is in conflict with themselves, to find peace, harmony, truth. They have a mission toward perfection, toward this connection with the divine. I smile when I think of this concept as it is so powerful to me. In reality, these warriors are fighting the mind and, as I mentioned before, this little green guy is very persistent. As you become aware of the strength of the mind, you will find it is not only a daily battle but you will laugh at the mind's persistence. What are your thoughts on the last passion – Vanity or Egotism?'

'Sure, people think highly of themselves. I don't see this one as relevant as some of the others,' you shrugged.

'Fair enough, these destructive passions bind to each person at different levels. However, you do not see a world, or at least the United States, as a society that is completely superficially driven?

This society is focused on how people look, what they drive, how big their house is. We spent a lot of time on this one already with respect to TV, billboards, and magazines when we discussed the inner 'you'. I am saddened that our young children idolize the skinny, drug-induced starlet in Hollywood. Why is this person idolized, because they superficially look good? Buy some diet coke and cigarettes and you have the Hollywood diet and then you too can look like a movie star. Vanity is everywhere. In essence, Vanity is an enlargement of the ego. A normal ego in a way is fine. I could not distinguish between you or I without one. In the end however, we need to let go of any ego and be connected to everything in the universe, connected to truth and thus let it completely go. In our immediate existence it is the abnormal enlargement or inflated ego where the problem exists. This is a very powerful passion and typically the last to let go out of all the passions. This green monster is very strong. This is when an individual sees themselves as the center of the universe, above others. This is where status, rank, castes, bigotry come in; the thought that 'I' as an individual am better than another living being, and 'I' deserve these things because of who 'I' am. I think we discussed in depth that this is NOT the real 'you'. This superficial, egotistical 'you' is typically driven by fear, something inside, some inadequacy that is masked through some action or belief.

I worked with a guy once who would not go to a barbeque because his gardener was going to be there. He said 'I am not going to eat with my *GARDENER*'. I thought he was kidding. I really didn't understand how an individual could believe something as drastic as this, and then I read Gandhi's biography and he was discussing his interaction with the 'Untouchables' of India and his love for these people was overshadowed by the remainder of the country's hostility and treatment of them. India, the place many consider as the most spiritual on earth, has a distinct and oppressive caste system. You are born into a status or rank just like in feudal Europe. This system has been around for thousands of years, placing an individual in a distinct social class from birth. This thinking comes from a God who discriminates and gives to certain people based on certain traits and even position in life. In this thinking, you can create societies where you take over their land, establish a belief that these people are below you and use these people and their resources for your benefit as you are above them. This is how slavery, wars, rape, oppression to women and children are built.

The book *Guns, Germs and Steele* by Jared Diamond gives a vivid account of the why and how the northern Europeans advanced and controlled the entire world, destroying people and cultures along the way. If you understand the root of this thinking you can see this egotistical point of view everywhere.

How about being an African American person in America? Malcolm X used to ask people to look up the word 'black' in the dictionary. He is right, check it out. Black in the dictionary is defined as a bunch of things, but look at some of these definitions: 'gloomy, pessimistic', 'deliberately harmful', 'disgraceful', 'sullen or hostile', 'without any morality or goodness', 'illegal'. Were you aware of this?'

You stopped walking in deep thought, 'No, I guess I haven't really thought about it.'

'No offense to you, but of course, you are white. If you are a black man or woman in America you think about it every day. Now look at the definition of white as it will blow your socks off: 'decent', 'honorable', 'dependable', 'without malice', 'fortunate', 'morally pure, innocent'.'

'Wow... I had no idea. I am speechless. I guess fortunate sums up my feelings,' you said jumping in.

We began to walk down the path again engrossed in the conversation, completely unaware of the chaos surrounding us.

'Egotism manifests through self assertion, bigotry, displays of wealth or power, status, showcasing titles and degrees, and public speeches for the extent of showing off self.' I said. 'The 'I' is manifested everywhere. It is the person that says 'OK, let's talk about me.' This passion consumes a person into believing they are never at fault, nor do they have any imperfections; the fault is always another. The one big assumption of this passion is 'I am right, and those that oppose me are wrong, and to sustain this way of thinking I must destroy my competition.' Can you think of any examples on this one?'

'Hmmm... Let me think about it.' You paused looking up to the sky in deep thought.

'Any political examples?' I asked again.

'Oh, I am getting your hint now. You mean the famous George Bush quote, 'Either you are with us or you are against us'?'

'Ding! Ding! Ding! Bonus points, you got it. This is an easy one, but if you are aware of this concept you will hear and see this everywhere. It is pervasive and consuming. The mind is like fire as it is a good servant but very destructive when it is out of control. Until we exhibit the humility and understanding that all living beings are the same as the rest of us and we are all connected, we will suffer through this destructive passion. We will always want more. More power, more money, better looks, higher rank. It doesn't end until you destroy this illusion. We must lose judgment in order to have selfless love. If I have no attachment and belief that I am better than any other living being then I can live in harmony, live in truth. The first step is awareness; awareness of these destructive passions; awareness of the inflated ego; awareness of the fear that drives this behavior.'

I stopped talking to catch my breath and allowed the two of us to walk in silence for a few minutes. I was giving you a lot of information and I was worried it was too much all at once. We turned the corner and headed south on the final leg of our lap around the lake. As we neared the parking lot, I checked in with you, 'How are you holding up?'

'I am hanging in there,' you said with a sigh. 'Physically I am fine, however, I had no idea how much emotionally these conversations would take out of me. Where do we go from here?'

I smiled understanding the weight of these conversations. I had gone through your experience before in feeling the emotional weight of the world upon you as you try to break free in a spiritual birth. 'Well, once we have awareness with our mind in its destructive form we need to understand tools we can use along the journey, the tools of positive intent, words and action. From here we will discuss how to actually take the journey in cleansing our mind and body and then actually tuning into the vibration of the divine. However, I think we have taken in a lot today, why don't we hold off until Monday?'

'OK, this sounds good. I could use a break to absorb some of these thoughts.' You said lacking energy.

'OK, I think we covered the main concepts with the mind out of control. It is important to understand this major obstacle in our path to truth. I will send you a meeting request on Monday when we are both free. Agreed?'

'Agreed, see you Monday.'

You slowly walked off toward the parking lot; your head was down looking at your feet, deep in thought. You crossed the street without looking for any traffic, got in your car and drove away.

I sat back down near the dock at the small craft center awash in light and with the wind on my face. Various teams were stretching and motivating each other near the shore ready to launch their shell and start training. I watched a crew already on the water head into the final leg of their training run some fifty feet off the shore. The coxswain called out the tempo over and over again pushing the team to maximum effort getting the most of each moment until the team crossed the finish line completely in the *zone*, at peace with the integrity of their effort and with just being. They collapsed from exhaustion indifferent to any stimulus, alone in their own existence.

I smiled in this moment embracing everything, the sights and sounds of the boat, the team, the smell of the water, the warmth of the sun, and feel of the wind. I close my eyes blessed for this moment, smiled and walked away.

Chapter 4

Fear

Monday came with a great deal of consternation. I hadn't slept much since we spoke on Saturday morning. I couldn't get the monkey out of my own mind. My own little Hulk was taking over. I guess revisiting these topics gave the mind something to grasp onto away from a state of peace, almost as if it was trying to justify itself, or rationalize its unruly behavior.

My mind had been dwelling on the destructive passions and the source or fuel that drove these passions. I was intent on discussing this major instigator in the mind being out of control and wanted to discuss this with you as soon as possible. I checked our schedules and found the first available slot for both of us at three in the afternoon. I sent off an urgent mail to you, 'meet me at the Lenin statue at 3 pm, important topic to discuss!'

You immediately replied, 'see you there, can't wait.'

I struggled through my busy day as I had so many things on my mind that I needed to discuss. My day sped through in a daze until I burst out of the office and practically ran to our meeting. I grabbed a couple of teas for us to drink and took a seat under the shadow of the 16 foot high bronze statue of Vladimir Lenin.

This cold war relic was nearly turned into a bronze scrap heap in the middle of the Soviet's Perestroika movement in the 1980's only to be saved by a Seattle English teacher who saw the historical and creative value of the piece. The Lenin statue had now become a centerpiece of the eccentric Fremont neighborhood, leering over a central downtown intersection.

I embraced the air outside, happy to be out of my office and peered up at Lenin hovering above me like a giant marionette.

He was in mid stride and positioned on the move to show the progress of the Communist party. I pondered the use of symbols in our society and how the mind grasped onto certain ideals to push one's agenda. I snapped out of my daydream to notice you walking across the street and upon your arrival I handed you a cup of tea and we both sat down.

'Thank you for the tea, what's on your mind? You sounded like you needed to get something off your chest.' You said.

You looked tired and withdrawn. I guessed this was from the weight of our conversations. 'I do, I have been thinking a lot of the mind and its destructive tendencies. I have been thinking a lot of the root of its destructive behavior and I keep coming back to one core element or fuel that pushes the mind off balance.'

'Yeah, what's this?'

'The fuel that typically drives the destructive passions and desires, the instigator of the little green Hulk if you will is *FEAR*. I wanted to make sure we discuss this topic at a deeper level. It is important to both recognize when you feel fear within yourself, but also when you feel fear and guilt used as a tactic on you. Fear is an instrument of the mind to keep control. If you look at any of the destructive passions or desires in general, fear is usually the gasoline thrown on the fire. Let's take jealousy as an example. What do you think is ultimately driving this?'

'Possession... Control... Right?' You said jumping in.

'Sure, these are components of jealousy. At a deeper level, jealousy is driven by fear within you. Fear that you might lose someone you care about. Fear that they might choose another person to be with. Fear that you are inadequate. Fear that you might not be able to 'control' the situation or the individual. Right? Life is a little scary in the status quo world when you cannot control it. With this fear, the mind is going to implement strategies, manipulations, lies, anything to keep the world permanent in this illusion. Remember, this is the Buddhist concept behind ignorance in clinging to the static, permanence of life.

Life is not permanent. Life and the world change. One must flow with this change to be in harmony with it. If my partner in life chooses to be with another, I can do nothing about this. This is their choice. This is their path in life. Sure, I will be hurt by this but in the end this person does not define me, nor do they ultimately create my happiness. To love, one must truly let go.

As I mentioned a few days ago, one must let go of all attachments and thus one will love everything. I cannot control life. I can only flow with it and understand the beauty in everything the universe provides. My happiness comes from within myself. Once you come to peace with this, life becomes very easy. No external circumstance or person will upset you as this peace and harmony can only come from within. I alone choose my existence. If you come from this place in life and you are connected to everything else then fear dissipates. There is no need for fear. There is no fire to fuel these destructive passions. All relationships are just additive to this state. Does this make sense?'

'Sure it makes sense, but as mentioned before it is much more difficult to practice than a theoretical discussion.'

'As I have said, this is your journey; you either do or you do not. It is simply your choice. Saying it is too hard is simply the mind putting out doubt to keep the existing illusion intact. Guilt is a major component the mind uses to establish this doubt. I was recently having a discussion with a woman who held onto a marriage for many years through abuse, through a husband that could not shake an addiction to alcohol, through lies, all because of her guilt in what her family would think if she divorced her husband. In her mind, she had 'stood before God and everybody' in this marriage commitment. She felt as though she was quitting; she felt as though she would be punished by God and judged by her family. This is an interesting example as I am not suggesting you leave a marriage or a relationship at the first conflict or difficulty. However, if you have given a full commitment and effort and in the end you still have an environment that keeps you from peace, from love, from truth, then this decision is fully understandable. As I mentioned before, this life, this human life, is such a precious gift we must make the most of it. If you have an obstacle to your purpose, your path in life, then in the end you choose to let go of your purpose, or let go of this obstacle.

We need to live without fear of judgment from others. I will talk a lot about judgment and removing this from within ourselves to cleanse our mind; however, we also must live without fear of judgment from others and be the best possible person at all times. If you come from your heart, from your inner self full of integrity and love, then you cannot ask for more. Either way we need to love a person exactly the way they are, no judgment. All decisions in a person's life were made with the best possible intent at that time. If another person judges you for your actions remember this is not your choice; it is their inner little Hulk driving this reaction. You can only control yourself. Once you are aware of this you will notice fear and guilt as a tactic all the time. These controls are used to 'eliminate the competition' to one person's beliefs as we mentioned earlier around the inflated ego. Thoughts?'

'Again, this is a tough one, as we care about what others think of us, in particular our family. This is just human nature, isn't it?' You asked.

'Again, I would argue this is the mind fueled by fear. This is the 5 or 6 identity rating that you mentioned the other day. This is feeling that either you are inadequate or someone else believes you are inadequate. Listen again to the words of Lao Tzu in the Tao Te Ching:

'Chase after money and security
and your heart will never unclench
care about people's approval
and you will be their prisoner.' (Mitchell, 1988)

From my point of view, I am a 10 and always will be a 10, full of love and integrity. If another cannot accept me, then I cannot help them. I will still love them exactly the way they are, and, sure we will all make mistakes along the path, but love is acceptance. Love is forgiveness. Love is gratitude. Just like you will love your children no matter what they do in life, our love for another individual or living being is exactly the same. We are all perfect, exactly the way we are supposed to be. If I understand this then I can love freely. I can love everything. The path toward truth and finding the inner 'you' will expose this. At some point, you will not care if another judges you. It will not bother you in the least. You will not hold bitterness, or anger toward this person. You will accept and love them exactly the way they are.'

'I guess you are right. I would love to be in this space where I can feel confident enough to feel this way. I know this is the right path; I just have not been able to feel this way,' you said.

'Of course, don't beat yourself up. I have had and still do have these feelings. Just remember this is the little green guy trying to pull you away from love. Rule number one is to stop judging yourself. You are beautiful and full of love. Our mind is holding onto what it has been told is correct, or ethical, or without sin, indifferent to our intuitive voice inside. The previous example of the woman not wanting to leave her husband was driven by her background, her belief that God would judge her if she divorced her husband after her commitment to God, to her family which was inside of a church no less. Not to keep beating the same drum, but as you will see, these examples come up all the same time with the Western monarchical mind versus an intuitive mind in harmony with a changing, flowing universe. Fear in itself, like your ego, is normal. Fear, inflated by or corresponding to the ego, is not.'

'What do you mean that fear is normal?'

'Well, fear is a natural instinct to protect our physical self. You know – Geez, there is a bear or tiger over there. I should probably walk or run in a different direction. It gave us the fight or flight mechanism to survive. However, abnormal fears associated with the out of control mind oppress us. It is these fears that I am referring.

These could be as simple as fears that curb our behavior within ourselves. For example, as I mentioned earlier, I know people that are scared to eat or go to the movies alone. When pressed further, I find this fear relates to what other people will think of them. They feel that others will judge, or feel sorry for them. This thought is a blow to their ego. They are scared to put themselves out there for others to judge. Fear could also limit ones life by altering behavior. For example, a person scared of dogs, or scared of heights will alter their lifestyle because of this ingrained fear. Public speaking has been rated higher than death as a fear within an individual. Can you believe this?'

'Yes, I can believe it. I can do it, but I typically avoid it unless I have to.'

'Why? Because someone might judge you, or in reality, you might judge yourself?'

'I haven't really thought about it. I just know what I feel when I get up there, and it is not fun.'

'I understand. I used to feel the same way. I was terrible and I was terrified. I felt so controlled by this fear that I insisted on finding comfort in public speaking so I confronted it directly by joining Toastmasters and other speaking clubs or classes. Now, I am at least serviceable, but more importantly, I am comfortable. I consistently evaluate my fears to understand the root of them and to develop strategies to eliminate. I do not want to be controlled by anyone or anything in my life. Life is beautiful and pure.

There is no room for negative energy or fear in my life. This is the choice I am making. How about external fears? Do you ever feel like someone or something is trying to use fear to get you to act in a certain way?'

'I am sure this happens all over; however, my vivid thought of fear used upon me was in Sunday school with the discussion around the devil. You know, 'The devil will get you'; 'You will burn in HELL'. 'You better do this and do that', and so on. I would have nightmares of this big, red, very scary devil chasing me. I can still see the horns. Look at my arms; I have goose pimples right now. I would dream I was being burned alive in *HELL*. I would wake up in a sweat. Wow, I guess I see your point about control. Look at me, twenty-five plus years later and it still invokes a vivid emotion in me,' you said softly.

'You used one of the best examples, as very often religion uses fear as the basis of their playbook. It is a very compelling way to control. Ultimately, this is about control. It is very hard to implement a good marketing plan if those darn people keep asking questions and thinking independently. Can you imagine? People thinking for themselves – crazy, right?'

'Yes, crazy, imagine that. I actually remember asking questions either in Sunday school or regular school and getting chastised for this. 'Stop questioning', they would say. 'Just believe what you are told'. I guess I didn't fully realize the product of control.'

'Oh, it is bigger than you can imagine.' I paused in reflection. I looked up toward the sky and lower profile of Lenin and then looked at you and nodded upward. 'The entire concept of control is epitomized within the culture that originated with this big guy here,' I said nodding at Lenin. 'I think everyone should read George Orwell's book, *1984*, as this premise is fully explored. This book breaks down this playbook of fear, of control really well. Are you familiar with this one?'

'I remember this one from school; however, I cannot

remember if we read this or not.'

'The premise of this book is a look inside of a communist state, and how the government controls the people. The central character works in a place called the Ministry of Truth where all news is distributed. These people in this Ministry of Truth lie, embellish and manipulate the news to control the people. Even the name Ministry of Truth invokes a feeling of control as this place is the emitter of lies. They use billboards to convince people of things like 'freedom = slavery', and 'ignorance = strength', as the truth. It was a crime to actually think. You were put to death for these thought crimes. A war was always going on, against whom no one could even remember. The people were led to believe that they needed 'Big Brother', the government, to protect them. There was even a slight indication that the government was actually bombing their own people; could this be possible? The most interesting point to me about this book was when the central character asks a question concerning all the general people out there; if they would just rise up then they could have their real freedom. This character, Winston, was told that controlling the people, the 'Proles' in this case, was easy, just give them their beer, and their sports (football), and the threat that they need protection from 'Big Brother' and they will not question, as it is assumed this is just the way things are supposed to be. This book will blow your socks off. You will begin to see this playbook everywhere.'

I paused taking a deep breath and inhaled with a sip of tea content in my metaphor.

You looked Lenin and then me up and down clearly wanting more. 'Like where? Give me an example.'

'OK, it seems to me the administration in the White House here in the early part of the 21st century uses this book as their standard operating procedure. Look at the use of color schemes and threats of attacks and war to get people to do things, even vote for bills because of this. They name things like the 'Patriot Act' and 'Freedom Fries'; this is right out of the Ministry of Truth.

Look around, it is not just our government. It is TV, movies, and more – fear is pervasive. The Michael Moore movie, *Bowling for Columbine*, explores this fear-induced society in America. Watch TV, the news, read the paper and you will see this. We have a shock-based culture that uses fear to manipulate and control. If you remember our conversation about how to combat the mind, combat the little Hulk, we can use our magic blue ball with positive intent full of selfless love. Reading the newspaper and watching the majority of TV and movies promotes the opposite thought inside of us. It brings in anger, fear, bitterness, violence, all destructive forces. We need to remove these from our thought patterns to stay in a state of peace, a state of love, a state of truth.

It truly is an important exercise to understand when this is happening. Only *YOU* can control YOU. Be curious; be aware of fear and the destructive passions. These points are essential to stay in a state of truth. Our thoughts become us. It is our ability, our choice, to produce a positive environment full of truth. If you are not in a state of love, if you are full of fear, full of the destructive passions, it is your choice to change this and be in a state of harmony.

One of my favorite quotes comes from the Tao Te Ching; it addresses leadership and talks about one of the worst type of leaders – those that lead out of fear. Listen to this beautiful quote:

'When the Master governs
the people are hardly aware that he exists.
Next best is a leader who is loved,
next, one who is feared.
The worst is one who is despised.
If you don't trust the people, you make them untrustworthy.
The Master doesn't talk, he acts.
When his work is done, the people say, 'Amazing: we did it, all by ourselves!' (Mitchell, 1988)

Beautiful, isn't it?' I asked.

'Yes, this is great.'

'The Tao Te Ching talks quite a bit about fear,' I said. 'Here are a few more passages:

'When we don't see the self as self
what do we have to fear?' (Mitchell, 1988)

And another:

'Whoever can see through all fear will always be safe.' (Mitchell, 1988)

'I have seen many people and environments that use fear to control the situation or the individual. I have seen individuals use fear to control another human being; I have seen this in business, and I have seen this in politics consistently. I see this in the media everyday as this sells newspapers and ad space. I, myself, have been consumed by this. I was caught up in the debate prior to the Iraq war and found myself reading and listening to as many newspapers, websites and radio talk shows as possible. I was spending three to four hours a day on this exercise. I filled myself with anger, frustration, bitterness, outrage. I had trouble sleeping. I finally understood what was happening to me. Like a huge wave, I was surfing this monster negative energy swell. It truly consumed me, oppressed me. I was not in a place of love, a place of truth. I immediately stopped all this activity. To this day, I will just browse the paper for interesting articles. If I find that I am being pulled away from a place of love, a place of truth, then I stop. I will not allow another to put me in this state. This is my choice.'

I stopped here letting you have a moment. Lenin continued his dominance over the two of us, casting a shadow across our bodies. The street in front of us was a main thoroughfare between

Fremont and the adjoining neighborhood to the west called Ballard. The afternoon traffic was beginning to pick up on the street and the noise escalated in turn. You shifted in your seat putting together a question.

You sat upright confident in your thought and asked, 'doesn't this make you feel helpless? I mean, in a way you are being controlled, controlled in the fact that really the only information coming out is negative, and fear induced. From my point of view it looks as though those oppressing are winning if you ignore their action.'

'Well, the reality is that nothing can control me unless I let it. Think again of Viktor E. Frankl's *Man's Search of Meaning*. These people were in full oppression yet felt free as they refused to give up their attitude, their positive intent in life. They refused to let fear and oppression overtake them.

Our attitude is the ultimate choice in life. No one can take this from you unless you let them. Someone can physically hurt you, manipulate you, even take your life, but in the end, they have taken nothing from you. The inner you, full of positive, vibrant energy and love, will never die; it will just transform into something else. Thus, they can take nothing from you. You are in complete control. With this, just like the mind, fear becomes comical. However, you have brought up a valid discussion around the oppressed 'winning' if I choose to ignore it. This is worthy of more discussion. From the big picture, no one wins, everything is impermanent. Everything will change one day. Those in control will not control in the future. Life is a cycle in constant change. Every oppressor has eventually died off, from the Egyptians, to the Greeks, to the Romans. Look at this statue, not that long ago Russia was known as the dominant, world power Soviet Union and 'controlled' Eastern Europe.

Look at these words from Chief Seattle in 1851 toward the white people buying the surrounding Native American land:

'You must teach your children that the ground beneath their feet is the ashes of our grandfathers. So that they will respect the land, tell your children that the earth is rich with the lives of our kin. Teach your children that we have taught our children that the earth is our mother. Whatever befalls the earth befalls the sons of earth. If men spit upon the ground, they spit upon themselves. This we know; the earth does not belong to man; man belongs to the earth. This we know. All things are connected like the blood, which unites one family. All things are connected. Even the white man, whose God walks and talks with him as friend to friend, cannot be exempt from the common destiny. We may be brothers after all. We shall see. One thing we know which the white man may one day discover; our God is the same God. You may think now that you own Him as you wish to own our land; but you cannot. He is the God of man, and His compassion is equal for the red man and the white. The earth is precious to Him, and to harm the earth is to heap contempt on its creator. The whites too shall pass; perhaps sooner than all other tribes. Contaminate your bed and you will one night suffocate in your own waste.'[2]

This cycle has been true since the beginning of time; the oppressors will too one day fall. Ultimately I can only control myself and lead by this example. With this I look at the true meaning of wealth and how I can give back beyond setting an example within myself. The words of the Tao Te Ching exemplify this:

'The Master has no possessions
The more he does for others
The happier he is.
The more he gives to others
The wealthier he is.'(Mitchell, 1988)

I can lead by example within myself and give through love. This love will lead to selfless giving to those that cannot help themselves. In this I cannot be oppressed. I cannot be controlled. Fear is powerless to love.'

I stopped here to catch my breath and took in the energy of the moving vehicles and people. I looked at you and smiled. I felt a connection between us, a bond that can only be understood by those upon this journey toward truth. You smiled back still in reflection upon my words.

Checking my watch I shook my head. 'We are making a habit out of this,' I smiled.

You laughed and stood to stretch your legs. 'I have to run and pick up my boys,' you said. 'I do want to continue on this thread of our discussion. I feel like we are in the middle and I can't stop now.' You shrugged, 'what's next?'

'Well, we explored how the mind out of control is fueled by fear and is our major obstacle to truth. We need to get to how to quiet this mind through meditation and the tools we can use along our path. As I have mentioned, one of our tools on this journey is the magic blue ball. Our magic blue ball is using positive intent, positive words, and positive actions. Intent, words and actions are very important to understand as these could be either a tool or an obstacle depending on your approach and attitude. So, exploring this further is what's next?'

As we briskly walked back to the office, your mind seemed distant and cluttered. I imagined you were concerned with getting to your boys on time. I let the silence hover over both of us until we arrived at the parking garage where I put an offer out to you, 'I am slammed at work for the next couple of days prepping for an upcoming trip. Why don't we take a breather until Thursday late afternoon? Is there any way you can stay a little later after work, we can run our meeting into appetizers and coffee somewhere. How does this sound?'

'This sounds great; I will make plans for someone to pick up my boys for me on Thursday night, this is perfect. Thank you again, I really appreciate all of the time you are giving me.' You waved at me on your way into the garage.

'I give nothing to you; I only share with you as you do with me. In this, we are present with each other, and I am grateful.' I called out to you.

You smiled and rushed to your car.

Chapter 5

Positive Intent, Positive Words, Positive Action

Tuesday and Wednesday were a blur. I was heads down planning for a business trip to Edinburgh, Scotland the following week. In addition, I was on the verge of a big decision in my life and I needed time alone to ensure if this was the right decision or not. I volunteered for the Scotland trip for this very reason.

I didn't think much about our meeting until Thursday morning when it hit me we had plans in the late afternoon to continue our discussion. I sent you an e-mail late morning asking if you could pick me up outside of the Interurban Sculpture on 34th near the Fremont Bridge. My last words were 'Fieldtrip, let's take curiosity on the road…..I will tell you where we are going at three, see you then, Thomas.'

You immediately responded, 'of course, see you at three.'

I had asked you to drive as I knew I would be running back and forth between meetings and in my case between buildings in the afternoon. Rather than running all the way back to the office I chose a notable spot to meet that was convenient to quickly jump in the car. I arrived a few minutes early and explored the artwork in front of the intersection. It was a piece of art called *Waiting for the Interurban* featuring five cast aluminum human statues and a curious dog waiting for the now defunct interurban light rail train. The statue was noteworthy as locals continuously dressed up the characters in various attire ranging from birthday hats to team colors to poetic or very often political statements. The statues were a constant topic of discussion in our office with only one sentence needed to prompt a reply, 'so, what are *they* wearing today?' This question did not need description and always brought a smile.

Today, the statues were bare of any messages outside of the artist's creative intent. I looked at the bland, nondescript faces of the statues staring blindly with their eyes open and their feet stuck aimlessly in the ground. They looked lifeless and even confused as statues should; however, I began to see the resemblance to many of the 'living' people in this world walking by me on the street and in life.

Perusing the artwork, I froze in my spot. Peering between the legs of the people was the perfect body of an attentive dog with a *human* face, beard and all. I had heard of the rumor that the sculptor, Richard Beyer, modeled this face after the unofficial mayor in the early Fremont days, Arman Napoleon Stephanian, the pioneer of modern day curbside recycling.

Whoever's face it was on this statue it certainly woke me up from my slumber the past few days. As I inspected the human face on the dog my mind was drawn to the Karmic wheel, the continuous cycle of birth and death from one living creature to another until one frees themselves from this illusion of the permanence in life. In a way, the human faced dog reminded me of the monster or demon that the cosmic dancer Lord Shiva, in his divine dance Nataraja, stepped on to rid the world of ignorance, of self and the persistent ego. I smiled in the thought of Shiva with his upper right hand holding a small drum symbolizing the sound or vibration from the origin of creation, his far left hand held fire representing destruction and death, his middle right hand held the gesture of assertion representing 'be without fear', while his final middle left hand pointed to his raised foot representing liberation.

Shiva represented this endless cycle of suffering and illusion unless one can liberate, and in this case 'squash' the demon of ignorance immersed in the desires of the mind that cling to the permanence of a static world. My mind drifted in thought now convinced this dog was the demon of ignorance.

I snapped out of my trance with a honk from a bus, the doors opened and the driver asked if I was getting on. I smiled and shook my head no. As the bus drove off, I decided to have a little fun before you arrived by placing my coat and scarf on one of the statues. Next, I stood to the rear as if I was a late addition to the group. A few cars slowed and took notice driving by with looks wondering if I had officially 'lost it', until finally, a silver BMW SUV slowly drove up and your head stretched out from the driver side window. You scanned the statues, smiled and finally spotting me called out, 'hop in Mr. Comedian.'

I grabbed my scarf and coat and jumped in the passenger side door.

'Where to?' You said nodding my way.

'Top of Queen Anne hill, on Queen Anne Ave.' I pointed across the bridge and up the adjacent hill called Queen Anne just south of Fremont.

You made your way up the steep road, zigzagging past ornate Victorian style homes and magnificent oak trees. Your car was meticulous on the outside but well worn on the inside, an obvious takeover by your two boys, with toys, DVD's, and food covering your back seat.

Catching me inspecting your car, you called out, 'sorry my car is so dirty.'

'It is of no difference to me. Remember, I have kids too. I am still trying to dislodge a sticky substance out of the back drink holder in my car.' I said.

We made our way onto the main street of the Queen Anne neighborhood past numerous restaurants, yoga studios and coffee shops. Queen Anne was the sophisticated neighborhood in Seattle sitting next to the Space Needle and on top of the hill holding a 360 degree view of the water, mountains and city all in one. This community housed a more professional, upscale population indifferent to the other adjacent 'city' neighborhoods like eccentric Fremont and the gay and counter culture hub Capitol Hill.

'OK, where are we headed?' You called out snapping me out of my day dream.

'Park anywhere, we are going to a café right up the street.'

You backed in your BMW to an available parking spot and we walked up the sidewalk.

'Here it is,' I called out, 'El Diablo Coffee Company.'

'Are you trying to tell me something?' You said with a half kidding, half truth smirk.

'Ha ha....funny, well, in truth since our topic today is about the influence of intent, words and action I thought this place would appropriately set the tone for us today. Besides after your Sunday school story and how the image of the devil and hell brought fear to you, I thought we could address this head on.' I said smiling opening the door.

You ordered a café Cubano to go along with my decaf soy Mocha, causing you to tilt your head, 'you are not one of those guys are you?'

I nodded with indifference. 'Yep, I am one of those decaf, soy, no whip guys.'

We grabbed two cozy sofa seats seat as you eyeballed me looking for any more surprises and sipped our coffee taking in the essence of the café. El Diablo billed itself as the only Latin style coffee shop in Seattle complete with Latin food and drinks. The walls were filled with vivid murals most with bright red flames, and some sort of a devil image.

I nodded to one of the murals, 'that is the café's mascot, Bettie.'

Bettie was a painting of a cute girl devil with a long tail, bobbed hair cut and spiky horns drinking an espresso as if she was at one of the tables.

I looked around at the rest of the café, devils and skulls were artistically painted on the top of tables and trash cans throughout. In the back corner of the café was the 'Love Grotto' an area sheltered from most of the café filled with a loveseat and huge mural of kissing cupids below a banner of the famous Latin song *Bésame Mucho* (Kiss me a lot) by Consuelo Velazquez.

Feeling our small talk was coming to an end, I jumped back into our conversation from our last meeting. 'A few days ago I brushed on the topic of intentions, words and actions along the path. I discussed how these can either be a tool or an obstacle. All of this is dependent on choice. Our paths are a product of choice. Our thoughts and intentions are a choice that ultimately becomes action. In action we choose to lift ourselves and thus others up or we can choose to bring ourselves or others down. Words are tools we use in conjunction with our choice. In this they either inspire or destruct. Buddha stated this very clearly:

'All that we are is the result of what we have thought.
If a man speaks or acts with evil thought, pain follows him.
If a man speaks or acts with pure thought, happiness follows him,
like a shadow that never leaves him.'

I paused sipping my coffee engrossed in the energy of the café. 'Let me ask you something, do you remember this quote? *Worms, Roxanne... Worms.*'

'Yes, the movie with Steve Martin... Roxanne. Very funny,' you said.

'Right, the character Chris in the movie was supposed to be saying 'Words, Roxanne, Words.' This is a great example of the importance and potential destruction that can be caused through wrong intent, words and action. So many conflicts, from wars to marital disputes, are started because of negative intent, miscommunication, assumptions and lack of clarity in speech. Intent, words, and action are the byproduct of our state of being.

Remember, we are what we think. If our goal is to be a vibrant beacon of positive energy, love, and truth, then we must emit this energy, this frequency, out to the universe. Quieting the mind is the vehicle to this state of presence at all times. The magic blue ball is the exercise to make the mind aware that the inner 'you' is conscious that the little green Hulk is getting unruly, and for the inner 'you' to emit selfless love. If the mind is controlled by the senses and the destructive forces are filling your thoughts, your words, your actions, then you will receive back the same energy you emit. If you are filled with anger and jealousy, then you will receive this same energy back. This was the main premise in the book, *The Secret*. Did you read this book?'

'No, but I've heard about it', you said.

You sat back in your chair getting comfortable. I smiled inside knowing you have now grown accustomed to our 'talks' and these were not short conversations. These conversations needed to find their own way without structure, with the openness of a child seeing things for the first time. They were not black and white nor did they have a time limit.

'The concept for *The Secret* has been around for thousands of years and was put into a current perspective very well in this book and movie. The secret is, in a way, the magic blue ball. You can fill this ball with any thought and thus it will be a reality. This is the important point. Do you want to fill your intent, your manifestations, with instigating the destructive passions? Do you want to fill your energy with attachment to material things and purposeless tasks away from truth? I laugh when I watch this movie and some have filled their magic blue ball with getting good parking spaces, or in having the biggest house on the block. Again, I choose not to judge, but we have this gift in this human form to connect to the Divine, to connect to love. If we are connected to love, there is no greater gift. Does this make sense?' I asked.

'Yes.'

'The book and movie did talk about connecting to the universe, to a state of love; it wasn't all from a superficial standpoint. There were a lot of good messages in the book and movie. In order for us to connect to this state of love and quiet the mind we must understand how to take this path and the obstacles along the way. My goal is to fill the intent in my magic blue ball with love, with truth at all times. As I said, there is no greater gift to me. In this state of love, I am connected to the universe. All doors open. I am everything. Life is beautiful. Understanding the importance of positive intent, positive words, and positive action are instrumental in reaching this state. If we do not use this tool, this magic blue ball, in the appropriate way then this intent, these words and actions are simply an extension of the destructive passions driven by fear. Are you following me?'

'I understand what you are saying. Give me some examples around intent and words used to fuel the destructive passions,' you said.

'OK, let's talk about it. Intent is very important to understand. We have mentioned this a few times, but I will state again, intent takes the same energy as actually speaking or acting on the thought, thus, to the Universe, intent is the same as actually doing the act.

In India, they have elaborate spiritual plays where men play both the men and women parts. The reason is to limit the possibility of accruing negative karma that may occur if women are on the stage. Even though no action has taken place, men may fill their minds with desire while watching a play filled with women. I would argue that to control these desires, this intent, then one must quiet the mind instead of removing the potential desire. You cannot run from the destructive passions.

Sure, you can go live in a cave away from society and feel a perfect state of bliss, but in the end you cannot run from your mind. You cannot hide; these destructive passions are always with you. They will find you eventually unless you quiet them from within, changing your environment can only assist in creating a more positive atmosphere. Ultimately, the environment is meaningless. If you conquer the mind, you conquer the environment, you conquer everything. Remember the Guru Nanak quote, 'conquer the mind and you conquer the world.' In addition, once you remove yourself from the cave and reenter society then the Matrix will always be in full effect with the sensory overload persistent in controlling the mind. You cannot run from this. You have to battle this within yourself and bring in love. Love is the supreme law; the senses cannot compete with this. You have to remember that thoughts are things. The anger, lust, or any other desire that you hold in your heart controls you. You cannot connect or emit love when you hold this negative intent or action. Thoughts?'

'Again, the discussion is practical and makes sense, but to apply is difficult. These just come up... I know... I know, we either do or we don't, right?'

'Close enough,' I said laughing. 'Remember, this is part of the journey. It is not easy. It takes time to quiet the mind and fill yourself with love. Do not beat yourself up; you are perfect in your best way right now. You are putting forth positive energy this moment and I am blessed to be near you. Thank you.'

'You know a few days ago you made similar comments and I could not understand where this love, this positive gratitude, was coming from. I may not be in this state of mind yet, but I understand where this is coming from. It is a choice made by you, and in this, I too, am thankful,' you said.

'Yes! I am so glad you see this. I am blessed for your awareness and curiosity. Thank you.' I paused in reflection sipping my coffee smiling at you for your awareness. 'Now, in addition to intent, I want to discuss words, as very similar to intent, words are either an extension of our fear and destructive passions or they are an extension of love. We either bring others up or bring others down with them. This is simply our choice in life. Buddha stated, as one proposes to speak, ask yourself; is it true? Is it necessary? Is it kind? (Johnson, 1939)

The Tao Te Ching comments on the importance of words, or non words:

'Those who know don't talk
Those who talk don't know.' (Mitchell, 1988)

I think about this quote a lot because it comes up so often for me in being around other people. I think sometimes people just like to hear themselves talk, to build upon their ego. I think they are, in turn, afraid of silence, because in silence they have to interface with the 'real person' inside and not the artificial role created persona they wrap around themselves in a cloak. You remember the Alanis Morrissette song *All I Want*? The lyrics touch on this point:

'Why are you so petrified of silence?
Here can you handle this? (SILENCE)
Did you think about your bills, your ex, your deadlines,
Or when you think you're gonna die,
Or did you long for the next distraction?'

Words hold context or connotation for people. They have a defined literal meaning but they also hold specific context to each individual. For example, I might say 'you look skinny' or I might say 'you look slender'. In the dictionary these might have very familiar definitions; however, they could be perceived as one positive and one negative. Add tone or inflection to these words and you can really create a stir. A study by Robert W. Schrauf showed that people express more negative than positive words.[3] He did this study across two different countries and asked the individuals to write as many words in two minutes that expressed emotion. After the two minutes he had them rate whether they felt each word was positive, negative or neutral. Over fifty percent of the responses in the study were of negative words, thirty percent were positive words, and the final twenty percent were neutral. I think this research is a testament to the power of the little green Hulk. Our senses control the mind and in turn we output constant negative energy.

We are inundated with this negative energy from everywhere. We see this insistently from other human beings. We see this across all forms of media from print, to video games, to movies, to TV. It has been estimated that by the age of eighteen, the average person will have viewed 200,000 acts of violence on TV alone.[4] The American Psychology Association has studies that show a typical child in America watches roughly 28 hours of television per week, and by the time a child finishes elementary school at age eleven they have seen as many as 8000 murders.[5]

Now, take this and add in violent music, movies and video games, and our existence in the Matrix is consumed by violence and negative energy. Again, remember we are our thoughts. If our thoughts are constantly in a state of disruption filled with anger, jealousy, violence, and lust, to name a few, then we are continually away from truth, away from a state of love. As mentioned, we need to either remove the obstacles or let go of our purpose. Ultimately, this is the choice and the battlefield is within ourselves. We can choose to live in the Matrix, in the illusion of a life that doesn't change, and thus suffer deep within ourselves; or, we flow, we adapt with the universe and under-stand the impermanence of all things, the interconnectedness of everything and live in truth. Have you seen the movie *What the Bleep do we know?*' I asked.

'No. I have never heard of it.'

'You should watch this; it dives into the Quantum Physics discussion we had a few days ago in addition to the role of positive intent. In one of my favorite scenes, bottles of water are innocently shown one by one. Each bottle of water was given different concentrated thought by an individual, some with positive words such as love and harmony and another with negative words such as hate, and murder. After some time with these words placed in front of the water, pictures of the molecules were taken. The bottles given positive blessings and thought had a distinctly different look than the negative bottle. They showed clarity, structure and beauty. The pictures of the molecules in the hate bottle were in complete disarray, chaotic, and not pleasant to look at.

This reminds me of another study around positive and negative energy with plants. Researchers were doing a study on the growth of plants with positive reinforcement and soothing music versus negative reinforcement and loud, rock music. They found that the plants with the positive and soothing energy thrived, and the plants from the negative environment struggled. I can recall a photo of two plants, one exposed to classical music and the other rock music. The classical music plant was upright and thriving while the rock music plant was actually growing away from the speaker, trying to get away from the vibe if you will. Other studies have shown that human IQ scores are at a higher level after listening to classical or soothing music versus rock or angry music. We are living energy; the same as the molecules of water and of the cells of a plant. Our inner being is affected in the same way to a negative environment. Thoughts?'

'A very interesting concept, but also a very new concept to me, I will need to absorb this before I can comment further. Again, the concept makes sense; I need to see the application of this change in real life scenarios.'

'Fair points, I think you will begin to see valid examples all around you now that you are aware of this concept around energy. Your example with your children from the other evening summarizes this point. Rather than choosing the energy around anger, you chose love and the result was drastically different.'

'You are right! I see your point,' you said in sudden clarity.

I rested here for a minute letting you absorb the clarity of your actions with your children. The café was beginning to fill as it looked like an event was planned for the evening. One of the baristas assisted an overweight man with a scruffy beard, black vest and matching brimmed hat and red converse hightops, in moving two chairs from the corner of the room to set up a microphone and amplifier.

I turned my attention back to you and continued the conversation. 'Negative intent and words bleed into negative action. This is an inevitable consequence of our energy. We begin to fill our thoughts with the destructive passions, we put this energy outward to other living beings, and then we act on this energy. We act entitled; we act superior; we act far away from truth. We label and stereotype other living beings. We generalize. We make assumptions. We judge.

Sit at a lunch counter or turn on the TV right now and you will hear judgment. We criticize and put others down for our own internal satisfaction. I remember reading the press coverage of Angelina Jolie at the SAG awards where Jolie was nominated for her incredible performance in the movie *A Mighty Heart*. In addition to her amazing acting in the movie, Jolie had taken on a leadership position around the globe in supporting UNICEF, the United Nations Children's Fund and had donated millions of dollars to various charities around the world. Rather than writing about these positive actions by a person with incredible depth, I read negative press contemplating how they hate her dress, speculation of her pregnancy, and the latest in her relationship with Brad Pitt. The mind is programmed to pull down, to find the negative, 'glass half full' thoughts and actions. This is unfortunate as there is so much beauty and good in this world. It is right in front of us if we are willing to see it. Again, we either bring people up, or bring people down, don't you think?'

'Yeah, but come on, this is natural. What harm is in it?' you asked.

'The harm manifests; it builds and grows until it is all too consuming, just a constant output of negative energy. Add this output from everyone else in this world and there is a lot of negative energy going around. It really is amazing when you look at it. Our life within this illusion is completely consumed with negativity. If we are all beacons of energy, we have a choice. We can output positive energy and thus receive this back, or put out negative energy and be mired in this muck, this Matrix, this illusion filled with suffering. In the book The Path of the Masters, Julian Johnson quotes one of the laws of the Masters from a philosophy called Sant Mat that applies directly to this point:

'Never criticize, never find fault, never abuse; Never blame anyone for anything either to their face or behind their back; Never hurt the feelings of anyone, man or animal; Never let a harsh or unkind word escape your lips, But speak always words of love, truth and kindness.'(Johnson, 1939)

'Pretty compelling, huh?'

'Yes, this all sounds good, but I am living in a different reality where things happen. I am beginning to feel like I am back in church again.'

'Understood, this is lot to grasp. To me it was like this unattainable perfection, kind of 'be like Jesus' message. You know what I am saying?'

'Yes. Like it is almost depressing because I know I cannot do this,' you said defeated.

'Well, we either do or we do not. This is your choice. Everything I am talking about throughout our discussion is attainable and attainable today. It is simply a choice. I look at it like this. I have a blueprint or a model that I am trying to attain. Every day I do the best I can to reach toward this blueprint. If I make mistakes I don't judge, I just move forward. Think of it this way; wouldn't you like to be around people like I am describing?'

'Of course, who wouldn't?'

'Now add in compassion and love, genuine love, and someone who is present with you and you have compelling relationships. My friendships up until recently were, at best, arm's length. We talked about sports, women, cards. We cursed, drank, and in some cases, after 25 years, I honestly don't think I knew them very well at all, at least the inner person outside of the material persona. It is sad to believe 25 years if not lifetimes go by and we do not even have a connection with these people, we do not know the most important aspect of them, their inner being. Once you realize this then you try to build this type of life, and have these types of relationships. At some point you begin making decisions in surrounding yourself with people that build on truth and love or remove those that don't. It becomes the whole 'sponge worthy' criteria with our time that we mentioned earlier?'

'I understand, but isn't our number one priority in our lives to avoid the inevitable, the thought that we are actually going to die? We mask our lives and fill it with superficial things. This is a full-time job for most people. They buy Corvettes in their fifties, add a twenty year-old blonde, get facelifts, hair implants. I mean some people even freeze themselves in the hope of coming back. It is our obsession. It can't change.'

'Ah... along with the act of JUDGEMENT, one of my least favorite words,' I jumped in with a deep sigh.

'What....Corvette?'

'No, of course not... *CAN'T!* 'Can't' is right up there as my least favorite word. I want to talk more about this word in a minute but let me first say that I understand where you are coming from and it certainly looks like these things can never stop. We are bombarded with it every day. However, in the big scheme of things, we cannot worry about this as the only thing we can control is ourselves. As I keep saying; it is our choice; we either do or we do not; this is our decision. I will not judge you either way. Have you heard about the book *The Four Agreements* by Don Miguel Ruiz?'

'It sounds familiar, but I have not read it.'

'The book is very compelling and really focuses on what we have been discussing here. Every time I begin to think of a negative word or thought, Don Miguel Ruiz's first agreement shouts into my head: 'IMPECCABLE WORDS! IMPECCABLE WORDS!' This book focuses on four simple agreements to transform your life. Listen to this summary:

'Be Impeccable With Your Word
Speak with integrity. Say only what you mean. Avoid using the word to speak against yourself or to gossip about others. Use the power of your word in the direction of truth and love.
Don't Take Anything Personally
Nothing others do is because of you. What others say and do is a projection of their own reality, their own dream. When you are immune to the opinions and actions of others, you won't be the victim of needless suffering.
Don't Make Assumptions
Find the courage to ask questions and to express what you really want. Communicate with others as clearly as you can to avoid misunderstandings, sadness and drama. With just this one agreement, you can completely transform your life.
Always Do Your Best
Your best is going to change from moment to moment; it will be different when you are healthy as opposed to sick. Under any circumstance, simply do your best, and you will avoid self-judgment, self-abuse and regret.'(Ruiz, 1997)

'Perfect, right?'

'Yes, again, all beautiful, but is it practical?' you asked.

'There is another one of my least favorite words... 'BUT'. Again, we will get to this in a minute. Let me tell you a quick story about a friend of mine. Every time she has the urge to curse

or get angry toward either herself or others she blesses them.
Funny right? I thought so at first and then I heard her a few times
and it completely transformed the energy in the room from
tension, and possible anger to peace, and calm. I still smile
hearing her bless someone that just cut her off in traffic. A little
different than 'jerk', right?'

'Point taken, I understand. It just seems so out of place. It
seems like people will start calling me a *Holy Roller* behind my
back. What do you *think*?'

'You are talking about a big issue, which at least for me took a
considerable amount of time to get over. I was extremely self
conscious of other people's opinions. I was always trying to
please or conform to fit others. I was very concerned how others
would look at me when, say, I became a vegetarian, someone who
meditates, and so on. It literally took me years. Today, I don't care
what anyone besides myself thinks, or in this case 'feels'. I specifically remember when I decided to eliminate curse words. It was
not that big of a deal at my house as I didn't do this very often
outside of some conversations with a few friends. When I quit, I
was concerned with these friends. Cursing was just part of our
speech. These were adjectives to add color to the discussions
around sports or women. I thought I would get called out right
away. At the time I decided to do this, I was already at the point
where I didn't care what they thought anyway so I forged ahead.
I just stopped cold turkey. And, you know what? Not even a
notice or comment. Can you believe this?'

'This example is not a hard one for me as I was never a big
curser anyways. My issue is subjecting it to my children as I hear
this language all the time on TV, and in music, such as Hip Hop.
It just gives a negative vibe.'

'Right, if I was a woman, I would be more than offended with
some of the language used in these songs. This is beyond disrespectful. Speaking in this way is shouting to the world 'I DO NOT
DESERVE RESPECT OR LOVE.' We have talked a lot about the

negative energy, intent and actions surrounding our interactions with people; however, we have not explored this at a deeper level outside of the persistence of the mind. Let's look deeper at the fear, or driver behind this in people. Let me ask you a question; have you ever watched Jerry Springer or a soap opera?'

'Not a soap opera fan, but I have to admit to watching *The Jerry* a few times. Why?' you asked, suddenly perking up.

'Well, any of these shows, or even the newspaper or news is geared toward misery. Remember the song about dirty laundry on the TV news? There is a reason for this. Why is it that little or no positive news is shown or written about?'

'I never really thought about it. Why?'

'There was a newspaper that tried to launch once containing only positive news and it didn't sell. Only the negative survives. I cannot turn on FOX News or even CNN as the news is simply sensationalism: 'Where is the missing white girl?' Not that this is a bad thing but there are hundreds of people missing. Let's do a show on all of them. Let's do a show on veterans from the war and the cutbacks in their disability pay. The news is handed to these networks; little to no investigative reporting is done, and all news in America is done for ratings. The networks just report off the newswire in what story will grab the most sensationalism. You know, the whole 'car wreck' theory? People have to look and their attention span is short so the next 'car wreck' is presented. The media does not get to the curiosity questions we asked in the beginning of our conversation. The 'Why is the world the way it is?' question. Or, 'Why do I feel this way?' 'Where does my food come from?' 'Why are we at war?' 'Why is the economy bad?' 'Why does the rest of the world despise American politics?' 'Why are people so angry?' Honest and open discussions with deep investigative reporting are rarely done. Media is a business. Global media is owned by roughly six individuals. They appeal to the bottom line, which is, in essence, ratings. Investigative reporting is expensive; it is too much information for our 'car wreck' attention span. We are always looking for the next wreck or storm of the century. This is the heart of the concept around *The Jerry*, as you called him. Looking deeper, I am sure you can see the destructive passions working diligently. Our inflated ego is alive and well looking down upon others. Our attachment passion is burning our 'sponge'-worthy hours on minutiae.

Exploring this concept further, I want to relate a very compelling book and sales training approach by David H. Sandler called *You Can't Teach a Kid to Ride a Bike, at a Seminar*. In his sales training, they teach something called the NOT OK technique which I will discuss in a minute as it is very interesting. David Sandler was a sales teacher who really dove into the psychology of people and how they react in certain situations.

Psychologists have begun to understand that human beings feel better about themselves when another person is suffering. It is kind of like this: Your day isn't great; you need money; you are tired; you hate your job; but you turn on Jerry Springer and – bam! – You feel better. Your life is certainly a lot better than those people on TV, having sex with both sisters, beating each other up, you name it.

Soap operas are the same concept; the news, reality TV, I could go on. We are programmed this way. It really makes us feel better to have this misery below us. On the flip side, we do not like people to be too happy. You know the ones; everything seems to be going their way, and you cannot stand it. You hear the people in the office after they leave the room. They tear them up: 'Can you believe that person, going to Hawaii again? Hawaii isn't even that great. I hope it rains the whole time.' This happens all the time. When you step back and look at it, the mind is not only obvious, but pretty comical. The mind filled with the destructive passions and the inflated ego constantly obstructs your path toward love. Coming from a place of truth, you will only want love and happiness for another living creature. What do you think?' I asked.

'This is really compelling. I have never thought about this concept before. I am kind of feeling a little like a vulture as I too have enjoyed these stories, these shows. The 'Julia Roberts really isn't that pretty' stories, you know, bring them down a notch. Wait, you didn't tell me what the NOT OK technique is?'

'Oh right, so anyways, with the starting point that we like to bring people down a notch, the opposite is also in effect; we like to rescue people if they come across in a non-threatening, suffering way. If someone is truly 'not OK', we feel better about ourselves by helping them out. David Sandler talks about the reception desk of an office where a sales person walks in looking perfect with a $1000 suit, smile and confidence to hold the world up. Well, guess what? The receptionist doesn't exactly have the best job, everybody pushing stuff down to her or him. When this 'polished' salesperson walks up to the desk and in effect talks down to her or him by saying 'I need to talk to the President', what does he or she do? They table him, throw him out, and then talk about him the rest of the day with a smile on their face. I have been in sales where this happened to me over and over again. It is not fun as the sales guy. Then I tried the Sandler 'I am not OK' approach with respect to needing to be rescued. I still do this today. Instead of walking up polished and making state-ments like 'I need this' or 'I need that', you come from a completely different approach. Walk up lost, looking disheveled; put your hands up and ask, 'I don't know if you can even help me out, but here is my situation'. It might not work, but it removes the ego from you and people want to deal with you on this basis and truly see if they can help. If they cannot help for whatever reason they will feel incredible empathy for you.

Interesting, huh?'

'I will have to try this one,' you said.

'Well, you do not want to come from an untruthful place, you are just removing the 'I need this', or 'I need that'. Mostly you are removing the 'I am entitled' persona. You will see an incredible change of character with the people you are communicating with,' I stated. 'Let's discuss key negative words that come from within ourselves such as 'ifs, buts and can'ts'. What do you think?'

'Sure.'

'Whenever my sisters or I would say 'if' or 'but', my mother would begin singing the song, 'Ifs and buts were candy and nuts… everyday would be Christmas'. I still cannot get this song out of my head; it still gets me fired up,' I said smiling. 'I just touch on this briefly, because certain words will come up in your head as you head down this journey and you need to be aware of them. Don't judge them, just notice them. You will hear them… 'If I just do this once then it will be ok', or as we have already heard, 'But, this guy cut in front of me', or 'What if my doctor says I need more sleep or to eat meat', or my personal favorite, 'I can't do that; that task is impossible'. Again, being king for a day, I would outlaw the word 'CAN'T'. Your mind sparked by your will and spirit can do anything. The inner you can accomplish anything. The word CAN'T reminds me of one of my favorite stories out of the book series *Chicken Soup for the Soul* by Jack Canfield and Mark Victor Hansen. Do you know these books?'

'Sure, these are great books. I don't remember this story though. What is it?'

'It is about a first or second grade school teacher. Her students kept repeating the words 'I can't do this', or 'I can't do that'. Finally, she had enough. She came in one day and asked them to clear their desks and take out a piece of paper. She then asked them to write everything they cannot do in their lives.

'Everything?' they asked. 'Yes,' she replied, 'everything.' I believe one boy came up and said he would need more than one piece of paper. She told him to take as many pieces of paper as needed. Once they completed writing out their 'can'ts' she asked them all to fold their papers and place them in a shoebox, where she then marched them all outside carrying a shovel. She asked for any last words for all of the things they cannot do and then they took turns digging a hole. The kids really got into it. Finally, they buried their 'can'ts' that day. Every time she would hear the words 'I can't' from them during the school year she would point to the wall where a 'R.I.P. I CAN'T' sign stood. Great story, right?'

'Good story, a little simplistic for this world though isn't it?'

'Maybe, but I bet you remember it the next time you say the words 'I can't'. If I hear any of these words, in particular the 'if I do this', I always then ask 'AND THEN WHAT'. Let me go back to your example a few minutes ago: 'If I stop cursing, then I will get called a HOLY ROLLER', remember?'

'Yes, I remember.'

'My question to you then would be 'and then what?' They call you a HOLY ROLLER, and then what happens to you? What? They chase you down the street screaming at you, 'How dare you stop cursing? How dare you?'' I said. 'When you really look at your fears they are ridiculously simple and overblown. Nothing will happen to you. At worst, you will begin to simplify your life, and surround yourself with quality people. Thoughts?'

'It makes sense. It will be hard but I see the point.'

'Again, not to state the obvious; we either do or we do not. Just as we discussed the importance in awareness around fear and guilt; awareness around negative energy is just as important – both from outside toward us, and within us, understanding that we are our thoughts, and, thus we need to remove the external obstacles, or change our energy within. It is this simple.

The magic blue ball is our tool. Control it and the world is yours. Truth and love are the result.'

I stopped here mentally tired in exploring the destructive mind and the instigator of fear. The café was buzzing now. The brimmed hat, red tennis shoe man popped up to the microphone and introduced himself as 'Donny' and the MC for the evening's open mic poetry night.

He prepped the room on the events of the night and encouraged anyone to come up to the microphone with their own 'poetic voice'. With this he shared a few of his own poems. We sunk into our chairs absorbing the words and a fresh cup of tea. A few people from the audience made their way up and courageously shared their poems filled with a little piece of their heart and soul. I looked at you engrossed in the moment.

'I am going to share a poem and then we can head out of here so you can get home to your children,' I said smiling.

You looked at me as if I couldn't be serious. The mic opened and I walked to the front of the room for my turn. I paused letting the eyes sink into my body. I embraced the room, the connection with the audience and I introduced myself and began.

'Hi, I'm Thomas, in the spirit of the great Sufi poet Hafiz, this poem is titled *When I am Alone*:

'When I am Alone
No eyes upon me
I feel your presence
at my side like a warm embrace
No judgment or expectations
this moment holds no time
bridging yesterday with tomorrow
No clothes upon my back
I am naked to the world
for all to see nothing and everything
No fear
within me
I am what I am
when I am alone'

I walked back to my chair to a smattering of applause as the next person started on their own poem. You looked at me like I had just kidnapped your children. 'Where did that come from?'

You said in disbelief.

'From my heart, from the universe, from love, this is all.' I shrugged, put on my jacket and began to head for the door.

We headed back down the hill to Fremont in silence. I think we were both mentally tired wrestling with such a serious topic. Getting close to the office I offered another meeting time, 'Why don't we meet for lunch tomorrow? We can meet under the Fremont Rocket. I think we are ready to actually discuss how to take the journey. What do you think?'

You paused, not sure what to take of my comment. My guess was that you were uneasy about actually taking the journey. It was as if you were looking over a cliff, all the discussions and prep time in the world could not prepare you for the actual jump off the cliff. I smiled with this thought knowing you had already jumped.

'Sure, this sounds great.....I will meet you there.' You said finally breaking the silence.

I thanked you for the ride and waved goodbye ready for some rest.

Chapter 6

Tuning Out: Cleansing Your Mind

Friday came and my mind was still heavy. I blocked time on both of our calendars for 'lunch and a walk' and continued to prep for my trip to Scotland the following week. This was a big trip for me. I had told management a few weeks ago I was considering moving on from the company and I wanted to use this trip to sort out my decision. They offered their full support. However, this decision was not easy for me. I had been in the business world and the technology industry my entire life, part of my own existence was tied to this fact. As much as I thought I had disassociated myself from the workplace I still found the thought difficult to ascertain. The morning flew by in my heavy mind and I finally needed to breathe. I left the office and walked along the water for some time before heading north and then back east toward the Fremont Rocket.

I could see the Rocket a few blocks out, it was hard to miss at 55 feet high. This relic of the cold war, a real 1950 era rocket saved from the scrap heap was now one of the defining landmarks in the neighborhood complete with steam released on the hour to signify lift off. I thought it was both an easy spot to meet as well as an appropriate metaphor for the discussion of launching or taking the journey toward truth.

You arrived right at the scheduled time and I nodded to the east and we began walking down the sidewalk. 'I have a great, quiet lunch spot for us to explore.'

We headed east for a few blocks and then north on Fremont Avenue to one of my favorite stomping grounds, *The Flying Apron* vegan and gluten free bakery and lunch spot. We secured a table as I prepped you for possible options. 'OK, so this is a vegan spot, but trust me the food is really good, perfect for our upcoming discussions.'

The bakery was simplistic with a few tables and counter service. Its main purpose was the huge kitchen in the back where the staff was consistently at work putting together creative and beautiful food. We both ordered a soup and salad in addition to a vegan dessert and settled onto a table. After a few moments in eating the delicious food, I asked for your opinion, 'What do you think?'

'In full honesty to you, this food is incredible. I am not sure what vegan actually means but this food and dessert is out of this world.'

I smiled with your 'out of this world' reference symbolically blending with the rocket ship metaphor. 'Great! I am so glad you enjoyed it. Nothing better than breaking bread with a friend and an interesting topic,' I said. 'I will admit I was trying to show the possible flavor of nutritional food. We will talk more about this a little later. But, for now, I am glad you enjoyed it.'

'Sounds like you love food,' you said smiling still engrossed in your meal.

'Plants, vegetables, nuts and fruit represent the divine in nature. Eating them in their raw state is the best as they are living energy. I see and feel tremendous truth and blessings in their presence. I will talk more about food as energy later when I talk about cleansing our body; however, we are now at the crux of our journey. We are now at the 'how to take the journey' portion of our discussion.

Before I get into the details around the journey, let's recap our discussions up to now. Everything we have discussed so far culminates with our next two topics about 'tuning out' and 'tuning in'. At the start of our discussion we talked about truth, and although ultimately this is self defined, we discussed concepts of truth, and the connection with a state of selfless love. We then discussed our 'inner self', the real you. The 'you' that equates to truth, the 'you' that equates to love. We talked about this place where this real 'you' comes from, your naked soul stripped of all labels and roles, full of integrity, full of absolute positive energy and love. We talked about how the perceived you is not the real 'you'; it is not 'truth'. This external, superficial reflection of you is driven by the mind, driven by fear, driven by desire. The mind and the inflated ego focus on meaningless things such as vanity, lust, anger, attachment, and material things. We discussed how fear is an extension of the mind out of control, a tool to keep us away from truth. We talked about the importance of our intentions, words and actions. And, now we are here, does this give a decent reflection on our discussion?' I asked.

'Well, it was certainly much more in-depth than this, but, yes, as a summary, this does a good job.'

'When you came to me a week or so ago, you had a very simple question, 'How is it that you are happy all the time? Where does this positive energy come from?' Do you remember?'

'How could I forget? I thought this was a cup of coffee conversation and here we are more than a week later.'

'Yes, and I hope I do not disappoint you further as I do not have a special 'key' in my pocket that I am going to use to unlock all of your secrets, no hidden Celestine Prophecy manual here. This is a journey, a journey without an end point, a journey that we take every day, doing the best that we can each and every day seeking truth. This is the beauty of it. It takes tremendous hard work, discipline, patience, and perseverance. The Buddhists used to tell individuals considering a spiritual path that their desire must be the same as a man with his hair on fire searching for water. Otherwise, the journey is too hard. The universe will constantly challenge you, challenge your beliefs, and challenge your quest for love. In the end you will have to decide if the journey is worth the effort. I have found that taking the famous thousand mile journey truly does begin with that first step, every day. However, each day, after taking a step, eventually you cannot see that point where you started. You find immense value in the journey and cannot look back. You begin to look at your old life with disbelief, as if this was a different person, a different place. Life begins to slow down; you find beauty and grace in everything, and you begin to smile. You smile all the time; how could you not, as life is this wonderful journey that you get to partake in? This is how I see it, anyways. So, I hope I didn't dampen your spirits in the journey. We really are ready for the heart of the discussion with the 'How do we take the journey?' Are you ready for this?'

'Sure. I am not discouraged by your statements. I guess I originally had a thought that you could give a few pointers in how to be happy, maybe a great book, or some things to reflect on in life. The more I think of it, however, is that I have been doing this my whole life and I am receiving the same results. At some point you have to change, right?'

'Well, the famous Benjamin Franklin quote states that 'the definition of insanity is doing the same thing over and over and expecting different results'. We have all done this. Let's take a look at a different approach. So, getting back to the 'How to take this journey' conversation, we really break this down into two main buckets – 'tuning out' and 'tuning in'. In order for us to get to this place of truth, to get to this inner self, this place of boundless, uncompromised, selfless love, we have to do some things.

First, we have to cleanse our vessel – our mind and our body. If we want to become this boundless, beacon of energy, we need to clear any obstructions for us to radiate, and 'tune out' this energy, this love to the universe. Does this make sense?'

'Sure. I guess this is why cell phone towers are on top of the highest points.'

'Or why radio telescopes are on top of the mountains or unobstructed in the middle of nowhere listening to the depths of the Universe, as you will see when we discuss 'tuning in'. Either way, it is the same point; we need to clear any obstructions or junk for us be in union with this energy.

So, let's look at how we can do this. In India the Yogi's go through some interesting exercises to 'cleanse their vessel'.'

'Such as?' You asked sitting up in your seat.

'Well, I am not sure you want to hear this. They do things like swallowing strips of cloth and then pull them back out of their bodies to cleanse their stomach before they meditate. They sit in pools of water and 'pull in' water up their anal cavity then hold it and try to dispel anything blocking – kind of a homemade colonic. Interesting, huh?'

'Let's just leave it at interesting.'

'Well, I am not going to suggest you follow this plan; however, there is some method to their madness. The colonics part alone is an interesting topic. Many people love to quote that 'John Wayne died with 40 lbs of impacted feces inside his colon'. This information is near impossible to verify outside of an interesting story. However, I have seen photos of impacted colons that reabsorb these toxins back into the body. It is not a 'cleansed' environment, and in essence is putting poison back into your body. Another way to look at this is that we cleanse our hair, our teeth, yet we do not think of cleansing our insides. If we are to follow a proper diet we can scrub or 'cleanse' the inside of our body to act in its optimal, unobstructed form. If you hold the belief that we are this beacon of energy and you want to have the most polished, energy proficient beacon as possible to radiate positive energy and eventually pull in and be connected to this truth and omniscient love, then we need to do a couple of obvious things to unblock the path. First, we need to clear the mind and then we need to cleanse and continually cleanse and properly fuel our bodies.

With cleansing our mind, we have had some discussion on this already; however, let's take this a step further. In order for us to start and 'cleanse our palate' if you will, we need to let go of anything blocking love inside of us. We all hold some form of bitterness, anger, and resentment inside of us. For whatever reason, we hold onto this, carry it with us like a travel bag wherever we go. Why do you think this is?'

'I don't know. I guess we feel justified,' you said.

'Justified? I hear the ego loud and clear here. 'They did this to me. I will never forget. How dare they do this to me?' This is an external view of yourself in how people should see you and treat you. In the end, who are you really? You are no one. You can only control yourself. How people want to react and treat you is up to them. Either they do or they do not; this is not your concern. Your only concern is the energy you will project, and in this, you will attract this energy back to you. It is really simple.

So, guideline number one in 'tuning out' is letting go, FORGIVENESS. Look deep inside yourself and find anything holding you back from this beacon of positive energy and let it go in forgiveness. Sit down for coffee with these people, write a letter, e-mail, singing telegram, I don't care, just do it. The weight will rush off of you like a waterfall. You will smile; you will feel something from the inner 'you'. 'The truth will abide', as *The Dude* from The Big Lewbowski would say. What do you think?' I asked in full animation.

'This is a pretty big thing to ask.' You looked around the room growing self conscious. Although there were only two more people in the bakery, you moved closer in not wanting the 'world' to hear about your personal life.

'I didn't say it would be easy,' I said indifferent to your uneasiness, 'necessary, maybe, but not easy.'

'There are some things that have happened to me that I do not wish to discuss here,' you softened your tone looking around the room again. 'I don't believe I can let go, these memories are too painful, too deep.'

'I understand, and you don't need to share here. This is your luggage that you are carrying with you. However, in order to love, you have to let go. This is not a gray area. I think Mahatma Gandhi said it best when he said 'The weak can never forgive. Forgiveness is the attribute of the strong.' Or, we can use the quote from Jesus when Peter came to ask him 'Lord, how many times shall I forgive my brother when he sins against me? Up to seven times?' Jesus replied 'I tell you not seven times, but seventy-seven times.'[6] Forgiveness is the ultimate blocker to love, to truth. We have to do this in order to truly love, no matter what the circumstance. At the very least, if you are having trouble with forgiveness, perhaps this quote from Oscar Wilde will serve you better: 'Always forgive your enemies – nothing annoys them so much.'

We both laughed at this last quote.

'OK, I can use that last one,' you said.

'Well this last quote doesn't exactly come from the best place, or a place of truth. However, it does work. I remember I owned a business and we would send out a lot of marketing information. We would get these calls from irate people, because they received a letter in the mail, yelling and screaming, how could we do this to them? How could we waste their time like this? Initially, I was taken back and gave the same energy I received. I would hold my ground and say things like, 'Well, you know most of our customers who are not interested in our services just throw the envelope away versus actually taking the energy to call us and get upset.' For an instant this made me feel better. I mean it is true, isn't it?'

You nodded.

'However, this would just fuel the fire, and they would get angrier. So, I changed my tactics. When these people would call I would smother them with kindness, with forgiveness. I would say things like 'I am so sorry you had to be put through this trouble. I am so sorry you had to go through this.' At first, they thought I was tempting them, ridiculing them and they would try harder. The harder they tried and nastier they got, the nicer I became. Every time they would end up backing off their comments and anger, and apologizing for calling, stating that it really wasn't that big of a deal. Forgiveness is a monumental step in cleansing the vessel.'

'Sure, but this is an incident that really isn't personal in nature. These are different.'

'Are they? Ultimately, are they? I understand where you are coming from. I can still remember when I got to this point I am at today. I was leaving someone I truly loved; someone I really felt connected to, and had tried so hard with this relationship for over five years. I had to leave as I felt my inner self, my truth, was being compromised. I felt I was catering to this person and not being myself so as not to receive anger or bitterness. When I left, I began to smile deeply inside of me. I cried. Emotions came out; I started to listen to my 'self' again. I sat down and wrote numerous e-mails coming from my heart to people I had let go long ago because of bitterness and anger. I forgave. I radiated love. I called family members I hadn't talked to in years and let it go, just positive vibrations of love. A lot of these people still emit judgment and criticism, but in the end I do not care. This is their baggage. I love them for who they are as they are exactly who they are supposed to be at that moment. In forgiving, emotions flowed from me that I didn't know were even inside of me. I felt lighter. I felt alive. I felt a rebirth in knowing another individual will never put negative energy in me again. This is such a beautiful thought to me. You cannot love without forgiveness; this is the first guideline.'

'I understand, and this may ultimately need to be done, it is just such a hard thing to *ask*,' you said.

'I am not asking you to do anything, as only you will decide one day if any of our conversations are important and you will decide either way, nothing more, nothing less. This is neither right nor wrong, it just 'is'.

I got up and put on my coat, and nodded toward the door,

'come on, let's stretch our legs.'

We headed north out of the bakery and took the next right heading east under the Aurora freeway. I felt better in talking to you. I realized I had been immersed in my own head the past few days and sharing with you had allowed me to let go again. In this I was very grateful for our meeting. We walked up a steep hill and found ourselves face to face with the Fremont troll. This concrete statue stood 18 feet high and was a play off the old Scandinavian folk tale called 'Three Billy Goats Gruff' about an ugly, angry troll who lived under the bridge. He was ugly, only one of his eyes was visible and looked to be a used hub cap. His left hand swallowed a real, old VW bug with California license plates. I laughed to myself in this site. Having grown up in the state of Washington I could remember the anti California mentality in the 1970's and 80's. Seattleites thought the California folks were taking over and there was a real negative sentiment. Times had changed, the city had evolved and with the growth of the high-tech industry the city was now multistate, International and multicultural.

You smiled in seeing the troll, 'so this is my mind destroying the love inside of me, you said nodding toward the crushed Volkswagen.

I laughed and nodded yes as we took a seat on one of the troll's fingers and continued our discussion.

'So we were talking about forgiveness as guideline number one in cleansing your mind. Guideline number two is to always COME FROM A PLACE OF TRUTH, full of integrity, and honesty. This seems obvious on a journey toward truth; however, look at this one closer. You will find people often make decisions on what either best serves their interest or what they feel will lessen the pain or circumstance of another. The 'white lies' – see there we go again with words – the 'white' lies, I guess, are not as bad as the other lies. Come from a place of truth, and integrity and you will be treated the same. If not, this is not your issue.

Stand up for integrity; live from a state of honesty at all times. People will begin to be pulled to you, pulled toward your positive and truthful energy. How many times have you heard 'I would rather just know the truth'? This is the respect that we deserve. This comes from love; this is the basis of truth. Does this make sense?'

'Sure. This one seems fairly obvious if our intent is a journey toward truth, toward love.'

'OK, this leads us to the next guideline in letting go: NO JUDGMENTS. As discussed, everything is exactly the way it is supposed to be. How can we judge something that is exactly the way it is supposed to be? Again, I asked, 'who are we to judge?' We are no one, but we are also everything. Remove all the labels, intentions, comments, negative 'VIBE' that comes out when someone doesn't fit your 'model'. Judgment is a direct reflection of our ego thinking we are above another living being. When you stop judging people you will free yourself to love. People expect you to judge; it is so common that it is practically in our DNA. When you stop judging, people will feel emotionally close to you; they will feel safe; they will want to be open and give love just as you are giving love. Remember, every decision a person has made was made with the best intent possible at that given moment. This is all. How can I judge someone with this in mind?'

'I guess I need more time to wrap my mind around this one,' you said crossing your arms.

'Remember don't think... FEEL.' I said laughing trying to lighten the moment. 'Do you remember the movie Phenomenon with John Travolta?'

'Yes, I liked this movie. Why?'

'This movie sums up judging people when you do not understand them. Fear drives the ego to judge and treat people below ourselves, completely outside of a state of love. John Travolta was this normal guy, a mechanic; people were fond of him as he was like everyone else in town. All of a sudden, after his tumor began to take over and utilized more of his brain, he didn't fit into their model anymore. He was different. The townspeople were scared of him and judged him because he was different. Rather than getting to truly know him and understand that he was coming from a place of love they ostracized him. So many times in history we have done this; we immediately want to destroy, or kill that which is different to ourselves. I always think of the Spanish Inquisition. These people couldn't be farther from God, The Great Spirit, Allah, The Divine Source, or whatever you wish to call the creator or source of energy. I am truly saddened at the waste of living spirits because of this mentality. Removing judgment is a huge step toward truth.'

'OK, I am on board on this one. These points are certainly impossible to debate. I understand.'

'OK, so after we FORGIVE, COME FROM A PLACE OF TRUTH and STOP JUDGING we flow easily into the next big cleansing of our vessel and guideline number four: POSITIVE INTENTIONS, POSITIVE WORDS, POSITIVE ACTION.

We spent some time on this one last night as this guideline is extremely important. If we are this beacon of positive energy and we want to receive positive, vibrant energy back, then we have to emit positive energy, pretty simple, right? They say once you start on this path three things happen: you sleep less, you eat less, and you talk less. You will understand this more as we go along; however, the talk less is absolutely true. I find myself searching for more quality words, meaningful words than just talking. Especially negative words, such as cursing, which are in essence you stating to the world you do not deserve respect or positive energy coming your way. Positive intent is just as important as positive words as you are creating the energy either way. A negative thought invokes the same energy as actually speaking it. In other words, in just thinking these thoughts you put them out into the universe. Ultimately your inner self is driven by your intuitive 'self' that is driven by your feelings or intentions. So, when you feel good, you emit and receive positive energy. Thoughts?'

'I think you hit this last one home earlier. Again, I think it will take some more reflection on my part to fully understand. I am not sure I understand how deep of an issue this really is.'

'I understand as I still reflect on all of these thoughts almost daily. I catch myself with negative thoughts. As we mentioned earlier no one is perfect. I have tried very hard not to speak or act in a negative manner; however, I do catch myself thinking negative thoughts at times; these usually come when I am tired, or irritated, or whatever excuse I give myself at that moment. Just the other day, I was at the coffee shop and this guy, you know the one, not aware of any of his surroundings, he keeps grabbing other people's coffee, cutting in front of people, and then he knocks a coffee off the stand and it spills all over the floor. My immediate reaction in my mind was 'What an idiot!' Right? I mean that's funny. Jump on someone's misery and feel better about yourself; you know, a complete Jerry Springer moment.'

'Well, that is funny though,' you said.

'It is funny but still a negative vibe I am putting out into the universe. I will receive that vibe back. This is all, nothing more, nothing less. I had another coffee shop moment the other day; I was in deep thought, writing in my journal, and I felt this lady 'projecting' onto my space, looking over my shoulder, fiddling with our joint foot rest; it really was annoying. I was about ready to leave, or say something negative to this person, when I stopped, took a deep breath and looked her in the eyes and asked her 'How are you doing today?' This turned into a wonderful, very fulfilling conversation with a person I still communicate with today. Again, we either pull up or pull down. It is our choice.'

'So, are you saying we shouldn't laugh?' you turned and

looked intently at me.

'Great question,' I said. 'At the root of our true self, is laughter, wonderful deep fulfilling laughter as we have such joy for life. Laugh at life, if you really look at life from the outside in, it is comical. During some of my most challenging moments I just began laughing to myself, uncontrollably. Why not? I cannot do anything about it so why not laugh about it. With respect to laughing at others, I have a guilty pleasure in this. I love the comedians Ellen DeGeneres and Kathy Griffin, and *The Daily Show* with John Stewart. Kathy Griffin in particular is brutal; she makes fun of everyone. I guess at the root of my enjoying this laughter is that it is typically directed at someone who is driven by some sort of an EGO issue. I can hear my judgment.' I said shaking my head. 'If we are really about projecting our energy and our energy is driven by our feelings, then laughter fits well into this as it makes you feel good. I personally choose not to project this negative energy at others, but I laugh at myself constantly.

This leads into the next guideline for cleansing our vessel: REMOVE ALL NEGATIVITY THAT SURROUNDS YOU. What do you think of this?'

'It makes sense but seems impossible. Just look around,' you said shrugging.

'Sure, the negative, ego-driven vibe is everywhere. I will agree with this comment. However, we can make choices to limit the amount of negativity in our lives. I have personally eliminated or, I should say, extremely limited the news. Before the Iraq war started I became so wrapped up in the news that I found I was constantly angry and on edge. Even the 'anti-war' message generates a negative vibe. It just overwhelmed me. I believe in Mother Theresa's mantra that if there is ever a pro-peace rally then invite me, as this is appropriate use of energy. So, I went from this 3-4 hour a day news junkie to nothing.

In fact, I removed the whole thought vacuum (TV) from my

life outside of a few moments here and there such as movies. You can choose to eliminate negativity in a lot of places such as limiting playing too many video games, or violent, negative TV, movies, or music. See yourself as a receiver of the mood or energy that is being projected at you and what feelings are present in you at all times. If you are feeling overwhelmed, angry, or any other negative emotion then do your best to remove yourself from the environment. This could also mean major things such as people, or your job. Is a job worth the negative emotions that are present with you all day to earn a living?'

I paused in thought at this last statement. I felt a twinge inside of me, knowing this was my subconscious talking directly to me. 'Joseph Campbell used to say 'follow your bliss'. Follow your heart and happiness will follow. If you chase the superficial, you will chase this to your death. Surrounding yourself with positive people is another major energy 'intake' or energy 'outtake' with respect to being around negative people. Negative people will suck out your positive energy. You will feel drained. You will begin to absorb their energy and in turn act in a similar, negative manner. Remember, you are a beautiful person full of value and love. When you choose to emit this wonderful positive energy, you deserve to receive this back. This is why I love being around animals; they are pure love, pure positive intentions, pure beautiful energy. Once you realize how you feel at all times, you will understand innately to remove yourself from negativity. You will become the plant with the negative music blaring. In order to grow you will grow in a different direction to the negativity. Do you see this today?' I asked.

'Probably not to the extent you are discussing. Of course you notice it as it is everywhere in life. I guess you learn to adjust or just deal with it. I understand this concept as some things put me in a bad mood and then I am an enabler, if you will, of this bad energy. As you say, I guess it will be interesting moving forward as I will try to monitor this at all times.'

'Once you are aware, then you are well on your way toward finding peace and the truth. Once you start to 'tune in' you will not want any part of this energy; it will become obvious to you,' I said. 'OK, so we have asked for forgiveness within ourselves, come from a place of truth, passed no judgments, we have worked toward positive intent, positive words, positive action, we have removed as much negativity as possible in our lives, and now, we move to our next guideline – NO FEAR.

As we discussed, fear drives so many negative emotions in our lives such as anger, jealousy, bitterness, vanity, and many, many others. Be aware of fear. Feel your emotions. If you have a negative emotion, most likely it is driven by a fear inside you fed by the ego. Make a note of unsubstantiated fears and work toward eliminating them. These can be externally driven fears such as public speaking, as we discussed before, or perhaps you have a fear of water; take swimming lessons and get past this fear as it will control you. Women often are very fearful of being attacked. Take a self defense course or a number of courses. This, of course, does not guarantee safety but it will build confidence and lose the fear within these individuals.

Be aware of external fears that come from people or institutions in positions of power such as the church or government; be aware of the emotions inside of you and how you feel when confronted by these circumstances; once aware, look inside of yourself to understand your intuitive feelings. Be curious; ask questions; find out answers for yourself and in the end believe what you feel is right.

This is also true of internally driven fears; take, for example, jealousy. What ultimately are you afraid of? Losing your partner? If my partner chooses to be with another person and disrespects the truth and love we have between us, then it is best we are not together. Being afraid of losing this person and building up animosity, bitterness, anger and jealousy is simply unjustified and does not come from a place of truth. Understand this and you will begin to find clarity around your fears. Confront these fears, control them and eventually lose them all together. In order to love, you cannot come from a place of fear. Most of all monitor your feelings as this is where the inner 'you' and truth comes from. When you feel bad, fearful, bitter, anything outside of peace, love and truth, then you need to understand why you feel this way and either remove yourself from the environment, or change the environment within your mind.'

I stopped talking here letting you take in these thoughts. The two of us watched car after car pull up to the troll, jump out, take a photo and drive off. I wasn't aware of the troll's magnitude as a tourist attraction until now. I stood and nodded toward the sidewalk. 'Let's start walking back to the office.'

We picked up the sidewalk again and began making a circle back toward the office heading down the hill toward the waterfront.

'The next guideline we need to understand to cleanse our mind is having NO CONTROLS.' I broke the silence. 'Eliminating controls in our life concerns losing any item on which we have become absolutely dependent upon and cannot do without. We ultimately should not be attached to anything or anyone. In this way, we can love everyone and everything. Often we find ourselves in a routine that begins to drive the external, perceived self. We must learn to eliminate any of these controls, or ensure that these are not actually controls. Listen to a few of these comments as I know you have heard them: 'I don't know what I would do without my coffee', 'I have to watch my TV show', 'I can't do without my Jimmy Choo shoes'. OK, the last one is from Sex in the City. Do you know what I am saying?'

'At a high level, but I am still missing the issue with owning a pair of Jimmy Choo shoes?'

'Nothing, as long as these shoes do not control your life, would you be willing to give these shoes to a stranger on the street? If the answer is no, then these shoes control you. Think of this indifferent to Jesus when one asked him for his shirt and he said please take my coat too. These are just 'things', ultimately not important. If you are stopping yourself from doing things or more importantly if you find that you cannot get through your day without a certain 'thing' in your life, then you have a control issue.

Let me give you one of mine to explain further. This is a relatively small issue but it is still a control none the less. I am from the Northwest and have spent a considerable amount of time here in Seattle. As you know this place can be dreary in the winter and coffee serves as a balance point to get through these winter months. As you heard my order yesterday I have an affinity for a soy mocha. However, I had developed both a mental control and a caffeine control with this drink, this 'thing'. If I didn't have my drink I became agitated, annoyed, and in a bad mood. Plus, I was spending a lot of money on these drinks. Finally I looked from the outside in and I realized I had a control. I stopped these drinks cold for months upon end. As you have seen, I still go to the coffee shop and even have my soy mocha; however, now it is decaf and it is not controlling me. Just to be sure, and with other things in my life I will cut them off cold just to monitor the control.

Be attached to nothing, love everything. I have a friend who has to have a glass of beer or wine every day after work. This is a control. Controls will limit your ability to love, to find truth, as these are attachments keeping you from this divine state. OK?'

'Sure, I see your point. It seems as though this is less of an issue than say positive thought or forgiveness, don't you think?'

'Each of these will be valued differently for everyone. It may seem like a lower priority; however, in the end, if we want to be this 'naked' element of truth standing full of integrity, openness and love then we cannot have anything or anyone that ultimately controls us.

Next on our list of cleansing our mind, we need to live in a state of COMPASSION, filled with ahimsa, or non violence. If we truly are everything and connected to all and we hold atoms in us from trees, ants and every other living thing, then how could we harm in essence our brothers and sisters? We are everything.

With respect to non-violence, we are actually nothing. What I mean by this is who, outside of our human ego, would defend that humans are above or in dominion over plants, animals, and other people. The statements in the Bible explaining that God has put upon earth animals for the sustenance of human beings have done more damage than you could ever imagine. Our ego is why we are out of balance in this world. We, speaking collectively, believe that we are entitled, that we deserve, and that we are justified. We speak words that we are the *TOP* of the food chain.

We will discuss animals for food production at some point; however, I need to call out the necessity for non-violence and *COMPASSION* for all living beings. Most of my examples to date have been around plants and animals; I haven't even touched on the injustice we do to our fellow man with the oppression, slavery, violence, rape, murder, and much, much more that we inflict on our fellow man, our fellow brothers and sisters, is appalling. War is such an intense negative energy with side effects that extend well beyond the battle field. The maimed twenty-four year-old soldier who will never have a normal life; the stress induced soldier who returns home and beats his wife and his animals; the innocent people caught by a wayside bomb; lives extinguished in an instant. Eddie Veddar states this very well in the song *Here's to the State*:

'The bombs that fall on children don't know which side, don't care which side, that they're on.'

Mahatma Gandhi denounced any violence against the British in India's fight for independence. This was done even though the country was controlled and oppressed by the British utilizing the cheap Indian resources; 'cheap labor' to FEED the GREED. His countrymen had every right to fight back; however, they persisted and under ahimsa they succeeded.'

Your face turned to a frown in deep thought. I paused waiting for your response, knowing something was on your mind. The light changed and we crossed the street and down a hill again finding the waterfront trail.

You straightened, confident in your thought, 'at some point, I might need to protect me or my children. I will not allow this to happen under some concept of nonviolence?' Your tone was serious and direct.

'Good point....; non violence must be used at every opportunity possible. If you must protect yourself or your children then do so. Do it with the least amount of force as you can possibly use. I have been around a lot of martial artists in my life and typically these people are the last that would ever be in a fight or use violence. They are centered, at peace, and realize violence is not the answer. They train to lose the fear in fighting. They train not to fight unless there is no other choice.

This brings us to our last core point for cleansing our mind,' I stated. 'GRATITUDE.....Live in a state of gratitude at all times. I like to think of two big bookends in cleansing our mind – FORGIVENESS and ending with GRATITUDE. Gratitude is love. Gratitude is telling the Universe that you are filled with love and you want more. I keep a gratitude journal to express my thanks for each day. It is my love affair, my love diary with life.

Expressing this attitude at all times is the ultimate expression of love. I send notes, call people, ensure that I am absolutely present with them and tell them 'Thank you for sharing, for being here with me.'

Understand your emotions, and if they are not coming from a sense of gratitude then you need to adjust them. It has been stated before to live everyday as if it is your last. Why wait for that moment of death to remind us? Life is beautiful. It truly is. Give thanks for the opportunity to be in this wonderful life. Thoughts?'

'I guess, no one gives gratitude enough; however, the more that you mention it, I realize that being in a state of gratitude in my mind would make it impossible to be in a bad mood, or angry, or even fearful. Gratitude is extremely powerful.' You said.

'Yes, you have it. If we use patience and perseverance and abide by the cleansing of our mind, using activities of forgiveness, come from a place of truth, use no judgments, positive intent, positive words, positive action, remove all negativity that surrounds us, eliminate fear and controls, live in a state of non-violence and compassion, and finally give gratitude at all times, then we will be emitting clear, unobstructed love into the Universe. In this we will receive the same wonderful, positive energy and love back. What do you think?'

'I understand. These may be difficult but the concept makes sense.'

I stopped just short of the office and shrugged, 'this is the first step in taking the path, living with integrity and love while cleansing your mind to emit positive energy into the universe.'

'So, where do we go from here?'

'We have two big topics left, tuning out in cleansing our body and finally tuning into the universe and accepting the vibration and love back into our inner being. I am leaving on Sunday for nearly two weeks out of office to Scotland. If there is any way you can clear some time tomorrow on Saturday we can cover these topics in depth. What do you think?'

'I will make time, we can't stop now.' You shrugged knowing the truth of this statement.

'Excellent, let's meet at the south entrance of the zoo at 10 in the morning tomorrow.'

'The zoo? Sounds great,' you waved and began walking back to the office.

I waved goodbye and continued walking along the waterfront reflecting in my own thoughts. The sun's rays finally broke free from the embrace of the clouds and shined on my path while creating diamond like glitter along the water. I breathed in the fresh air, filling my lungs and exhaling long into the air giving life to a nearby tree. I smiled in this connection, happy in this moment.

Chapter 7

Tuning Out: Cleansing Your Body

I arrived early on Saturday morning, partly out of respect for your time as I didn't want you to wait, but mostly out of excitement. I was anxious to continue on our conversation from yesterday with the building blocks of living the path and taking the journey toward truth. I spent Friday evening finishing the prep for my trip so I felt relaxed and present for your arrival. I was excited for the day, parked the car and began to explore the surroundings of the zoo.

I walked past the rose garden to the southeast of the zoo and took note of the tightly manicured hedges and fresh buds starting to gather on the bushes. As I neared the entrance of the zoo I felt the energy and excitement of the children waiting to enter the complex. I remembered feeling this when I was a kid, the zoo was always the best field trip. I guessed even as children we have an innate attraction to connect to animals. To add to my point I saw a group of children gathering around 3-4 bronze statues representing a small baboon family in front of the zoo entrance. The kids swarmed and climbed on the statues blending and connecting with the baboons creating a new, surreal family dynamic. From a distance I heard a loud humming noise that sounded like a loud extended 'AUM' or 'HU' as if I was at an Ashram in India. As I got closer I realized it was the group of kids vocalizing an extended 'cheeeeeeeeeeese' sound while they got their picture taken.

I bought our tickets and sat out front for a few minutes near a small bronze sculpture of the earth with an elephant, gorilla, mountain goat, turtle and beetle on top who seemed to be saying in their own Rodney King voice, 'can't we all just get along?' I guessed this piece signified the animals were on 'top of the world'. I couldn't help in finding the irony in this depiction as it sat outside of what amounted to an animal prison and the direct antithesis of the statement in the Bible that God created animals for the dominion of man.

In looking to the west of the entrance I noticed a sign stating 'this way to the War Garden'. This must be the morning of irony I thought. If a garden was a place to cultivate herbs, fruits, vegetables, flowers and trees, then was this a place to cultivate war? I walked up the trail and immediately noticed one of two large gun barrels pointing at me on my way up to the park, I dodged the barrel and meandered through the cut grass and cedar trees to find a statue of a soldier dedicated to the veterans of the less notable Spanish-American War from the beginning of the 20th century.

I took a seat on a rock and pondered the scene. This park was on the edge of over 92 walled acres to hold in animals from around the world, some on the fringe of extinction while military guns blossomed in the War Garden to honor those that died in battle. I shuddered in thinking of the power of the destructive mind. The scene was surreal to me; the guns looked like they were guarding the zoo as if keeping the inhabitants 'safe'. These guns came off as overcompensation for something, kind of like the insecure man driving a Corvette. They were almost stating, 'yes, your loved ones died in the war, but look at us, the mightiest war power of them all.' It reminded me of the war parades that have existed long before we were writing words, highlighted later by the likes of Hitler, Stalin, and Mao in a show of strength to strike fear in any who might oppose. I grew sad in these thoughts remembering the words of Smedley Butler as I sat in a peaceful garden trying to reflect on those who passed in the act of war.

I snapped out of my reflective moment by a galloping Labrador retriever pulling a determined, small woman on a morning jog. She had attempted to restrict the dog's movement by tying his leash around her waist which led to a free for all run by the dog and a woman running as fast as she could to keep up, it was almost as if she was skiing along the path. I smiled in thinking she would reach her personal best today, and grateful for the reminder of being present.

It was about 10 a.m. so I walked back to the entrance and waited for your arrival. As usual you were right on time at 10 o'clock on the nose. You smiled as you approached me, visibly excited for the day.

I hugged you and nodded toward the entrance, 'let's go explore, I already have the tickets.'

'I am excited; I can't remember the last time I was here without my children. It was a long time ago, that's for sure.'

We entered and I took an immediate left to the Family Farm area. We walked in amongst a group of children stalking the animals around the pseudo 'farm'. First on the farm were the pigs, fat and happy with their curly tails. I bent down and looked at one who stopped exploring looking me up and down. He was too shy to come to my open hand, but I keep trying wanting to touch this beautiful, smart creature.

I looked over at you, unsure in the moment as if you were anxious to see the big ticket items such as the gorillas or elephants. Indifferent I continued my exploration at the farm. I followed some children to the sheep and pet the face and back of one of the animals. The sheep looked pleased to have the connection and followed me along the rail as I began to walk away. I looked back and noticed you trying to pet him, briefly touching his back before pulling back unsure of yourself.

We continued around the farm to the last section with the cows. At first they ignored our presence focused on their own activity, until finally one of them came over to the rail to look at us closer. She looked us up and down, smelled us and began to nuzzle her head into my hand. Petting her was not an option, she wanted a hand on her head and it was going to happen, slobber and all. I stroked her cheeks looking deeply in her eyes and smiled, pleased to have such as moment. You took to this animal petting her neck and feeling the attention she nuzzled her head into your hand. I noticed you uneasily wipe the slobber off your hand while smiling in the beautiful energy of this animal.

I led us over to a bench to watch the interaction with the crowd and the animals. The children crowded the rails followed a few feet behind by their parents. The kids were so excited to have the opportunity to interact with animals, the moment was precious. Then I noticed a group of kids eating hot dogs and hamburgers as they pet the animals. My day of irony had continued. I smiled in disbelief at this scene, wondering if these kids even knew what they were eating.

In looking at you, I wondered if you noticed the symbolic act. 'What are your thoughts that these kids are eating the same animals that they are petting?'

You looked at me in disbelief, found the crowd of kids eating the food, thought about my statement and smiled. 'I hadn't even noticed this.'

'Exactly, this is how we live life with our bodies.' I paused reflecting on this moment while thinking of a more vivid way of expressing this sentiment. Inspired I stood and asked, 'Do you know of the Quentin Tarrantino movie *Pulp Fiction*?'

'Sure, Great movie.' You sat up engaged as usual in my movie metaphors.

'There is a wonderful scene between John Travolta (Vincent) and Samuel L. Jackson (Jules) concerning why Samuel L. Jackson doesn't eat pork.' I began walking back and forth with an attitude channeling the characters for you and the growing crowd to hear. 'The exchange goes like this:

'Vincent: Want some bacon?

Jules: No man. I don't eat pork.

Vincent: Are you Jewish?

Jules: Nah, I ain't Jewish. I just don't dig on swine, that's all.

Vincent: Why not?

Jules: Pigs are filthy animals. I don't eat filthy animals.

Vincent: Bacon tastes gooood. Pork chops taste gooood.

Jules: Hey, sewer rat may taste like pumpkin pie, but I'd never know 'cause I wouldn't eat the filthy mother******. Pigs sleep and root in sh**. That's a filthy animal. I ain't eatin' nothin' that ain't got enough sense enough to disregard its own feces.

Vincent: How about a dog? Dogs eats its own feces.

Jules: I don't eat dog either.

Vincent: Yeah, but do you consider a dog to be a filthy animal?

Jules: I wouldn't go so far as to call a dog filthy but they're definitely dirty. But, a dog's got personality. Personality goes a long way.

Vincent: Ah, so by that rationale, if a pig had a better personality, he would cease to be a filthy animal. Is that true?

Jules: Well we'd have to be talkin' about one charmin' mother****** pig. I mean he'd have to be ten times more charmin' than that Arnold on Green Acres, you know what I'm sayin'?'

I sat back down to a smattering of smiles and confused looks including yours. I had begun to think you either thought I was crazy or you had begun to accept me like that one odd uncle everyone has in the family.

'Beyond my strange act, this is a very funny exchange in a great movie. However, if we look deeper at this one, it really doesn't make sense. We don't eat dogs, cats, or typically horses, but we eat sheep, cows, chickens, and more. Interesting, isn't it?'

'I guess, I haven't really thought about it. I guess we just do what the norm is in society.' You said still looking me up and down.

'Ahh... What is the norm? I cannot help but think of controlling the 'Proles' in *1984* with this one. Do you remember in the beginning of our conversations, I said our journey starts with curiosity?'

'Sure, I remember very vividly.'

'OK, well this curiosity extends to more than just intellectual questions. It extends to everything. In order to exude vibrant energy from our vessel, our body, then we must be curious in everything about our body. Curious about what we put into it, curious about what we expose it to, curious about how to optimize the energy within it. This curiosity is important in cleansing our vessel. This is important to understand as we need to optimize this physical vessel or shell of ours to connect to truth. If we understand that our bodies are simply a carrier of our energy, our spirit, then we can look at our bodies differently. In Tibetan the word for the body is lü which means 'something you leave behind' like baggage. (Rinpoche, 2002) To a Tibetan the body is simply a carrier of our true self, nothing more than luggage. Great metaphor, huh?'

'Certainly gets to the point.'

'From a western point of view, another way to look at the body is to think of a physical temple or church. We treasure this physical building considering it the literal versus metaphorical 'house of God'. One would not think of putting junk, or trash in this building or mistreating it in anyway. This would be a catastrophic act to most Judeo/Christian followers, yet these same people drive to a fast food restaurant and put the equivalent of 'junk' in their bodies. I just described the body as the carrier of our vibrant energy, our truth. This truth is the connection to the universal love, to the divine, so thus our bodies are in essence the real 'house of God'. If we think of bodies in this way we wouldn't think of damaging it in any way, we would treat it with the utmost care and respect. In addition, we want to extend vibrant energy out to the universe and therefore we need to feel good. An aching, or mistreated body will convey pain and displeasure far from the vibration of love. Does this make sense?' I asked rising to stretch my legs and heading north toward the Gorilla exhibit.

'Yes, this makes sense at a superficial level, however, at what depth are you discussing?' You raised your voice trying to keep up with my stride.

'At the deepest level possible, whatever you ingest does directly into your blood stream and has a direct impact on your body, whatever you place on or expose your body to will eventually make it into your blood stream and have the same negative or positive effect. Your body recreates every cell over a process of seven years, so in essence your body is completely regenerated every seven years. Everything you do influences these cells at the deepest layer, from the food you eat to the mood you choose to take. These cells are a reflection of your vibration.

We have already discussed the unimportance of the exterior of the body. The facelifts, the external superficial driven activity surrounding the body is of little interest to those on the journey to truth as these are a waste of energy. The real 'you' is beautiful, radiant, glowing. This is the 'you' that I am interested in. Now, when it comes to the 'inner' body, if you will, if we want to ensure that we optimize our energy and remove all obstructions to connect to the source, then we need to look at our bodies in a different light. We need to optimize the energy of our vessel, get this finely tuned body running as efficiently as possible.'

We arrived at the Gorilla enclosure, and I paused to view these beautiful creatures. About two feet from us sitting next to the glass were two females, one holding a small baby on her lap, next to them was the dominant Silverback male Gorilla. He must have weighed over 500 lbs. I thought to myself. The male was holding a bushel of branches stripping away the bark and leaves eating them in one big suck from his lips. He looked at us unmoved by any judgment.

'If we look at our bodies holistically and understand that we are simply animals, not much different than these Gorillas, then we need to understand the first rule in optimizing and cleansing our bodies in that *FOOD* is simply *FUEL*.' I said.

'This is the purpose of food, to put energy in our bodies. When not thinking in this way, food can actually control our lives as we mentioned earlier with the destructive passion of lust. We build in routines and thought around the supposed necessities that food provides us. Think of the coffee example earlier or, usually at a subconscious level, many of us are addicted to the feeling that stimulants such as sugar, and caffeine provide. At the very root, food is fuel. If we equate our bodies to that of an automobile, we wouldn't even think of putting a big chunk of sludge or waste into our car's tank of gas. This is what we do with food. We are constantly putting in 'junk' and then we feel horrible, through allergic reactions, sluggishness, and constipation. It is impossible to feel love and happiness when you haven't had a good bowel movement in three days, or when you constantly have a headache. Believe it or not, food is a huge component of our dissatisfaction in life not to mention long term disease and death. Food as fuel is a very hard one for people to come to grips with as they ultimately 'have to have the sweets', 'have to have meat', you name it. As we discussed earlier, this is a component of the lust passion. In order to feel radiant, feel love, we must feel good within our bodies and not just follow our desires. What do you think?'

'I guess I haven't broken it down to this level. I mean, I haven't had too many conversations around bowel movements,' you said laughing. 'At times we want to have some enjoyment in our lives, right? At least personally I try to follow guidelines of healthy living and do the best that I can. Isn't this the best that any of us can do?'

'Sure, we can only do the best at any given moment. Remember, I am discussing a blueprint we can point toward. The biggest suggestion I am giving you is to put your curiosity to work here. If you start with the premise that you are a race car and you want to optimize your performance then you would be very aware of what you were putting in the gas tank, right?'

'Sure. I can buy this.'

I started walking down the trail again north and then east toward the elephant and orangutan exhibits. We walked slowly without a purpose focused on the discussion indifferent to the chaos surrounding us.

'From a spiritual standpoint, as I already mentioned our body is our temple, the container of our vibrant energy, the vehicle to connect to the Divine within. If you look at your body in this light, then what we eat and do with our bodies changes dramatically.' I said. 'I am going to take you to a great raw food place today for lunch, I really look forward to your feedback, but let me ask you, did you enjoy the food from the café yesterday. This was vegan without any animal products.'

'The food was amazing. It really was, I was skeptical going in but I have to say the food was delicious. However, food is such a difficult topic; I hear conflicting information almost on a daily basis. One minute coffee is bad for you and the next it is great for you. I am so confused; I end up just eating whatever is easiest,' you said in full defeat.

'Fair statement, and in a way the information you hear will probably always be conflicting. Fear sells news, and even worse, most of these studies are funded by those who benefit from the results of the information. Makes you think, right? I would encourage a couple of things here. First, trust your intuition. Your intuition will get better over time as you continue to 'tune out' and then focus on 'tuning in' which we will discuss later today. Second, let your curiosity out. If something seems out of place, look deeper.

I couldn't believe what I found out. My two big 'wow' topics were milk and sugar. You know the two big 'staples'. I grew up in a country-type atmosphere. Small town; we ate a lot of meat, usually covered it with gravy, drank lots of milk, and had sides of some type of sugar usually represented in the form of a pie. When I first became curious with respect to food, I looked at milk first. Growing up I was an addict with milk drinking a minimum of a couple thirty-two ounce glasses of chocolate milk over dinner. This was on top of a whole day with milk and cheese. I used to chomp on blocks of cheese for a snack; you remember the cartoon telling you to snack on some cheese. I couldn't get enough of it. I started to feel like this intuitively didn't feel right, even though we are constantly bombarded with comments that we needed milk for calcium, or to lose weight. Remember the celebrities advertising 'Got Milk?' A lot of this money to run these ad campaigns comes from our tax dollars. Interesting isn't?' I rhetorically asked.

'Now, outside of the advertisements and dairy association backed 'studies' look at this intuitively. A cow produces milk for an obvious reason, right? This is for a baby cow. Breast milk is the perfect food for that particular animal at that particular age. I mean, if we intuitively looked closer at the issue, a better alternative would be producing human breast milk versus cow breast milk for production in our stores. Can you imagine this? Continuously impregnating women, pumping them with hormones and other drugs so they produce ten times the amount of normal milk production, and in the case of cows, after they begin to decline in milk production (typically five years), then we slaughter them as they are no use to us. So, a cow that typically lives around twenty-five years lives a life of five years, constantly pregnant and under stress so we can drink a product that, from an energy standpoint to our body, is inefficient at best, and at worst is extremely damaging to our bodies. Oh, and the babies that the dairy cow produces are another interesting point of reflection. The female calves have the fortunate life of following their mother into the milk production business. The boy calves are not so lucky; they are typically sold for veal where they live for 18 to 20 weeks in a wooden crate so small they cannot turn around, fed a diet to make them anemic so their flesh is white and then finally slaughtered.'

'I think I am going to be sick.' You said wincing.

'Look, as I said before, once you go down the rabbit hole you see reflections of the human race that will absolutely amaze you. I am not trying to use fear to change your behavior; I am just trying to discuss reality. You can choose to do anything you wish in life; it will not bother me in the least. I am simply trying to expose the importance of curiosity and some of the things I have come across in my journey. Fair?'

'Fair... I am still with you for now.'

'Without curiosity, we walk into the store and our senses control the mind. We have no idea what we are putting into our bodies. We let taste alone drive our decisions. We buy pretty shrink-wrapped packages of meat, cans of food filled with preservatives, and item after item filled with sugar. We go home, cook up this food filled with chemicals and inefficient energy, destroy most of the positive nutrients, if there are any, and then we put this sludge into our bodies. Then, we still do not understand why we feel terrible and have no energy. I have always said we, as humans, should have to find and kill our food; this would give us a different perspective on our diet, and an appreciation of exactly what we are putting in our bodies. However, we can do this with a curiosity, with awareness in what we are putting into our vibrant, beautiful bodies. We would never put inefficient fuel into our real car, yet we constantly do this with our bodies.

With the auspice that food is fuel, giving up milk was the best thing that I ever did in my life. I went from consistently having a minimum of two or three colds a year and at least one flu episode to not getting sick at all. Today I will get a twinge in my nose for perhaps a day and then it will disappear. I see it. Others around me will get the bug and be very sick for a week to two weeks.

Milk produces mucus in our bodies and mucus helps facilitate keeping bugs in our system. This includes allergies. I know plenty of people who stopped dairy and the allergies went away. Even medical doctors promote taking children off milk if they are suffering from allergies. When I stopped drinking dairy my nose ran with mucus for over a month straight. It was as if my body said, thank you, let me get rid of this non-productive stuff. But, I digress. Sugar was another big 'eye opener' for me.

I read the book by William Dufty called *Sugar Blues* and became aware of how pervasively processed and manufactured our foods really are. This book discusses the history of processing foods, in particular refined sugar. Refined sugar equates to a poison we continuously put into our body. We 'polish' off any of the natural or whole components of the sugar cane and when eaten, it infuses directly into our blood stream spiking our insulin levels. Diabetes in this country is a major issue and a major component of this comes from eating refined sugar. There is an example in the book of a sugar plantation owner who became extremely overweight, had major dental problems, and suffered from diabetes. However, the workers in the field who chewed on and sucked on the sugar cane in its natural state were lean with no health problems and had incredibly white teeth. It was the processed sugar that caused the problem.

These empty, no value calories are everywhere. I urge you to go to the grocery store at your next opportunity and try and find products without refined sugar. I searched for half an hour one day to find one pasta sauce without sugar. Typically these foods without sugar are made with fresh, whole, simple ingredients. Good chefs know the fewer, simpler the ingredients, the better the product. I was blown away at this revelation. Refined sugar is NOT good at all for our bodies. This book talks about this processing that happens in most of our foods.

Rice is a big one. We, again, strip away the whole grain and 'polish' the rice to this nondescript nutritionally meaningless white rice. I highly encourage reading this book as it will open your eyes. Just to quell your fears, I am not suggesting you give up sweets, I am just suggesting there are better alternatives than refined sugar, such as honey, my personal favorite agave which was in your dessert yesterday and brown rice syrup. Pumping your blood with any sweetener is not great; however, if you use it, it is better to use a natural source which your body has to digest and process prior to it getting into your blood stream, kind of a natural release versus the 'heroin' like example of pumping the refined white sugar into the blood. Take at look at how much sugar is in soda drinks, or what is actually in 'fake' sugars on the market. Read some reports on diet colas and what is actually in those products. This will blow your socks off. Again, I digress,' I said with a shrug.

'To get back to the 'food is fuel' discussion; I have a friend, Matthew, who is a great example of someone following a path of truth. Not just from a positive mental example, Matthew also has a health education and nutrition background. Whenever I think of food as fuel I think of him. Matthew has divided his day into multiple meals, all pre-made to be eaten every two hours. He eats the same thing every day, down to the ounce. He is like a professional bike rider taking in the perfect amount of fuel for his energy machine. He doesn't waste time finding food, or eating inefficient food. He is the most productive person I have been around. Oh, and he is one of the most peaceful, happy, radiant people I have ever come across. This might be the extreme for you, but we all must truly understand ultimately that food is fuel. Thoughts?'

'Well, eating the same thing everyday doesn't sound very appealing to me. This seems a little extreme for me.'

'Understood, we each choose our own path. I do not follow the path of eating the same meals everyday like Matthew, but he gives me a blueprint to look at and understand and realize that food is our energy – nothing more nothing less.'

I veered off the path and entered the butterfly exhibit with you close behind. The enclosure was filled with tropical plants and trees and the greenhouse like atmosphere was humid even on this overcast, dreary day. Specs of color emerged everywhere, blue, red, purple and yellow fluttered across the room. We walked through and inspected these beautiful creatures floating around the room. After a few minutes I noticed 3-4 butterflies had gathered on each of your arms and a few on your back immersing your coat with specs of vibrant color. You smiled taking in your visual transformation as the butterflies moved on with their curiosity filled journey.

We continued our way down the path to the elephant exhibit trying to get a glimpse of the large mammals. Most had gathered far off from the view point, we could only see one large male peering his head around a tree looking in our direction. He put his head down and charged for a few paces until continuing his slow walk to the rest of the herd. I smiled watching this moment.

You caught my smile and curiously asked, 'what's so funny?'

'I am smiling as I am reminded of a story with Buddha and the charging elephant.' I said. 'An elephant had become enraged in a small village creating tremendous destruction and fear. As the villagers ran for their lives, The Buddha took a seat in the middle of the road directly in the path of the charging elephant. He sat calm with his eyes closed in meditation. The elephant enamored by his calm presence stopped charging and laid down in front of him while The Buddha stroked his trunk. This is why you see The Buddha pictured with an elephant in a lot of sculptures. Whether this story is true or not, it still brings me great pleasure in thinking of the power of love and the connection to all living beings.'

I nodded toward the path and we continued again toward the orangutan enclosure and picked back up our conversation concerning tuning out and cleansing the body. 'A big topic beyond the 'food is fuel' discussion is that in order for us to truly have a clear vessel we must choose a VEGAN DIET, or at the very least a vegetarian diet. I am going to discuss this in depth as you may have great consternation of this cleansing initiative. Again, think of this as a blueprint. Be curious to understand how the body operates. Be curious to understand that the choices you make in life are connected to everything in the universe. Every decision holds implications for other living beings.

The simple answer for eating a vegan diet is twofold: one, it follows the act of ahimsa (non-violence), and in a deeper context from an Eastern philosophical standpoint, it brings to you the least amount of karma with respect to eating animals versus plants; second, it is both the most fuel efficient and least intrusive on the universe.'

I paused here feeling out your state of mind. You were silent and look disinterested in this topic. I decided to continue with the goal in trying to reason with your mind knowing this was a requirement for you to let go.

'I know this is a big topic and at first one that seems impossible or impracticable with a family. I can hear the famous words 'CAN'T' and 'BUT' ringing in your mind so let me break this down further. There are multiple reasons for a Vegan diet: spiritual, health and universal.

We have talked at a high level in why from a spiritual standpoint, however, let's explore this further. In living a Vegan lifestyle one chooses to eliminate all consumption or product containing any animal meat, animal by products (such as gelatin), or any other animal product such as milk, cheese or eggs. Most vegans also try to eliminate animal products from their lives completely such as leather goods, cosmetics tested on animals, or that use animal products. In living this way we are choosing to live in a state of ahimsa. In order to have a clear vessel that radiates energy we must abide by this principal. How can we possibly come from a place of love when our ego is telling us our lives are more important than another living being?

From a spiritual standpoint, for us to take on the least amount of karmic load, we need to take in the least karmic material which is a nut and plant based diet. I believe a book every person in the world should read in their lifetime, *A Diet for a New America* by John Robbins, is one that will 'blow your socks off'. Robbins is one of the sons to the Baskin and Robbins ice cream families. The courage John Robbins took to write this book even though his family had built its fortune on the very back of the dairy industry is stunning. Robbins noticed his family members were dying extremely young, most often from heart disease. He opened Pandora's Box and became curious. What he found was simply a must read for everyone who puts an animal product into their bodies.

I took you to the Family Farm for a reason. I wanted you to look in the eyes of these animals and feel their presence. I challenge you to tell me these beautiful animals are not filled with a spirit. They are filled with curiosity, personality and love. Instead of buying our shrink wrapped package of meat, become aware of the process it took to put this beautiful animal into the flesh you find packaged at your local grocery store. Become curious in animal food production and what you are putting in your body.

Animal food production is a business. There are no considerations for animal rights or that animals have souls and a living being. Animals are a widget thought of as how to optimize top line revenue while minimizing costs. Neither the animal nor our health is considered in this equation.'

We finally arrived at the orangutan exhibit where we took a spot up high to watch the animals. The sun had now broken free from the clouds and we stood embracing the warmth while we watched the beauty and power of these animals. We spotted two large red orangutans below us. They were play fighting chasing each other across the enclosure. They were pure joy in their moment below us. I looked at you to see if you were still with me and engaged. Your eyes still looked present so I continued.

'If we look at the big picture in thinking of animals as our dominion, as a food staple we incur huge negative karma. We kill the equivalent of 8 animal lives per person on this planet each year. This amounts to over 48 Billion animals killed each year, with 9.5 Billion animals (excluding fish and other minor farmed animals) slaughtered for their flesh in the United States alone.[7]

We treat these living creatures horribly, confining them in small spaces; chickens in less than half a square foot of space where they cannot even stretch their wings; pigs in crates so small they cannot turn around; farm fish are raised in filthy, confined spaces so difficult that most develop parasites and/or disease and up to 40% may die prior to packaging for production. Animals are cheap, cages are expensive.

Broiler chickens are selectively bred and genetically altered to produce breasts and thighs at over twice the normal size making it even difficult for the animals to stand; most have serious heart, lung and liver issues. Their beaks are clipped at birth so they do not 'harm' other chickens during confinement with tens of thousands of other birds, typically in darkness. These super chickens pumped full of antibiotics and drugs are taken to slaughter at six or seven weeks old, whereas a normal chicken would live around twelve years.

Laying hens are often stacked at least four or five crates high on top of each other where the excrement falls on the animals below. In their early years they are kept in complete darkness until feeding time. Once they reach maturity to lay eggs they are kept in continuous light to maximize egg laying production. At around eighteen to twenty months, as their levels of egg production begin to decrease, the entire lot of egg laying chickens are taken to slaughter where the meat is used in pot pies and soup as the meat is too bruised for anything else.

The male chickens have a different fate. They are useless to egg laying production so, at birth, they are either suffocated immediately or just thrown into a grinder with their shells to be fed to animals on the feedlot or for dog and cat food. Over 100 million baby male chickens are killed each year in this way alone in the United States.

Pigs do not have it any better. After two to three weeks, they are ripped away from their mother, their tales are cut off, typically some teeth are removed and the males are castrated, all without any pain relief. Over 105 million a year are killed alone in the United States. Estimates are that over 1 million alone die on transport and over 420,000 are crippled on the way to the slaughter house. Over 80% have pneumonia at the time of death. All this from an animal that is naturally clean, curious and incredibly smart. It has been stated that a pig is smarter than a three year old human being. Perhaps we should revisit the Pulp Fiction argument.

Veal calves are an incredibly difficult story even to tell as I mentioned earlier. These male calves are taken from their mothers at birth and put in a crate where they cannot move and purposely given a diet deficient of iron. In this way they cannot move and their meat is tender and white for slaughter anywhere from two to twenty weeks old. Bon appetite!

Although numbers are tough to come by in animal testing, rough estimates put the numbers close to 115 million each year that are subjected to painful and fatal product testing in the United States alone.[8]

Over 50 million animals, including over 1 million cats and dogs, are killed each year for the use of their fur.[9]

I cannot go on. I am feeling too much negativity in me to continue. How do you feel?'

'Not good, obviously, I have heard some of these numbers before. I feel horrible, yet, I also feel I am being manipulated by fear to live a certain life,' you said.

'Fair enough, I don't want to scare you; I am just trying to state reality. We can hide from this all we want, buy our shrink wrapped food in the store and not think about it. You know, out of sight, out of mind. This is your choice, your life, your body. It truly doesn't bother me. You can sit down next to me right now with a huge steak, smothered in bacon with a side of chicken nuggets. It will not bother me whatsoever. I choose to live life filled with love. I choose to live as an example of this love for all life. This is all, nothing more, nothing less. I will not judge you. The obvious point in stating these examples and understanding the reality of the situation is first how this makes us feel. If we FEEL bad, then it is impossible to express love. If you truly do not feel bad and are aware of the impact on animals, as well as the environment and your health, which we will talk about in a minute, then we are on different paths in life. This is OK. Again, I do not judge you. I just saw an anti PETA movement T-shirt which said PWEETA (People Who Enjoy Eating Tasty Animals). These people feel justified that humans are on top of the food chain. Again, this is their choice. I choose a different path. I do find it interesting that we can have pets such as cats and dogs yet eat a pig or a cow. In China, they would just eat all of the animals. Right?'

'Understood, this is all new information to me so it is difficult to change patterns or behaviors that I have done all of my life. I wonder how people will view me; how I could actually live this type of life. I have an inner 'itch' if you will to pursue this but it seems nearly impossible.'

'This is your choice; you will ultimately choose to do this or not to do this. This impossibility is self defined, driven by your mind – anything is possible. Perhaps you will try your best and occasionally lapse and eat meat. So be it, you can only be the best that you can be at any given moment. With respect to how people view you; I am hearing the 5 or 6 rating coming out in you with how you view yourself without your roles. I can only point this out to you; at some point you must realize you only have yourself in your life to make happy. Everything else in life is an addition. This is you. You are beautiful. The rest of the world will fall in love with this energy. I will not spend much more time on this as I think I have made my point but I wanted to briefly talk about the universal environmental and health issues behind eating meat.

Remember the earth is an organism in itself so we must do our best to fit into this organism and be in harmony, in synch, with this being. In addition, we want to be at our optimal health so we can thrive, so we can be present, so we can love. Fair?'

'Yes, this is fair.'

'OK, let's look at the environmental impact on raising animals for food. Living in balance in the universe; as a business, animal production is simply inefficient. As I dove into this issue, I couldn't believe the impact eating meat had on the environment. I always knew deep inside that intuitively killing another soul was difficult for me, and I knew there were health implications; however, I could not believe the impact on the environment. These facts were truly astonishing to me.

70% of all the grains and cereals grown in the United States go to feed farmed animals.[10]

A major 2006 report by the United Nations, titled Livestock's Long Shadow, summarized the devastation caused by the meat industry. Raising animals for food, the report said, is 'one of the top two or three most significant contributors to the most serious environmental problems, at every scale from local to global. Raising animals for food is playing a major role is every environmental concern such as ozone depletion, and dead zones in our oceans.'[11]

In the context of the global water supply, the impact of animal agriculture threatens utter catastrophe. Factory farming is responsible for 37 percent of pesticide contamination, 50 percent of antibiotic contamination and one-third of the nitrogen and phosphorus loads found in freshwater.[12]

Farmed animals use more than half of the water consumed in

the United States. Animal agriculture uses 70 percent of the world's agriculture land and 30 percent of planet's total land area.[13]

According to the EPA, 35,000 miles of rivers in 22 states and groundwater in 17 states has been permanently contaminated due to this animal production run off.[14]

It takes five thousand gallons of water to produce one pound of factory farmed beef. It takes 25 gallons of water to produce one pound of wheat. In other words, if one chose not to eat one pound of beef you would save more water than by not showering the entire year (Robbins, The Food Revolution, 2001). A total vegetarian diet takes about 300 gallons of water per day to more than 4000 gallons in a meat eater's diet. (Robbins, 1987)

Farmed animals produce 130 times the amount of excrement as the entire human population of the United States. Factory farms do not have sewage treatment centers so the runoff from this excrement runs into our rivers, streams and oceans, polluting our water, depleting our top soil, and contaminating our air, some 89,000 pounds of excrement a second.[15] The run-off from factory farms pollutes our waterways more than all other industrial sources combined.[16]

Factory animal farms produce an estimated 18 percent of the greenhouse gas emissions worldwide, far outstripping the transportation industry. 37 percent of these gasses are from methane which has 23 times the impact on global warming than CO_2.[17] I guess the thought of a cow having gas isn't so funny.' I said smiling.

'In the past 50 years, fisheries have exterminated 90 percent of the large fish populations.[18]

More than 260 million acres of U.S. forests have been cleared to create cropland to grow grain and to feed farmed animals.[19]

According to the Smithsonian, the equivalent of seven football fields is bulldozed every minute to create more room for farmed animals. This effect has been highlighted in the Amazon

Rainforest where the clearing of the forest is directly related to the raising of farm animals.[20]

Livestock grazing is the number one cause of threatened and extinct indigenous plant and animal species in both the United States and across the world.[21]

It takes sixteen pounds of grain to produce one pound of meat, and even fish on fish farms must be fed five pounds of wild-caught fish to produce 1 pound of farmed fish flesh.[22] The world's cattle supply alone consume a quantity of food equal to the caloric needs of 8.7 Billion people, more than the entire population of earth.[23]

20 percent of the world's population, or 1.4 Billion people, could be fed on the grain and soybeans from U.S. cattle alone.[24] Yet, over 840 Million people in this world are hungry. If everyone on earth chose a vegan lifestyle we would produce more than enough food for the entire world.' I paused sighing.

'E, the noted Energy magazine, stated in 2002 that more than one third of all fossil fuel produced in the United States are used to raise animals for food.[25] We could tie many side components in here with respect to fossil fuels and the loss of human life and environmental impact from our involvement in the Middle East and the oil issues.

Depressing, isn't it?' I said.

'Yes. Back to my original question; how are you always happy when you know all of this?'

'Great question, makes you want to go out and get a bucket of KFC and a gallon of ice cream and drown yourself in the depression, right? No, not really,' I said laughing.

I nodded back to the path and we headed west again toward the tiger enclosure.

'To answer your question, I am curious; I read; I educate myself on the truth in our lives and I choose a path that I feel proud of and at peace with. I 'tune in' as we will discuss, and thus I am connected to the source with love. I can only take care of myself. If I am an example for others to follow, so be it. Ultimately, I can only choose happiness, peace, and living in harmony. This is all that can be done.

Of course, knowing all of this does not make me feel good. I don't ignore it. I donate money to causes, and when I have time I donate time or work toward efforts to educate people, but in the end, each person must choose for themselves.

Outside of the spiritual and environmental implications there are real implications concerning your health as well with respect to choosing a Vegan lifestyle. Again it is very hard to be happy and full of love when you feel bad.

Watching your health is not only being on a Vegan diet, but a diet consisting of whole, organic foods that are full of nutrients and deplete of poison and pesticides. I know plenty of vegetarians who really should be called 'junkatarians'. These people typically load their diet with processed foods such as refined sugars, and other simple carbohydrates.

There is a direct correlation to diet and disease. T. Colin Campbell talks extensively about this in his landmark book and research called *The China Study*. Campbell talks about the diseases of AFFLUENCE, those that typically touch countries from a western background such as the United States, England and Western Europe. These countries have higher rates of heart disease, cancer, and diabetes to name a few. Interestingly enough other countries that are starting to adopt a diet similar to western countries are now experiencing the same growth in these diseases. Campbell found a pure vegetarian (i.e. vegan) diet to be healthiest. Campbell estimates that '80 to 90% of all cancers, cardiovascular diseases, and other degenerative illness can be prevented, at least until very old age, simply by adopting a plant-based diet.' (T. Colin Campbell, 2006)

I know I am beginning to saturate this topic but let me give you a few other comments in how diet directly influences health.

The American Dietetic Association states that vegetarians

have 'lower rates of death from ischemic heart disease; lower blood cholesterol levels, lower blood pressure, and lower rates of hypertension, type 2 diabetes, and prostate and colon cancer' and that vegetarians are less likely than meat-eaters to be obese.[26]

Meat eaters are nine times more likely to be obese than vegetarians. (Robbins, The Food Revolution, 2001)

Vegetarians and Vegans live, on average, six to ten years longer than meat eaters. (Robbins, Diet for a New America, 1987)

Studies have shown that vegetarian kids grow taller and have higher IQ's than classmates, and they are at a reduced risk for heart disease, obesity, diabetes, and other diseases in the long run. (Robbins, Diet for a New America, 1987) (Charles Attwood M.D., 1995)

Vegetarians have been shown to have stronger immune systems and get sick less than meat eaters.[27]

The risk of death from a heart attack by average American man is 50%, whereas the risk by average American vegetarian man is 15%, and the risk from a pure vegetarian (Vegan) man drops to 4%.(Robbins, Diet for a New America, 1987) Unbelievable.' I said shaking my head.

'As I mentioned eating meat directly correlates to cancer as well. World populations with high meat intakes who do not have correspondingly high rates of colon cancer – None, world populations with low meat intakes who do not have correspondingly low rates of colon cancer – None. (Robbins, Diet for a New America, 1987)

Chlorinated hydrocarbon pesticide residues in the U.S. diet supplied by meat: 55%. (Robbins, Diet for a New America, 1987)

Pesticide residues in U.S. diet supplied by vegetables: 6%. Pesticide residues in U.S. diet supplied by fruits: 4%. Pesticide residues in U.S. diet supplied by grains: 1%.' (Robbins, Diet for a New America, 1987)

I paused here, mentally tired. We stood in front of the tiger exhibit and watched a huge male Tiger pace anxiously back in forth ignoring our presence. I nodded to the beautiful animal trying to extend on my discussion.

'Look at this animal. He is made to eat meat. He has a large gait, big paws and claws to chase and kill animals. Our body is designed for mobility not chasing or killing animals. This tiger's teeth and jaw are designed for meat consumption. His teeth are sharp and pointed for piercing flesh. Our teeth are flat for biting, crushing and grinding. His jaw mainly moves up and down to swallow his meat whole. In fact his saliva does not contain digestive enzymes; his stomach is filled with 10 times as much hydrochloric acid than our stomach. Our jaws cannot shear but move side to side for extensive chewing and grinding of high fiber foods. Our saliva contains extensive digestive enzymes and is alkaline in nature. This tiger is extremely acidic. Parasites cannot survive in the stomach of this animal due to this acidic nature. Back to our bowel movement discussion, this animal's intestine track like other carnivores is roughly 3-6 times the length of its body for quick expelling of meat which quickly rots. Our intestines are 10-12 times the length of our body like other herbivores and wind back and forth designed to extract as much nutrients from a fiber based diet. In addition this tiger has a liver designed to eliminate high amounts of uric acid which are created in the system to break down animal proteins. Our bodies do not possess this ability so our livers become extremely taxed trying to filter out this food.'

I stopped here knowing I had inundated you with data. I remembered when I first explored this topic my head hurt in trying to comprehend information that was new to me.

Your eyes frowned in thought until you were confident with your question. 'If all of this is true then why have I not heard of this before?' You said.

'A couple of reasons, the number one reason is that there are lobbies from various businesses, such as the American Dairy Association and Beef Industry lobby. They spend a lot of money to make sure we hear messages to benefit their products. Your tax money is at work; without subsidies a pound of meat would cost closer to $35 a pound.[28] I mean, look at Oprah, she makes one comment about giving up hamburgers and she is sued. Like most industries that make a lot of money, they are heavy hitters with money and lobbying efforts. The second reason is that you have not wanted to hear it. Again, it seems that life is easier to just live without questions. Why question what I put in my body, let me go to the store pick up my shrink wrap meat and buy my hamburger helper and feed my family; what is the issue, right?'

'I see your point. Just like anything, we are not going to hear the message until we are ready,' you said.

'Another reason is that western medicine typically does not focus on nutrition as a means to health. Physicians are not trained extensively on this topic. Western medicine is typically a band aid treatment. In other words, physicians in the United States rarely have the time to understand the root, or genesis of a problem. It is easier to prescribe a pill to solve the latest symptom rather than understand 'why' the symptom appeared in the first place. Our bodies are amazing and eating the proper diet can heal. Listen to the famous words from Hippocrates:

'Everyone has a doctor in him or her; we just have to help it in its work. The natural healing force within each one of us is the greatest force in getting well. Our food should be our medicine. Our medicine should be our food.'

This quote is over 2300 years old, pretty amazing. We have known this for a long time, and we have just gone adrift. Prescribing health through a proper diet is not big business; pharmacies run the American health system.

Buddha also talks about living a healthy life:

'To keep the body in good health is a duty, otherwise we shall not be able to keep our mind strong and clear.'

If you truly want to be happy, your diet is a huge foundation for this happiness. Again, we cannot be happy if we are not feeling well. Understood?'

'Understood, however, this is a lot of information to take in.'

'I understand. Take this as an overview and be curious yourself. Don't believe me; find out for yourself. Read *Diet for a New America* and *The China Study*. Read your own books, make your own decision. Just remember, anything that takes you away from a place centered in love and positive energy is an obstacle to truth.'

I turned and faced you with a big sigh. 'This is a big, overwhelming topic that comes from a very different place in how you were probably raised. Don't let it overwhelm you just think about the general theme of the discussion and let your curiosity take over.'

I turned and headed back down the trail toward the north meadow intent on soaking in the newly arrived sun and continuing our discussion. I was ready to lighten the topic away from this difficult discussion. I knew change was hard and a person's initial reaction was to fight and keep their existing lifestyle. Today's topic would take time to resonate, and more than anything it needed to come from within you, and not from my words. We crossed the meadow and found a park bench to take in the scene across the park. In the distance was the carousel and next to this was the stage for the summer concert series.

'In thinking of your body, you need to give it proper nutrients.' I said breaking our silence. 'I touched on this a little bit, but just cutting out meat is not enough; some vegetarians are far less healthy than those that eat meat every day. In order to maximize our energy we need to eat the right foods, *whole foods* full of nutrients such as organic fruits and dark green vegetables.

Just as in your mind, as you strip away layers with your body in getting more centered and at its core essence you will intuitively understand the balance that you need to feel healthy. This includes things like the proper amount of good bacteria, or probiotics in your body and vitamins. If you are eating a diet rich in fruits and dark green vegetables and whole foods such as brown rice and quinoa then you should not need to enhance your body with external vitamins, however, be curious about this topic and learn, understand the benefits of Vitamin C and Echinacea when you are sick, and ensure you are replenishing your body with minerals. Drink plenty of water; this is the core of your being. Water filters your blood. We need to move away from acidic blood to alkaline blood and this is done best through fruits and vegetables. Scientists have shown that cancer loves sugars and detest an oxygen rich environment. Ingesting dark green vegetables infuses your blood with oxygen and alkaline.

Understand enzymes the vital part they play in our health and well being. I have a friend who talks about them all day long. He is a man who had cholesterol over 240, and his prostate levels were so high they were going to put him on drugs for both of these ailments. He refused and went on a raw diet consisting of only fruits and vegetables that have not been cooked above 110-118 degrees. In this way, the food will have the optimal energy or life in the food source. This is pure energy you put into your body. When you eat raw food your body does not have to produce additional digestive enzymes to process it. When you eat cooked food your body has to use valuable metabolic enzymes to help digest this food. Eating raw food passes through your digestive tract in a half to a third of the time as cooked food. Pure energy is much easier on your system. In eating this way, my friend lost over 50 lbs, dropped his cholesterol over 100 points, and his prostrate levels went down considerably. This all happened in a matter of months. He went back to the doctor who couldn't believe it. They wanted to know what 'drug' he took, and could not believe this happened with food alone. Again, your body is amazing. It needs to be treated as a high speed race car. Don't put junk in it. Thoughts?'

'No, makes sense, I have no idea what raw food is about but I see your point,' you said.

'Well I will serve you a raw lunch here in a few minutes. There is a great place a few miles away. Also, in addition to understanding what we put in our body it is important to understand what you expose and put on your body. Whatever you breathe in your body immediately heads to your bloodstream. Breathe is life, it is critical to your well being. It is very important to understand what you are exposing your body to be it cleaning supplies to nail salons to your work environment. Another one is what you put on your body. Your skin is a sponge that is porous taking these elements directly into your blood stream. Everything from dying your hair, to skin products and deodorant should be analyzed as chemicals or ingredients that your body will have to process. I don't want to scare you just make you aware and encourage curiosity.

Next on our list of cleansing our vessel should be obvious in actually cleansing our vessel – BEING HYGENIC. I don't want to overstate the obvious here, but if our vessel is our energy giver and receiver, we need to keep this vessel as cleansed as possible both inside and out. I thought I was clean until I went to Japan. This culture thrives on cleanliness. It is appropriate to scrub yourself with a hard brush prior to getting into the bath. They get all of the old, dead skin off their bodies. Their bodies thrive; you can see it in their skin. Not to spend more time on colonics, but I have a friend who does this as her job. The stories I have heard concerning the lack of cleanliness inside our bodies is truly monumental. Research this yourself and look at colons from vegetarians versus meat eaters. This will blow you away. I think enough is said on hygiene as this is pretty straight forward, right?'

'Yes. I think I got this one down.'

I looked around the park and watched the energy. This meadow was the natural break spot to rest weary kids and for others to play or entertain. There was a group playing Frisbee and another in the middle of a Tai Chi routine, moving slowly and rhythmically in cadence with the leader. We watched this latter group flow from one move to the other without effort or thought, just like life I imagined to myself, one continuous flow with the Universe riding and embracing change and the vibration of love. I caught myself smiling in this thought.

I looked back to you unsure how you would take to our next conversation, 'OK, the next topic will deserve some comment back and forth. In order to cleanse our bodies and mind and extend this positive love vibration out to the universe we must follow this rule: NO MIND ALTERING DRUGS OR ALCOHOL. Thoughts?' I asked.

'Well, I don't do drugs so this is not an issue. I don't drink that much, but I am not seeing the harm with drinking occasionally. I am seeing studies out now even touting the benefits of alcohol. This one could be an issue.'

'Again, you will choose to live your life to the best of your ability I will not judge you. The purpose of this discussion is concerning the clarity of your mind and being completely present at all times. A single glass of wine or bottle of beer would seem not to disrupt this much; however, it is very easy to have one glass lead to two and two to three and pretty soon our clarity is gone and we are doing things not filled with integrity or love.

I have two stories for you on this one. First, concerning mind altering drugs. I have friends, who are very connected to others, full of love, and peace, yet for some reason they believe this connection to the earth includes smoking weed. I guess they believe they have 'met the farmer' if you will and have a connection with the earth. I recently went to a gathering at a friend's house. We talked, made food together, listened to music, and it was a great time. I had deep meaningful conversations with a number of people, more so than I had with any of my traditional friends, ever. At some point in the day, a few of them decided to light up and smoke some marijuana. The effect was immediate. They became so mellow, they stopped talking, leaned up against the coach, eyes closed, completely NOT present. They felt at ease and at peace but what they didn't realize was they could get this same effect and more within their own mind sparked by their spirit. Many others have claimed taking drugs as a path to God realization. Timothy Leary comes to mind here. I cannot give both arguments to this issue as I have not taken LSD or other mind altering drugs. However, what I can tell you is that the universal message across Eastern philosophies is that one cannot connect to the source without absolute purity and clarity of the mind.

This includes alcohol. Certainly a glass of wine or a glass of beer occasionally does not alter the mind, but it does affect its clarity. I was out with a friend recently who could not handle my not drinking at the table. I was having a great time, very involved in his conversation; however, as he continued to drink, his agitation to my not drinking increased. I am not sure if he felt guilt, even though I continued to reassure him I did not care if he drank or not. Perhaps, he felt I was 'left out' of all the fun he was having while drinking. I would challenge anyone to the following concerning alcohol. Drink water one evening while visiting a club, you will be amazed and very amused at what you observe sober. Bar staff are fully aware of this. The point is that you need clarity and purity for a cleansed vessel. Thoughts?'

'Fair enough, I see your point,' you said.

I looked back over at the small group engaged in the slow, fluid movements of Tai Chi and nodded their way. 'Exercise is another important topic in keeping the body tuned and vibrant. This is an interesting topic. We need to be fit and toned in order to maximize our race car and be the best that we can be so we can feel and extend truth in our lives. Getting outside, having the sun radiate on our skin is beautiful. Exercise is an important ingredient.

This concept is an important concept in eastern philosophy. You can see this concept in the Asana's of yoga, or martial arts such as the Tai Chi exercises this group across the lawn is practicing. In the east, it is believed that a rigid body, stiff and inactive, is a dead body. A supple, moving body is full of life. This group with their fluid movements is moving their CHI or internal life force throughout their body. Fluidity like water is the journey, soft, yielding indifferent to stiff and rigid. This is vibrancy.

I have a friend who walks around with a hula hoop as she constantly wants to be in motion. Exercise seems obvious, right? However, it is important to understand that exercise should be an addition to our lives after we fully 'tune out' and 'tune in' in our lives. It should not be the first priority, which we will discuss in a minute concerning 'tuning in' to the beauty of the universe. I have another friend who religiously exercises an hour to an hour and a half every day. This exercise in itself does not make her happy deep within her soul; this must be driven by other means.

I used to build my day around a jog in the morning, yoga if I had time, and finally meditation if I really had time. This meant I meditated about 10 percent of the time. I was not happy. Fit? Yes, and I had plenty of energy, but I was not happy at the root of my soul. As we have already discussed, we only have so many hours in our day, so many hours in our lives, spend them on truly important things. Exercise to get your body fit and energetic.

As I mentioned yoga, the physical forms, or Asana's are ideal as you will get supple and fit and can do this anywhere. In India this is one of the steps toward a spiritual connection; in fact, yoga actually means 'the union of the limited self and the divine self'. Yoga is the union between the physical body and the spirit. The physical forms in yoga are actually the most basic levels of a yoga practice. The ultimate state is the spiritual union with the divine source. Pretty similar to what we have been talking about concerning 'truth', right?'

'I have actually tried yoga and enjoyed it. I just couldn't find the time to attend classes,' you perked up hoping for a different possibility.

'Life has priorities as with anything else. I found buying a DVD and practicing at home helped me tremendously. Now if I do not have the time to attend a practice I just do my own yoga exercises whenever I have some time at home.'

I rose from the bench and nodded back toward the path. 'I don't know about you but I am starting to get hungry, let's head back to the car.'

We broke south back along the path focused on the conversation.

'The last cleansing exercise that I see as important for our body is to GET PROPER SLEEP. The term 'proper' will be relative as you will see moving forward; remember the comment of 'less food, less sleep, and less talking'. The important point is to take your sleep very seriously. This means not procrastinating over useless time delaying sleep. This means building a proper sleep environment that is quiet, dark, and filled with positive energy. One of the biggest items that disrupt our sleep is our animals. We have to make a decision toward ensuring that we get proper sleep. If the animal is disrupting this, then you must make a choice about allowing the animal in the room. Proper sleep rejuvenates our entire being. A tired individual is rarely present, or filled with love. Getting proper sleep is essential toward finding truth. What do you think?'

'I am just laughing over here, as I know when someone did not sleep well or enough their attitude directly reflects this correlation.'

'Right, sleep is a good thing,' I said channeling Martha Stewart.

We made our way past the penguins and the tropical rain

forest and stopped at the African Savanna for a quick look at the giraffes extending their necks searching for something across the park.

After a short break I found inspiration to discuss more around harmony in the body. 'Building harmony in the mind and body is essential for your happiness, for your peace in finding truth. The modern father of yoga, B.K.S. Iyengar, quotes the original father of yoga, Pantañjali, in a book titled *Light on the Yoga Sūtras of Pantañjali* on this very topic, 'for one who lacks ethical and perfect physical health, there can be no spiritual illumination. Body, mind and spirit are inseparable: if the body is asleep, the soul is asleep.' (Iyengar, 1993) Iyengar continues in discussing the attainment in cleansing the mind and the body: 'The impurities of the body and mind are cleansed, the dawning light of wisdom vanquishes ignorance, innocence replaces arrogance and pride, and the seeker becomes the seer.' (Iyengar, 1993)

I walked down the path again reflecting on this last quote, 'the *seeker* becomes the seer, beautiful isn't it.'

'Yes, however, this is a lot to take in, I feel as though I am at the beginning of this journey still trying to grasp the concepts.' You walked straight with your head down.

'I understand, this is a lot to take in. I think these words will shine the further you are on your journey.'

We made our way to the front entrance and I called in an order to go from Chaco Canyon, a raw and vegetarian food restaurant a few miles away. 'Let's get the food to go so we can talk about the most important topic of taking the journey to truth in an appropriate spot.'

'What's this topic?'

'TUNING IN to the energy and vibrancy of the Universe. Let's go get our food so we can focus entirely on this topic.

I offered to drive and you readily agreed. We swung by the restaurant and picked up our food and I headed west to toward the water.

Chapter 8

Tuning In

I drove past the zoo entrance and down a steep hill through the middle of the old Nordic fishing neighborhood of Ballard, which was now morphing into a vibrant young community with hip music, food and eccentric stores. The middle of the neighborhood held a small park filled with sculptures of trees and giant mushrooms. We passed the mushrooms, a Norwegian gift shop, the cliché fish and chip restaurants, and the Ballard locks to reach a sprawling marina on the expansive Puget Sound waterway. The road continued for a long period of time past this extensive marina to an obscure, hard to reach beach front park called Golden Gardens at the end of the road.

'This is the end, beautiful friend,' I said ominously in my best Jim Morrison tone parking the car.

'I have definitely not been here before.' You gazed like a child full of curiosity clearing missing my *Doors* reference.

We jumped out of the car with the food in our hands and made our way past a small wetland area filled with a large pond, ducks and natural habitat down to a narrow beach covered in sand and small rocks. I found us a seat on an old washed up log that was for now a permanent part of the park and broke out our food.

'OK, so we have a raw feast, a cilantro pesto pizza, green coconut curry and a raw nacho plate, with a raw chocolate brownie, a raspberry tart and strawberry lemonades. Enjoy.'

You looked at me then the food not sure what to think. I was beginning to think you were remembering my comment about Jonestown again; however, you tried the pizza and smiled. I smiled in concert with your enjoyment and dug in hungry after the emotionally tiring morning. We sat enjoying the food and the view. The park looked out across the Puget Sound waterway to the west taking in the Olympic Peninsula and a glimpse of the mountains through the intermittent clouds.

The beach sat at the end of Ballard, encased in a fence, rail road tracks and a large hill to the north surrounded by the waters of Puget Sound to the south and the west. The food and view were magical. We had this part of the beach to ourselves as no one else took the time or energy to make their way to this far edge of the park. The sun was still out mixing with non threatening clouds, and a stiff wind from the west that rolled in small waves to the shore. I closed my eyes in mid bite enjoying this breeze in my face and the sound of the water. I felt good, I felt calm. I chose this park for a reason in discussing the path of 'tuning in'. I wanted a quiet place surrounded by nature and in particular the energy of the water and waves.

After we demolished the food and both of us were brimming with newfound living energy I decided to take on our next topic in our journey toward truth.

'We are at the crux of the journey, the discussion of 'tuning in' to the vibrant energy of the Universe. Before I talk about the details of this I want to give you my background in coming to this place myself in my journey.

I had spent years stuck, reading every book I could imagine toward spirituality, finding *awareness* or truth and still I felt stuck, unhappy,' I said in reflection. 'In fact, the deeper I dug, the more complex the issue became for me. I became isolated, constantly in deep thought toward my purpose in life. I struggled with so many 'why' questions; my head spun.

My friends seemed so different to me. They thought about very worldly things. I had become a vegetarian; I dabbled in meditation. I became curious with life. No one I knew thought this way. I was certainly a black sheep, a fish swimming against the current. This was obvious. I was ostracized in a sense, as much as a white male can be ostracized.

With my family I just didn't fit; I was the outcast. No one understood, nor cared to understand so they would judge at a distance, make surface level comments and leave it at that. Same went for my friends; they just didn't ask. They knew I thought differently but just didn't have any idea or curiosity in what I thought. They just believed I was real serious about life and let it be. They would occasionally get the courage to challenge my political or personal beliefs, usually after alcohol was involved, and then they took the Bill O'Reilly approach in trying to bully me, and not have an open, intimate conversation without judgment. I was depressed. I went through relationships deep in thought, distant, and not spiritually connected. The normal expectations from life pulled me in again and again as I continued through this pattern. Do you know what I am saying?' I asked, clearly trying to gain more insight into your own internal challenges.

'To a point, I mean, do we ever fully feel understood in life. I guess in a way this was why I approached you.' You said staring at the water. 'At a deep level I knew something was missing. I had my moments of happiness, I have a great family and my job is pretty good, from the outside looking in I should be fine, but I didn't feel fine. I felt there was something more in life, something inside of me that I wasn't experiencing. For some strange reason I felt this innate draw to you as if you had this missing piece for me. It was intuitive as if I didn't have a choice in approaching you. Although I was nervous I felt calm in talking to you. I had no idea the depths that we would be exploring but looking at this situation I am very happy and grateful I am now exploring this side of me. I feel as though I am going through a spiritual rebirth.' You continued staring at the water deep in your thoughts. 'I could see a glow surrounding you as if a light was shining from within.'

'You are kind in your statements. I think the light you saw

within me was the reflection of your own light. Perhaps seeing your own light you were encouraged to explore a new path. I can relate to your spiritual rebirth. I too had uneasiness, a constant pit in my stomach that my life was unsettled. Almost as if I was on a chaotic carnival ride spinning from one task to another, one year after another and I couldn't get off. I couldn't shake these deep thoughts. I wanted to understand my purpose. I wanted to find peace. I wanted love. I looked within myself to find when I was happiest. Always, my thoughts were when superficial matters didn't apply to my life and I was at my most curious and spiritual self, all predicated by meditation. I still couldn't get past the 'what next?' or 'how to' questions until a friend of mine, led by his example, encouraged me to go on another spiritual quest. This time I was alive. I found several books to help explain the 'how' in getting me to a place of peace, a place of love, a place of truth, and then I explored and I continue to explore on my own. I am on this journey each and every day. Is this similar to your experience in feeling unhappy?'

'I guess to a point, I think we all go through it to some extent, don't we? Isn't a mid-life crisis just self reflection that we will die one day?' you asked.

'Right, right! In turn, we typically turn away from this self realization of our mortality and mask it with worldly superficial 'things' versus an exploration of our soul. Most of us turn to cars, women, affairs, bigger houses, something other than the reality that we are faced with. Or most often, we just ignore the question concerning our purpose in life until we are on our death bed. Why worry about something we can't control, right? Isn't that why we feel so lost and feel we cannot do anything about it?'

'Hmmm... I haven't really thought about this. This feels true. I mean, some of us go to church and try to build a relationship toward the afterlife in this way. I don't know. I guess this is why we are so afraid to die.'

'Of course we are afraid to die; we don't know what we will

find in there. It is a scary thought. I am not about to answer this question; however, I do want to revisit the purpose of our being here in life, our choice in how we can live in this life, today.

During my exploration, I would read book after book from those that had achieved this level of peace and happiness, this awareness, you know, the monk smiling looking at the flower. I would read Zen poetry and look at nature and just know or see the beauty in this. I wanted this feeling all the time. I knew this was my purpose to connect back to the divine source in this lifetime, connect my drop of water back to the big pool of water that we all belong to. Remember the Jack Johnson song:

'All of life is in one drop of the ocean waiting to go home, just waiting to go home'

I just couldn't find the way. And then, I found it. It was my vehicle to peace, my vehicle to truth. Life became very simple after this, very calm, very beautiful. I am so full of life, so full of love now, so full of truth. This is why you see me smiling all the time. How could I not?' I said in admiration.

'What was it? What was this moment?' you stared at me raising your voice.

'The realization of my purpose in life was a big part of it. 'Tuning out' to cleanse my vessel and my mind was another big part of it. The understanding of who I truly was inside, not my money, not my clothes, nothing but my naked soul full of integrity and love was another big part of it. However, the biggest piece that I was missing that took me over the edge and helped me see this all with such clarity was *TUNING IN* through MEDITATION.

In my journey I cannot see the beginning any more. It is as if I have started and finished. I am nothing but I am everything. I'm talking about focused meditation, not the five minute *I want to reduce my stress level meditation*, but focused, intense sitting or even standing meditation. Alone, building toward 'no mind' or 'no thought', this is it. This is how we control the rambunctious mind so out of control for all of these years. This is how we tame the little green Hulk. This is how to find the real 'you'. This is how to strip away all these layers of roles and labels, and this is how to come face to face with the real emotions inside of you. Just you sitting in this dark place coming face to face with all the demons or baggage that you have, dealing with them, stripping away all the dirt, all the layers that obstruct truth. This is where we come to terms with forgiveness, gratitude, and positive thought. This is where we find deep, meaningful love with everybody and everything. This is it – you, face to face with truth. What do you think?' I asked, full of excitement.

You pondered these thoughts looking out over the water. 'It seems too simple. I was expecting some secret handshake or code.'

'You are funny. No surprises, or secrets to learn, however, it is not as simple as it seems. This path takes persistence, and incredible will. You will feel lost at times; you will feel apathetic and even outright lazy as your mind tries to keep you away from this path. You cannot let this happen; this is the little green hulk getting the best of you. This path is hard work and it may seem like nothing is happening, or no progress is being made, then one day you realize how connected you are to your peaceful feelings and you cannot let go of this way of life. It is like going to the gym or jogging, it feels worse at the beginning, then you push through and eventually you get up one day and you just feel good. Every day is another step forward and you realize you cannot go back to your previous life. Does this make sense?'

'Sure this makes sense. In a way I feel as though I have my own form of meditation. I get this through jogging or time in the garden.'

'These in a way are forms of meditation. Understand that meditation typically starts as a noun, as an event or an activity.

When you instill this into your life, into the core of your being at every moment, then it becomes a verb, an action that becomes you. This is using the blue ball to constantly fill yourself with positive thought and love. In this you meditate at all times, jogging, gardening, listening, and just being.

However, it is important to understand you MUST find time to sit alone without any other activity or thought. No music or thought of running up a hill, or which weed to pull. These are beautiful moments but you must sit alone, calm and breathing, taking back the reins from your monkey mind and letting your spirit soar. It is essential you find time alone in this state.'

'I have to admit my naivety here, what are you asking of me?' Your gaze moved from a haze to an intent stare in my direction.

'I am asking nothing of you. I am simply explaining the key that I use to connect to the divine. This is the foundation mentioned across all Eastern philosophies. Meditation centers and quiets the mind, quiets the little green Hulk, moves us from the thinking mind to the intuitive self. This is the main tool toward oneness with the universe. I am not requiring anything of you. Only you can decide if this path, this journey, is for you. It is your choice.'

'I understand. However, what type of time commitments are you suggesting?'

'This is a question you will have to answer for yourself along the journey. More is always better, however, this is not a *do 5 minutes a day* and you will have fabulous abs infomercial.

Once you start, and begin to feel peace within yourself, you will continue to push for more. I can tell you about my journey, but again, your journey is yours alone. I meditate for at least two and a half to three hours a day. I can tell you I always want more; it is never enough. It is important to start slowly and once you build up time in meditation to find a quality teacher. A half hour at a time in the beginning is a good starting point. Perhaps a half hour in the morning and a half hour in the evening prior to bed would be a great way to start.

Consistency is very important. There is a saying in India that you know within yourself when you miss a day of meditation, your close associates know when you miss two days, and the entire world knows when you miss three days. I start every day with it. I consider it as essential as breathing. I cannot imagine a day without it. In order for me to give my love I must first love myself. To do this, I need to 'die every day' in meditation. I battle every day and every day I feel incredible. As I mentioned when you reach a higher state of consciousness, meditation will turn from a noun into a verb. This sense of clarity and presence will be evident at all times. It will become a way of life, living from this third eye, this state of truth and love, beyond just sitting alone every day. It will become an identity for you. Meditation will be your life; you will just live in this state.

Sogyal Rinpoche talks of this *gift* in his book *The Tibetan Book of Living and Dying*: 'The gift of learning to meditate is the greatest gift you can give yourself in this life. For it is only through meditation that you can undertake the journey to discover your true nature, and so find the stability and confidence you will need to live, and die, well. Meditation is the road to enlightenment.' (Rinpoche, 2002) Thoughts?'

'Hold on. Let me go back to the three hour comment. I cannot possible do this. This is unattainable with my schedule,' you said throwing up your hands.

I paused letting you rid yourself of this frustration. I grabbed the garbage from our lunch, walked back to the trail and tossed it into a conveniently located garbage can. 'Again, this is your choice. Life is about priorities. Everything in life, from getting up in the morning, to what we have for lunch, to our friendships, to our political opinions, is a choice. We either choose 'to do' or choose 'not to do'. Pretty simple, and by the way, I thought we buried that word 'CAN'T', didn't we?' I said.

'I think those were the second graders that buried that word,' you said laughing. 'But seriously, I only have so many hours in the day. How is this possible? I do not see how I can fit this in.'

'I can only tell you what I do and you can determine if this is a viable option. I have a simple strategy; I sleep less, simple as that, and to quote Jack Johnson again from his song, *Sleep through the Static*, 'Who needs sleep when we have love'. I believe in this statement. I get up somewhere between 3:00-6:00 am, meditate for 2.5 hours or so and do a few Yoga stretches and I am on with my day. When I have time I add in additional activity such as a full yoga practice, or a jog at some point during the day. In this way, I am finished with my needs for the day before anyone else is even awake. I can be fully present. I can give all of my love for the rest of the day. My personal 'work' is over. Again, start slowly, be consistent and you will find incredible benefits. Do not focus on the three hour comment; focus on the consistency message and the commitment to this exercise. What do you think?'

'Three in the morning?! Wow! I am not sure what to say,' you said in full defeat.

'Look, this comes in time. First you get comfortable with a half hour, then once you see the benefits and feel more comfortable, you build more and more until you reach a level that you feel is optimized. I need at least two and a half hours a day. My soul actually wakes me up every day. I do not need an alarm clock. My inner self does this for me as it craves this connection to the source. You will find that meditation will give you similar if not increased benefits as actually sleeping. Of course, you still need sleep, but you will find you can give more and more to meditation. I still sleep around five or six hours a night, followed by three hours of intense meditation.

The more you sit the farther you can go on this spiritual path. It really is a simple request. I am not suggesting you have to forgo life itself and give up everything to sit under a tree like Buddha.

I do not judge these people, but this may not be for everyone. I am giving you an attainable goal to fulfill your purpose in life and have inner peace and love.

I will tell you this. You will not replace any of your activities in life that obstruct the path unless you find something more fulfilling. In other words, I cannot tell you to do this or that; you alone will have to find fulfillment beyond what you are receiving to replace your existing activity. This is with anything in life. So, unless you find benefits from meditating more than sleeping an extra two or three hours, then you will not do this. Does this make sense?' I asked.

'Sure. Everything you are saying makes sense on an intuitive level; it will just take an incredible life change and enormous will power.'

'Of course, remember the blueprint: we do the best that we can every day and we do not judge ourselves. This is all. What do you think?'

'I have some questions as I have never meditated before. Help guide me.'

I looked you up and down and felt the sincerity in your voice. 'I can give you some pointers but ultimately if you want to proceed deep along the spiritual path you will need to find a teacher to educate and help coach or guide you. Does this make sense?'

'How will I know who is the right teacher?'

'Well, first off, an Eastern thought says that when the student is ready, the teacher will appear. My guidance was pretty simple. What path and what teacher show the embodiment of who I want to be. In other words, this teacher should be the perfect example of what you want to attain within yourself – kind of a walking blueprint, if you will, as this teacher needs to be alive to help guide you along the path. I would love to ask Jesus a few questions, but I will not get any answers, at least on this spiritual plane as his physical body is gone. I think Jesus has been misrepresented in this way as I believe he was teaching this same philosophy from India that states this very thing when he said,

'I am the way and the truth and the life. No one comes to the Father except through me' (JOHN 14:6).

This is a similar language to Masters in India who act as living guides for their students to reach the divine source. Think of them as a coach or guide who has already traveled this path, already connected to the source. It is as if you have the blueprint, or map in this case, and you have an idea where to go but there are no roads or directions to get there. The Master is simply a guide to help you along the way and become a 'Master' yourself. A Master is simply a living being who has connected to the divine. As with any Master, once his existing physical body is gone we must find another 'living' teacher, another guide to connect us to the divine. This is all. Some teachers will focus on items that will be far from truth, such as focusing your meditation on superficial areas such as the genitals, or tantric areas. I believe we only have so many hours; I would rather focus my hours on the third eye or the gateway to the source of love. Or, these teachers will act indifferent to the destructive passions. For example, if you find a teacher driving a Rolls Royce, I can assure you that you can find a better teacher. Does this help?'

'It is hard to say. I guess when that time comes it will feel right.'

'Exactly....In the meantime let me provide some thoughts to get you started with this gift to yourself.' I looked around the beach for the best possible way to explain the practice of meditation.

I settled on a spot in front of a large piece of drift wood about five feet away from the water. The sand was dry and flat in this spot, and it was secluded and next to the sounds and energy of the water. 'Come, let's go by the water and I will show you how to *sit.'*

We made our way over to the driftwood which was curved over time by the water, now polished white looking like a commissioned work of art sitting at the far north end of the beach. We sat on the sand directly in front of the log where I casually crossed my legs in front of me and gently rested my straight back on the driftwood. 'You do not have to sit in a full lotus position to gain the benefits of meditation. Sit in a comfortable position with your back straight. Often it is easier to sit on a pillow or even in a chair so that you are comfortable over a long period of time. Your mind will try to attach to the discomfort of your body so it is both important to create a comfortable position and to tune out the dissatisfaction from your body. Eventually you will get to a point where you do not feel your body. Remember you are not this body; we die every day to free ourselves from this connection. This moment is beautiful as you will feel your true self indifferent to your body. You will radiate with energy and vibration as if the shackles have been removed from your being.

It is important to sit with your head up and your back straight. This is for three reasons. One, this position optimizes the energy and chakras in the body. And second, it is a position to keep you alert and from falling asleep. Third, it facilitates the full benefits of the breath allowing you to expand the lungs to your fullest capacity.

We are going to close our eyes and sit in a minute, however, I want to try something first. Keep your eyes open and let's both sit in silence for a few minutes. I want you to feel this experience first.'

I stopped talking and broadened my gaze across the water gently taking in the wind and lapping of the waves. I breathed in and exhaled slowly in rhythm back and forth. My senses immediately sharpened as I took in the smells across the beach and the water. The salt from the water was now acute. The wind caressed my face blowing the occasional grain of sand across my skin. I heard the birds call to each other and soar by on the wings of the breeze. I was lost in this moment smiling within my heart.

After a moment I felt you adjust your seat and pull at your pants. Once the first shift happens you can't stop and you continued to pull at invisible gremlins. I could feel the chaos in your mind. Your body language stated the obvious discomfort you were in sitting in silence for an extended period of time. I let you feel the full brunt of this experience for a few more minutes before I asked rhetorically, 'How did that feel?'

'In a word, UNCOMFORTABLE,' your face grimaced.

'Remember no judging, just experience how this feels. This is new to you, it should feel uncomfortable. Your mind is stubborn, it feels threatened. It doesn't want to let go. It likes busy, it likes chaos. Let this remind you of persistence and patience. These two words are necessary on this path.

Now, let's remove another sense from you in having you close your eyes. This will allow you to focus on calming your mind. Remember other paths choose different methods, for example in Zen meditation they keep their eyes open while meditating. Do not worry about this for now. To me it is like the saying *all roads lead to Rome*. We are all headed to the same place but we may take different paths.

Once you close your eyes, I want you to focus on two things. One, focus on the third eye between your eyebrows and second, focus on repeating a mantra. Eknath Easwaran has a great book called *Meditation: An Eight-Point Program* that discusses the importance of a concentrated mantra. Easwaran mentions that the root of the word mantra comes from man (the mind) and tra (to cross) (Easwaran, 1978).

So, this constant repetition, this blue ball if you will, enables us to cross or control the mind. Use this mantra during meditation and throughout the day to keep you centered and filled with love. Again, this is the magic blue ball to keep the little green hulk under control. Easwaran recommends choosing a mantra that has been sanctified by long use, one of proven power such as OM/AUM, Om Mani Padme Hum, Rama, Jesus, Allah, or other spiritual words that have been used over the years. He also recommends to stick with this word and do not change. It takes a while to embed this word into the inner 'you'. As you find a philosophy and a teacher to follow, more details on this will be given as you progress along a spiritual path. In the meantime, use the mantra; repeat it slowly, silently while you concentrate on the inner third eye. This is it. This is the central component of tuning in. After a while 2 hours will feel like 5 minutes.

Let's try this, OK?'

You sat silent still distraught over the first exercise. 'OK...let's try this.' You said without conviction.

'OK, let's close our eyes; focus on the third eye and on silently repeating a mantra. We will go for a few minutes.'

I stopped here, closed my eyes and became immediately engrossed in my own space filled with peace. I burst inside brimming with warmth and love. This is my home I thought to myself. My senses were even more acute and I felt as though I was part of the wind. I dipped and rose and fell with the wind. I felt as though I was flying into the clouds. I felt light and part of everything.

I could also feel your energy. It had calmed, and your breath had slowed. Just as I am feeling you gain this connection with yourself a train barreled around the corner shaking the ground beneath us. The roar was deafening. I sat unmoved by this event wrapping myself in the noise and energy from the tracks ecstatically experiencing the vibration within and outside of me. As the train made its way past our secluded spot I noticed you had moved from your spot sitting next to me. Startled by the train you had jumped out of your spot and was now standing next to the water trying to calm yourself. I sat for another few minutes before joining you.

'How are you?' I asked.

'I was doing pretty well until that train.'

'Let's talk about it. How did it feel before the train?'

'I felt calm. I felt my breath slow. I felt really good. I found that my mind quickly wandered even while I was using a mantra; however, I just kept coming back to this mantra each time my mind drifted. I felt like I was in a wrestling match.'

I laughed. 'You are in a wrestling match. A wrestling match with a committed competitor. You have to be on top of your game to compete in this arena.'

'Then the train came and I completely lost it. I jumped out of my seat I was so startled. After this I was lost, the game was over for me.' You said.

'I understand. Your mind is difficult enough to deal with and then you add in external noises or activities and quieting your mind and staying still is extremely difficult. Over time you will tame both the internal and external challenges to sit still and calm the mind. Eventually nothing will be able to knock you out of this state of harmony.' I paused looking you up and down. 'Do you feel comfortable in being able to sit on your own?'

'I think so....however, I know I am going to make mistakes along the way.'

I smiled in your sincerity. 'There are no mistakes. You are following a blueprint, no right or wrong. We do, or we do not. Do the best you can with full integrity and commitment. This is all you can ever ask of yourself.

Each day will be a battle with the mind and anyone who has meditated knows; your mind will continually fight and try to pull you away from a point of concentration. You will think about yesterday, what you have to do tomorrow, what time it is, what the kids are doing, anything but where your focus should be. This is OK, just understand that this is normal and it will take considerable practice to get 'control' over this mind. Do not judge yourself. It is OK. Just take the reins back from the mind every time this happens and bring it back to center.'

'This seems simply enough,' you said relieved.

'Right, the practice itself is not hard; it just takes dedication to fight this battle every day. You will have days that are very difficult in trying to keep a focus. This is OK. I have found that even during these challenging days I feel incredible peace throughout the day. Do not judge. Also, remember as you go down this path you will be pulling away layers so get ready for some emotions that you didn't realize that you had.'

'I am not sure I want to pull away these layers.'

'This is your choice. When you are ready then you will open this part of your life. However, this is and always will stay inside you until you come face to face with the inner 'you' – truth. You cannot fully love until you open your heart to everything.

We cannot be afraid of these emotions. The real 'you' is trying to get out, to love. I know this is scary. I know people who are afraid to be alone let alone find out who they REALLY are inside. This is a scary proposition. This is truth. This is it, as real as it gets. You will peel away those layers and ultimately find truth, find love. It is there in all of us. Just listen, listen for that beautiful sound of the energy of the universe. It makes a sound. Did you know this?'

'Really?' you said.

'Yes, this is the reference I made earlier concerning the radio telescopes. This is what we are doing when we meditate; we are 'tuning in' to the energy of the universe. With this, energy is in the form of a wave, and thus can be heard while meditating as you progress along the path. This sound has been described across many philosophies for thousands of years including the 'word' in the Bible ('in the beginning was the word, and the word was with God, and the word was God' – John 1:1), to the 'Tao', to 'Nam', to the 'Shabd', to name a few. It is there; listen for it, and connect to it; be one with truth, one with love.'

'So, this is it? This is 'tuning in'?'

'Yes, just like the radio astronomer tuning into the energy of the universe, simple, isn't it? Just as when we cleanse our vessel in tuning out our positive energy and intent to the Universe, we need to accept this beautiful energy, this love back in by tuning into this energy from the source. This completes the circle. We do this when we listen, when we tune in. Do this every day and tell me how wonderful the world becomes. Life is beautiful. Cleanse your mind and body and then 'tune in'. Don't worry about waiting until you 'think' you are perfect. Do the best that you can and each day will get better, filled with love, happiness, and filled with truth. The first passage in the Tao Te Ching makes reference to this connection:

'Free from desire you realize the mystery,
Caught in desire, you see only manifestations.
Yet mystery and manifestations
Arise from the same source.
This source is called darkness.
Darkness within darkness,
The gateway to all understanding!' (Mitchell, 1988)

Meditation is finding the darkness within the darkness. It is a place to find truth.'

I stopped here and stared out at the water. The sun had made its way above the mountains journeying to another's sunrise leaving us streaks of red and orange across the sky. We both sat and reflected on this natural painting tired from the long day.

'Come,' I said rising and beginning to walk back to the car, 'let's get you back to your family.'

You followed in a daze as the day had finally caught up to you.

'I will be out of town for two weeks in Scotland. If you need to reach me send me an e-mail and I will get back to you. Other than this, let's block out some time when I get back. I think we will both have a lot to talk about.'

You agreed and blindly made your way back to your car after I hugged you goodbye.

I realized you were drinking from the fire hose and needed time to settle on the changes taking place in your life. This break would be good for both of us I thought.

I drove home restless now ready for my own trip, a new phase in my ongoing journey. I fell asleep early anxious for a new day.

Chapter 9

Follow your Bliss

The plane took off from Seattle at 8 pm on Sunday evening. My spirit lifted with the plane as I was heading back to my roots, back to the home of my ancestors. Not that I knew anything about this, I had only recently been made aware of my connection to Scotland. My known ancestral line reached only as far as my grandparents. My grandfather had worked in a mill in southwest Washington for over 40 years, my father at the same mill for another 45. My father's parents had both passed away from cancer when I was eight years old. My mom's father passed in a mill accident when she was 5 years old. She barely knew him. Her mother passed when I was eighteen. I thought about this grandmother as we reached altitude in our 10 hour flight. She was a remarkable woman raising 8 kids on her own. She never learned to drive, was constantly poor but I never saw her sad. She was always laughing. I could still hear her laugh and visualize her playing our favorite card game called Nertz. She was a beautiful woman full of warmth and always giving to her family. Her last name was Hamilton and combined with my surname of Craig and I was a full blown Scot with some Irish and English mixed in. In fact the town I grew up in, Kelso, was named by a Scot who upon seeing the region was reminded of home. He named the town after his own back in Scotland just as Aberdeen was named just up the freeway in southwest Washington. This area was filled with last names directly connected to a Scottish heritage such as Clark, Hamilton, Baker, Buchanan, Gordon and others. I guess the Scots felt at home in this region with the rolling green hills and mountains with streams filled with fish. Maybe it was just the rain.

I was beginning to get excited for my trip. There was something about finding your roots. Native Americans talked about a Sacred Tree to their people, a tree that had roots reaching deep into mother earth and limbs reaching into the heavens. I could feel this tree, this yearning to connect the past and the present, connect to the divine and fully let go. I had begun this journey some time ago but I had not completely let go. I still wrapped myself in one significant role, a role that masked my true self and confined me to this static world. I wanted to completely let go. I felt in my heart that now was the time.

For 20 years I had wrapped myself into the persona of a business executive following a path that I was no longer passionate about. My days were filled with discussions in how to sell and market Widget X. There was nothing wrong with Widget X; in fact, it was quite useful for many companies. However, the further I went on my spiritual path the more I questioned the 'sponge worthiness' of my time. I was spending 50+ hours a week on Widget X, often falling sleep with the phone in my hand, doing e-mail in the middle of the night with constant thought in my tasks ahead. I didn't mind working hard, this was not the issue. I just didn't care about Widget X. Discussions centered on how 'critical' certain events and projects were. I couldn't wrap my mind around this concept. Or, I should say, my intuition was clearly telling me that my passion laid elsewhere.

My time over the past 20 years was not wasted, nor did I see it as a mistake. It was just over. I knew this in my heart. The company had used me to the fullest extent and I had used the company. This was not right or wrong, it was just a fact. All events happened exactly the way they were supposed to, and now I knew it was time for me to move on. To what I didn't know, I pondered this thought as the plane landed in London.

I switched gates to make my connection to Edinburgh and caught a glimpse of London as the plane took off. I had been to the city before having visited the main attractions such as the

Tower of London, Buckingham Palace, Piccadilly Circus, Big Ben, The London Eye, and attended a few plays. I remembered a few things about London. One London had great Indian food, and two, the weather was the same as Seattle, cloudy and dreary. However, what I remembered most was the history. What the locals considered as newer buildings were older than America. I had walked through old town that was destroyed during World War II, through majestic cathedrals and marveled at the base of the Tower of London built upon an old Roman wall over a thousand years ago. I remembered the eerie silence as I walked through the Tower of London even as it was filled with tourists. Voices from the past still spoke here. The prison was covered in graffiti of the past inmates keeping their pain still visible and alive hundreds of years later. The Tower Green held the same cobblestones that had gathered the blood from Anne Boleyn and a few other wives of King Henry the VIII as well as other *villains* against the crown. The hairs on my arm stood at attention thinking of the stillness of this place.

I thought of the huge ravens, the protectors of the tower. It had been said that if the ravens ever leave the tower would fall. I thought of these grandiose creatures as we began to land in Edinburgh. Native Americans have long revered ravens as a metamorphic symbol, an icon of transformation. It seemed we were all ravens, constantly growing, transforming.

As we touched down into Scotland, the voices of the past rang in my head. The English writer George Orwell spoke of history, of the past when he said, *'he who controls the present controls the past. He who controls the past, controls the future.'* The English romantic poet, Percy Bysshe Shelley also spoke of the past, *'fear not for the future, weep not for the past'* and England's most famous bard, William Shakespeare reminded us of this connection in his play *Hamlet* when Ophelia says, *'lord, we know what we are, but know not what we may be.'* *We know not what we may be....*I dwelled on this thought. The past was gone. We should not forget the past so we do not repeat the future, but dwelling on the past is clinging to the static. This is avidyā, ignorance. We cannot change what had been, nor what will become. In this I was reminded of America's great voice, Ralph Waldo Emerson, *'with the past, I have nothing to do; nor with the future. I live now.'* Emerson was a Zen warrior at heart.

I cleared customs, planned to drop my luggage at my hotel and force myself to stay up for the day. I had learned this lesson long ago with the time change. Sleeping through the first day only made it worse. I grabbed a taxi and found I could not understand a word this man was saying to me. I may have roots from Scotland and we both shared the native tongue of English but I could understand only about every fourth word from this man. The tempo of his words combined with the heavy accent and localized words made his speech inaudible to me. I nodded my head as if I understood and waited for the car to arrive at my hotel, The Channings. The hotel was notable as it was a series of townhouses strung together in a quaint neighborhood just outside of the city's center. The most notable draw of the hotel was one of the former residents of this property in the early 1900's, Sir Ernest Shackleton, the leader of the failed Antarctic exhibition and captain of the ship *Endurance*. Pictures of the ship and crew as well as memorabilia were placed throughout the hotel. The upper rooms were named after Shackleton and his crew mates to further remind the hotel guests of the hotel's tie to the past.

I dropped my bags, grabbed a cup of tea and began walking the city. I followed my basic plan of every new city I visit; I found the city tour bus, grabbed a ticket and hopped on board. I enjoyed hearing the history of the city, but in turn could find my bearings for the days to come. At the center of the city the Edinburgh Castle towered over everything. It was strategically placed on the top of the highest hill, fortified from every direction. The castle was built on sheer cliffs on three sides with a narrow entrance, easily defended, on the final side. This final side was the castle entrance and below the 'old town' dispersed in what was known as the royal mile. This was old school serfdom at its best with the specialty shops immersed along the path that were run by the peasants to serve the royalty above in the castle. I jumped off the bus here fully recognizing the depth of history in every step.

I toured the castle and walked the Royal Mile hearing about Queen Mary of Scotland, the plague, pagans, witches and the English. Even through the stout Scottish accent I fully understood the distaste the Scottish had for the English. The Scots were not shy about this fact and mentioned it often.

At the end of the Royal Mile sat the Holyrood Palace. I glanced indifferent to the royal accommodations and continued down the trail to Holyrood Park. This was my target. I wanted to climb Arthur's Seat, an extinct volcano rising over 800 feet. The trail was an easy hike and on my way up I passed a few people heading down, and now at the top I had Arthur's Seat entirely to myself. The view was incredible. I could see the Royal Mile and the castle clearly from this vantage point, with the city spread wide in every direction and far off to the east sat a large body of water, the Firth of Forth. I sat here for a long period of time, tired both mentally and physically. The air was chilled as spring had yet to gain a foothold this far north. The wind whipped at this altitude filling my lungs with oxygen lifting my spirit. I sat here with my eyes closed for a long time fully taking in this moment.

It was late in the day now and the sun was beginning to hide beyond the far off hills. I quickly made my way down the hill and walked back toward my hotel. The lights of the city were dominated by the lit castle in the sky. Far up on the hill the castle seemed to float above an oasis of darkness filling the night sky with an ornately lighted royal city, almost like a lit crown from a distance.

I was tired but it was much too early to go to bed. I instead chose to explore the city, find some vegetarian food and hear some local Scottish folk music hopefully in the likes of their own Alexi Murdoch. Edinburgh was known for two things, writers and music. I wanted to embrace both of these topics. I stopped at Sandy Bell's the place of poets and musicians, found something to eat, sat back and enjoyed some local folk music amidst poets and students alike.

I walked back to the hotel exhausted having slept very little on the plane. I fell asleep quickly, pleased in my day. The words of Edinburgh's own, Robert Louis Stevenson whispered in my ear as I dozed off, *'For my part, I travel not to go anywhere, but to go. I travel for travel's sake. The great affair is to move.'* Ah, I couldn't help but think the trip, life, is about the journey not the destination. I fell deep asleep at peace and content that I was *moving*.

The next few days flew by as I was immersed in work. The conference went well. Each day and evening I was asked to join group events such as golf at St. Andrews and Distillery tours, I declined both. I don't play golf and I don't drink. I was at the birthplace of golf and the epicenter of the finest Scotch in the world and I had no interest in either. My workmates looked at me as though they wanted to disown me, I was unmoved by their reaction. Instead I walked the city alone. I paid homage to the writers from Edinburgh finding their writing spots, and marks across the town. There were many, Robert Burns, Robert Louis Stevenson, Sir Walter Scott, JM Barrie, Sir Arthur Conan Doyle, and even JK Rowling to name a few. I visited the writer's museum, Robert Burn's old hangout *The Beehive Inn*, and other notable locations.

I found where the less fortunate were shut in to die during the plague, buried below the ground to *save* the living. I explored the expansive Princess Street gardens filled with fountains and statues ranging from the famous explorer David Livingston, *Dr. Livingston I presume?*, to beautiful Ross fountain, and the ostentatious, gothic, Sir Walter Scott monument standing over 200 feet high. I was reminded of transforming an ugly past into a beautiful existence as I read the history of the garden. In the mid 1400's King James III fortified Edinburgh castle by flooding the ground between Old Town and Princes Street. Initially a beautiful and serene lake called Nor'Loch was formed which quickly became a toxic dump with sewer run off from old town. In the 16th century the country was obsessed with witchcraft and the now toxic Nor'Loch was the testing grounds. The accused witches were put on 'Trial by Douking'. The accused were put on a seat with their thumbs bound to their toes and ducked (dunked) twice into the loch for a period of time. If the accused sank they were proven innocent yet inconveniently dead. If they floated they were then burned at the stake as this was the *proper* way to dispose of witches. As I sat in the gardens I reflected on transformation. I reflected on how a place with such negative energy could now be transformed into a positive gathering spot for the people of the city. The past did not exist, only the present. In this I surveyed the numerous flowers blossoming in the intermittent sun. I shook my head thinking of the power of the mind. The same possibility existed for both incredible beauty or in vast destruction. The only difference was the intent, the choice of each individual.

The end of the week came and I was finished with my work responsibilities. At the close of my duties I sent an e-mail to management within the company. I had made the decision to leave the company. I was no longer worried what was to become of me. I trusted in Joseph Campbell, 'follow your bliss and you will find your way.' I didn't know what this was yet, however, I knew what it wasn't and I wasn't willing to put on a mask any longer. I told management I was leaving the Monday I returned.

I sent an e-mail off to you to give you a heads up and tell you I would mostly be offline over the next week while I was exploring the country. I didn't want to explain via an e-mail so I left my note bare of any details with simply the words, 'I am leaving the company effective Monday when I return. I will block anytime you wish to further our discussions.' I packed up before I received a response from you, most likely a victim of the time difference.

My time in Edinburgh was now finished I was ready to explore more of the country and clear my head after this decision. I was not afraid, I felt light and free as if my true life was just beginning. I beamed in happiness anxious to explore each day. My first stop outside of Edinburgh was the city of Kelso. My family would have my head if I didn't visit the inspiration of my hometown.

I drove the winding roads for close to an hour realizing a few things in driving outside of America. One, driving on the unnatural side was not as easy as it looked. I found myself screaming out loud 'left is right, left is right.' After a while I didn't even know what that meant. Finally I settled down remembering a trick a friend from London told me, 'just keep the driver in the center of the road, if they are not in the center then they are on the wrong side.' This worked. The second key thing I learned was that freeways didn't freely exist like they do in America. Most of the roads were two lane side roads. We would call these country roads back home. Third, I realized the Scottish didn't care too much for lights, they used roundabouts. I felt like Chevy Chase circling around and around until I sorted them out. Finally, I realized the roads had a margin of error of about an inch on each side of each tire. This may be an exaggeration but my point holds true. I was ten and two on the steering wheel the entire drive not relaxing one moment.

Kelso was a quaint town near the border of northern England. It was at the center of two prominent fishing rivers the Tweed and the Teviot. At the center of town were the remains of the Kelso Abbey, at one time one of the grandest monasteries in all of Scotland. The central marketplace was splendid. I snapped photos and grabbed post cards for the family and made my way out of town. I could see why the founders of my hometown named the town after Kelso. As a whole, Scotland looked identical to southwest Washington, cloudy, misty weather, green rolling hills and mountains. The only difference was a thousand year old castle would jump out of the landscape in Scotland to mark the borders of the feudal territory. Our 'old' houses were from the 1930's.

I made my way across the country over the next week stopping at the main attractions such as Stirling Castle and the William Wallace monument. Robert the Bruce stood proudly outside of Stirling castle again high on the hill. The William Wallace monument dominated the far hill towering 220 feet into the air. This was the location of his decision victory at Stirling Bridge. Inside I took note of his sword standing close to 5 foot 6 inches long. I laughed to myself leaving the monument as a very ill advised statue of the movie version of William Wallace, Mel Gibson, was placed exiting the complex. Mel stood above a fallen English *head*. The sword alone was about as tall as Mel Gibson.

The castles, abbeys and lochs began to blend into one. I made my way north into the highlands driving through beautiful Inverness and Loch Ness on my way to Fort Williams. This was quite a drive in what seemed to be the middle of nowhere. It reminded of an old logging town, Forks in northwest Washington. I made my way to this remote spot to climb the highest point in the British Isles, Ben Nevis. I had enjoyed the past week touring the country; however, I was here to reflect on self, on truth. I couldn't think of a better way to explore the topic of truth than climbing a mountain. Since the beginning of recorded spiritual writings mountains had stood as the gateway to the heavens above, a place to reflect in silence in concert with nature like the Tao poets of old. I was excited to get out of the car, out of manmade castles and *religious* abbeys. My temple was within and my voice was nature.

I arrived at the trail head early wanting to make the most out of this 10 mile hike. The trail was just outside of Fort William crossing pasture land, until the pony trail took a turn up into the rocky mountainside. The day was cloudy as usual and was slightly drizzling. I started alone on this trail that seemed to be at one with the clouds above, a blend of white and green in a constant mist of rain. I crossed the deep green pastures filled with grazing sheep and small brooks of water that trickled down the hillside. About a mile into the trail I came across a black lamb a few feet off the path. The mother was another 15 feet or so off the path and immediately locked eyes on me unsure of my intentions. Feeling no danger the baby made his way over to me without hesitation as I knelt on the ground encouraging contact. The lamb nuzzled my hand and looked deep into my eyes completely unafraid. I sat for many minutes thankful for this moment in truth. I realized that a week of looking at statues of conquering men and dark, cold castles held nothing to this moment, this connection.

I continued on the trail for another hour where I finally came across some additional hikers. A fit couple in their late twenties to early thirties and an older man around sixty slowly made their way up the trail.

'Aye right day for a hike, isn't it?' The older gentleman called out.

I checked for sincerity in his statement and finding it answered, 'Yes it is. This country is beautiful.'

The truth was we couldn't see a thing. We were in the middle of a cloud, full of a foggy mist and could barely see 100 feet in front of us on the trail. However, it was beautiful to me, every moment of the experience.

'Aye, an American.' The man called out.

'You are correct.'

'Welcome....I am Robert Armstrong. This is my son Bruce and his wife Annie.'

'Thomas Craig, pleased to meet you.'

'Aye, a good Scottish name there, welcome home lad.' Robert

called out.

I nodded with a smile.

'I do feel obligated to ask you a question Thomas. What in the world brings you all the way out here climbing *The Ben?*'

'This is where my journey brought me.' I said without further explanation.

'Aye...I see. Well welcome, you can join us for the hike if you wish.' Robert said with nods from Bruce and Annie.

I smiled in agreement and slowed my pace to keep with the group. After some time we began to get passed by a myriad of hikers determined for the top. I was not concerned in this. If and when I reached the top then it would be so. This was an experience not a feat.

I found that Robert had lost his wife a few years ago to cancer and he had shut himself in with bouts of depression, gaining weight and losing his health. His son Bruce was worried about him and began nightly walks and weekend hikes with him. Today was the goal they had set a year and a half ago the accumulation of their hard work and positive intention. I could see the pride and hope in Bruce. I could only imagine what the past two years was like for this family. I was blessed to be in their presence.

We slowly made our way up the path, slow but sure I said to myself as I provided encouragement to Robert. He would smile in between gasps of breath. Ben Nevis was just over 4000 feet high, back home this was a hill compared to the 14,000 foot peaks, however I was sure to Robert, *The Ben*, was a personal Mt. Everest.

The pace was slow and deliberate. As a group we would stop every 45 minutes or so to drink some water and have a snack. Annie would delicately cut what looked to be homemade cheese and salami and place on crackers for them to eat. She would offer me some each stop and I would politely shake my head no and eat my trail mix. After 10 minutes or so Annie would wrap up the food again in a cloth napkin place in Bruce's backpack and we would continue.

I noticed many things on the final leg of our climb. I noticed how proud Bruce was of his father. He couldn't contain his smile the closer we got to the top of the mountain. My guess was he didn't really think his father could make it and here we were less than an hour from the summit. I also noticed the genuine love in all three of them. We talked a lot on the hike and outside of a brief discussion in why I was in Scotland I didn't talk about work again with them. They were interested in my family, where I lived, how I felt. I was truly grateful in sharing this poignant moment with this family. I would never forget it.

We continued on for close to an hour and we could see the trail begin to level off to only a slight incline. It was here on the initial lip of the summit that we found small amount of snow covering the ground still clinging to the previous winter. We rounded the next corner and after another ¼ mile we could see the end of the trail. The summit was marked by the remains of an old observatory from early in the 20th century. Gathered around were 15 or so hikers resting on the snow at the apex of the hike. We reached the plaque signifying the summit and the four of us stopped for congratulatory hugs. Robert and Bruce held each other for many moments. I could hear Bruce call out, 'I luv you faither'. Annie wept in the moment. I snapped some photos and decided to give them some time alone.

I found the edge of the summit overlooking a granite cliff peering 1000 feet below. Mesmerized I sat near the edge on the snow pondering the scene. The sun was beginning to break through the mist and burn off the clouds leaving a blue sky above as the summit jutted into the sky as a granite island peering above the white fog below. I sat here for many moments connected to this moment, feeling the wind, the sun, and the cold snow below me.

Robert made his way over to me and seeing my location called out, 'Daen't go jumping off the ledge lad.'

I smiled knowing I had jumped a long time ago. I closed my eyes to encapsulate this special moment, stored for my existence before we made our way back to the car. I stayed with my new family and ensured all made it back safe. It was near dark by the time we got back to the cars.

Robert insisted I meet them in town for dinner and drinks to celebrate. Of course I couldn't refuse this invitation and after a quick shower I met them at a pub in the center of town. I tipped the server ensuring I was brought nonalcoholic beer and sat down with the group. Robert seemed to have a rebirth after the day's events. He burst with energy downing pint after pint each proceeded by a toast from either Bruce or himself. The two of them were giddy, laughing and getting lost in their pints.

'To my new friends and family for the day, may your life be as blessed as mine was today.' I called out in clinking glasses.

The group cheered, took a big swig, smiled and patted me on the back.

We stayed at the pub until late in the night where on the final toast, Robert called out a dedication.

'To my lassie, Mary, may God rest your soul; I shall sing you Rabbie Burns's song one last time.

'O my Luve's like a red, red rose,
That's newly sprung in June:
O my Luve's like the melodie,
That's sweetly play'd in tune.
As fair art thou, my bonie lass,
So deep in luve am I;
And I will luve thee still, my dear,
Till a' the seas gang dry.

Till a' the seas gang dry, my dear,
And the rocks melt wi' the sun;

And I will luve thee still, my dear,
While the sands o' life shall run.

And fare-thee-weel, my only Luve!
And fare-thee-weel, a while!
And I will come again, my Luve,
Tho' 'twere ten thousand mile!'

Robert hung on this last note for a long moment as tears came down his face. Bruce and Annie both hugged him sobbing. I made my way over to the group and hugged Robert.

'That was the most beautiful song I have ever heard sir.' I said.

'Dead brilliant da,' Bruce called out.

Robert just nodded still engrossed in the song. Finally he lifted his glass to me and said, 'Lang may yer lum reek.'

I turned my head trying to decipher any of these words. My face must have showed my confusion as Bruce translated. 'He means to tell you to live long and be well. It is a statement of affection here in Scotland.'

'Aye....' I said. 'Thank you Robert. To your lives, journey well.' I clanked their glasses.

The group gave one last cheer of farewell to me and we hugged and made our separate ways. I laid in bed for hours moved by the love of this man for his passed wife. I finally drifted off to sleep, tired and at peace in my final night in Scotland.

I woke early the next morning and began the long drive back to the airport. My mind was in a daze through the drive as I passed still lakes that looked untouched by human hands, green hills rolling across the landscape, and quaint little villages frozen in an earlier time. I caught my plane and transfer to Seattle in London and then I slept. I had let go of a lot of emotion the past two weeks and it was now catching up with me. I woke on the approach to Seattle ready to move forward from the past, ready to live in each moment, ready to live in my passion.

I will always remember Scotland for helping me find this presence. I went to sleep knowing the next morning would be emotional for me as I packed my office and said my goodbyes. I was ready.

Chapter 10

Conversation about God

I arrived early on Monday morning. I wanted to pack and load my boxes before anyone arrived so as not to make a scene. I filled my car and found a quiet place to set meetings and catch up on past messages on my computer.

I noticed three e-mails in a row from you sent on the day I gave you the heads up I was leaving the company. The last one sent said 'READ FIRST' in bold letters. Of course I passed this and read the first message sent. My message had stated I was leaving the company and we would discuss when I returned, and with this you had a one word response, 'WHATTTTTTTT???????????' This was quickly followed by another e-mail with the subject line 'Why are you leaving *me*? The body of the message was a long diatribe in how I had built you up and now I was leaving you and you would be lost. You asked questions like, what am *I* going to do *now*?' Your final message ecstatically pronounced 'READ FIRST' in the subject line and apologized for the last message. You hoped I was happy and that I made a good decision and looked forward to our discussion.

I knew you were dealing with change. People have a very difficult time in dealing with transition from the static. The first reaction is typically anger, 'Why me? Or, Why did *you* do this to ME?' The ego jumps out in the middle of change. I knew we would have a lot to talk about so I booked out the afternoon on your calendar, and set up a few other goodbye meetings with select management and employees. My official goodbye was scheduled around lunchtime, a quick get together with cookies and cake. I was expected to say a few words and then this chapter in my life would be over. I was worried how I would feel but I felt great. I felt at peace.

The day flew by; I held my meetings, said my goodbyes, made my public statement and walked out the doors without looking back. I sent you a text to meet at the coffee shop on 36th a few blocks from the office at 2 pm. I got to the coffee shop early and gathered my thoughts still dragging from the time zone.

You walked in with a busy mind. I could feel the questions jumping out of your head. I knew we had a lot to discuss. I was ready and looking forward to this. I had missed our connection.

'Hello again,' I said giving you a deep hug. 'How are you?'

'No......we are starting with you. What happened? Was this a sudden decision? Why didn't you tell me?'

I tried to decide which question I would answer from this firing squad. 'I have been thinking a long time about this decision and felt this was the right time to move forward in my life.'

'Were you mistreated? Was this job related?'

'No.....I found myself no longer passionate about my job. I was spending a tremendous amount of time *wasting* hours. I was no longer willing to follow this path of no passion. I found I was following a path toward *truth* yet I hadn't fully let go. In making this decision, I was making the decision to go ALL IN. Life is too short not to live with passion. In life, we play all in, or we do not. This is our choice. I chose to follow my heart.'

'What will you do?' You asked.

'I do not know. Isn't this beautiful?'

You smiled beginning to understand the existence of curiosity, of staying present, of taking the journey without expectation.

'Now....how are you?' I asked. 'I thought of you often on my trip and I am anxious to understand what has happened in your life since I left.'

'I am fine...OK, I guess.' You sat slumped in your seat. 'My mind has been filled with so many thoughts since you left. I am more confused than fine. I know I am letting my mind run wild, but I cannot help it. So... I am glad we are meeting again as I have all these thoughts on my mind and I really need to discuss them with you.'

'This is natural.' I smiled. 'This is your mind fighting back. It will not give up, remember persistence and patience. Remember the fact that we die every day to overcome this monkey mind. I am completely ready to listen. I have a cup of tea, a comfy chair; let me hear what is on your mind?'

'OK. I have been struggling with a lot of things. First off, I will tell you I am amazed at the amount of negative energy out in the world. The news in particular, people's comments, movies, you name it. We are immersed in it much more than I realized. Second, I wanted to tell you I bought a vegetarian cook book and snuck a few meals into my family. They knew something was different but it did not make a substantial difference. I was very pleased. Of course, I started with some basics, such as pasta and other items but I was pleased none the less. However, my biggest consternation over the past few weeks has been about your comments a few weeks back concerning God. The comment you made to me that God is within me, and that I am essentially God. Or, the comments you made concerning Jesus; these comments are radically different than my belief system. I am really having trouble coming to a middle ground on these.'

'Then don't, keep your same beliefs. This is OK. This is your choice. The only thing I ever suggested from you was to be curious about life, live a pure life filled with integrity from a state of truth and to connect back into this energy, this truth, via meditation. On top of this, believe whatever you wish. I do not judge you.'

'But you seem so confident about your statements. They really shook me. Do you know what I mean?' you said, looking away.

'Sure, I understand. As I have already told you, I come from the same background as you for the most part. I struggled with this dichotomy for years. I couldn't change my belief system as it was so engrained into my external being, or mind; yet I had all of these new, intuitive feelings that it should be different. I know exactly what you are going through. In all of the rabbit holes, this was the most difficult one for me,' I said in full empathy.

'Even though I am conflicted with this possible departure in everything that is my spiritual foundation, I am still curious. I found myself wanting to talk about this now in a different way than before. I have this 'itch', if you will, that will not go away.'

'OK. Let's talk about it then. Let's confront it head on. Be forewarned, these are just my opinions. In fact, in this matter, all we have are opinions. I mean, it is very difficult to hold facts up around a lot of these discussions, right?'

'Fair enough, however, I want to understand more of what you believe with respect to God, primarily coming from the Christian faith.'

'OK. Stop me at anytime if this is too much for you. Again, I do judge you for your beliefs; these are simply mine that I feel comfortable with. Let me give you some background and let's see where this takes us. Feel free to ask me anything, I appreciate your curiosity. I will give you my process in getting to where I am at today. I think at the end of the day I am much closer to your thoughts than you might think. At the root of every religion is love. This is wonderful. Most religions hold many positive messages that center on family, good deeds, helping and caring for each other in the community, and love. However, nearly every religion has evolved over time through different interpretations, backed by different motives and the need to add superstitions, ethical context and rituals. We have talked a little about this before regarding ethics. At the root of your being, in a state of truth, a state of love, you intuitively understand how to act and live in this world full of love. The 'thou shalt not' messages do not work. Fear does not work. Remember our conversation about fear and the dangers surrounding fear, the ego and the destructive passions. Most religions have evolved over time fueled by the destructive passion vanity and egotism, the 'you are either with me or you're against me' belief. This belief that we would have peace and harmony in this world if only everyone would believe my way of thinking is flawed. It is completely egotistical and full of judgment. This is the entire context relative to the problems in the Middle East. The context that I am right and you are wrong, and then have the belief that you are fighting for your God to prove the righteousness of your belief; this has been going on for thousands of years; we just repeat history, over and over again. As human beings, we are simply judging and holding onto attachments. Do you know what I am saying?' I asked.

'I understand the context. Again, on paper this is much simpler than reality. What attachment are you referring to?'

'Attachment to a lot of things, such as 'I am right and you are wrong' attachment to an area of land, attachment to words and believing them as the absolute, as black or white, without understanding your intuitive inner being, your inner curiosity, your inner truth to state a few. Look at the Middle East; most of this fighting is taking place over who owns the land. The belief is that the land holds significant value and symbolic context for all of the conflicting parties. Kind of, my symbol is the correct symbol, and thus more important than yours. Do you see this?'

'No, I don't. I completely understand the conflict. I would fight too over these important religious sites. They hold such meaning,' you said, flushed.

'Why do they hold such meaning?'

'The land is sacred. This is where Jesus walked, and important historical events out of the Bible; they hold considerable importance,' you said, continuing to raise your voice.

'First, I want you to tell you that I understand your point of view and I do not judge you for your beliefs. I appreciate your passion. On the other hand, I would say to you this is simply land. These are simply symbols. Look at this quote from Chief Seattle:

> 'The Great Chief in Washington sends word that he wishes to buy our land. How can you buy or sell the sky? The warmth of the land? The idea is strange to us. Yet we do not own the freshness of the air or the sparkle of the water. How can you buy them from us? Every part of this earth is sacred to my people.[29]'

The concept from the mind that you deserve this land, that you have a better reason to own this land. How can these people take these things from us? This is the little green Hulk pushing your ego. Do you hear it?'

'Wow! I don't know what to say. So, in your mind you would allow others to run all over you, take everything from you?' you said shaking.

'Remember when I said that if you let everything go, all attachments, then you love everything. These people have taken nothing from me. This is land. These are buildings. These are symbols.'

'What if it was more than this? What if they were harming you?'

'Again, I have every right to protect myself, but either way, they are taking nothing from me. So, they take my arm, they imprison me; they can never take the inner me. Remember our concentration camp discussion from Viktor E. Frankl. Even if they were to extinguish this body they have taken nothing from me. I know this is difficult to understand right now, but my body is simply a physical vessel. This is not me. My energy will move forward. I cannot control the actions of this divine play, this Matrix that we live in. Until one understands the impermanence to everything in this world, and understands that everything changes and that ultimately we cannot control this, then we will suffer; we will not have peace.'

'I am not sure what to say as I am far removed from this type of thinking.'

'Do not say anything; these are my thoughts, nothing more, nothing less. Let me shift gears and talk about my progression on my thinking toward religion per your original question. I grew up in a similar background as you in a Protestant church called The Church of Christ. We would go off and on, maybe one or two times a month. I remember three specific things from my church; one, the Bible was considered sacred – all fact – and one did not question this; two, church was both a way to wash away all the previous week's sins and ask 'God' for what you really needed in your life; and, third, church was incredibly dry and boring. With respect to the latter, at least in my very white, Church of Christ church. This church does not believe in musical instruments so hymns were sung A Cappella. Just a note for everyone involved, A Cappella should only be sung by really good singers,' I said laughing. 'Anyways, as you mentioned before in our conversation, like you I was taught not to question, to just accept authority and the Bible as fact, no matter how absurd this felt inside. We still have this progression from the church today. The church is still battling the recognition of evolution and the age of the universe and earth. It conflicts with the written word of the Bible; this is Copernicus and Galileo in the 21st century. Those following a black and white path have a difficult time with change. They cling to the static as if their life depended on it. History is filled with these moments such as women and civil right issues, to evolution, and global warming. Change requires independent thought. Thought that looks beyond a flat world, or a world where the universe revolves around earth. The concept that 'we don't know' is difficult for a black and white thinker. Back to the stories from the Bible, these innately didn't resonate with me, didn't 'feel right'. I was conflicted, until I took a course in college exploring Joseph Campbell. This was one of my first departures from the 'Bible as absolute word' track of thinking.

We looked at Campbell's books, *The Power of Myth* and *Hero with a Thousand Faces*. This was my first 'WOW' moment. The 'WOW' moment came from the thought that myths are engrained in our cultures for thousands of years. Remember we talked about our early ancestors writing on walls over 25,000 years ago. They were curious; they needed to explain things in order for them to make sense. Human beings have been doing this for thousands upon thousands of years. In a book I mentioned before from Bill Bryson, *The History of Nearly Everything*, he talks about when humans began finding fossils and our intellectual response to make sense of these findings. We would find a fossil in Europe that exactly matched in age and type to a fossil, say, in Florida. In order for our minds to rationalize these findings, and more importantly, fit into the context of the Bible and the supposed length of civilization at roughly 5000 years, we created stories to fit our existing belief system. The scientists at the time hypothetically built a land bridge from Europe to Florida. We began to have fossil findings all over the world and pretty soon we had all these hypothetical land bridges to 'explain' things, rather than look at the facts, and that the Earth might be much older than 5000 years old and at one time a single land mass. This didn't fit the biblical context and our 'minds' could not rationalize it. We completely dismissed our intuitive findings.

As I read Joseph Campbell it became very clear to me that the stories in the Bible and other religious texts were an obvious mix of facts and, more importantly, myths. This is not a bad thing, but myths none the less. Myths are incredibly important for a culture; they put our subconscious into context.

Let's take a look at a few that I felt were obvious, take Adam and Eve. If you look at various myths around the world there are similar creation theories. This one in particular is interesting as the word 'Adam' actually comes from a word meaning soil. This story was a direct metaphor that we come from the earth, just as a plant. Then, take Eve, coming from Adam's rib; again, if I was a woman I would be quite offended at this one. This one myth has created more misery for women than you can imagine. The belief that man has dominion over women and with other comments in the Bible also has dominion over animals does not come from a place of truth or love. Putting a Burqa over a woman as a means of control or giving away women in marriage is a direct reflection of this myth. Comments that humans are at the top of the food chain reflect this dominion over animal mentality, or the church statements that animals do not have 'souls'. Spend any time with an animal and you will adopt a different mindset.

Most animal lovers will accept this from a dog or a cat, but have trouble transferring this mentality to all animals and living things. This dominion over animals thinking does not come from an intuitive place, a place of love. Life is beautiful; just be; be in the middle of it without controls, or hierarchies. If we come from a place of truth, a place of love, we do not need to develop a story, a myth, to satisfy our intellect. I do not judge those who wrote these words as these words satisfied their intellect at the time. I, however, choose to take an intuitive approach versus the 'word' of God correlation. Does this make sense?'

'Yes, but this is a very difficult departure for me from my original belief system.'

'Right, as I had these thoughts initially, I intuitively couldn't follow the angry God – the white man with a beard, sitting on a throne watching our every move and pointing his staff when he wanted to make something happen, you know, like make that guy score a touchdown. Do you know what I am saying?'

'Yes. This model, or the blue-eyed Jesus model just doesn't intuitively fit, does it?'

'Not for me anyway, I cannot get into a God dictating his law and will upon us as *HE* wishes. Church is a reflection of this 'don't make him mad' or you will receive his wrath. You still hear these comments today. God does not want homosexuals, so if you accept them you will receive the wrath of God. This 'God on the throne' concept was portrayed by Morgan Freeman in the movie Bruce Almighty. At least they put a black man as God; I thought this was a nice touch to the original metaphor. However, the rest of the concept was the same; in this case they updated God with a computer taking in as many requests as possible. I am just not on the same page as this. It is almost like God taking in our orders, filled with a customer service department, and perhaps even a returns desk. Intuitively, it just doesn't flow. I never understood the 'I will ask for it', or 'I will pray for you' in my daily prayers, that God will answer my prayers. I was speaking to a family member the other day concerning their church service and during the ending 'testimony' this church member was asking God for a new TV. I am befuddled by this entire concept, as this implies the Morgan Freeman God model is a wish maker, almost like Santa Claus for those that are 'good'. In this case, directly appealing to our destructive passions, I cannot intuitively understand these concepts. When I give thanks or gratitude, or positive thought in meditation, I give gratitude for the strength to keep my positive mind, and energy so that I can connect to this energy and fill myself with love. I guess this is why I have trouble actually using the word God, as it typically conjures up the image of the old, angry, white robed, white man with a beard. I prefer to use 'the great spirit', 'the divine source', or sometimes one used in India – the 'nameless one'. My friend calls her God, Nature. This to me is as good as anything. To me God is LOVE. At the very root, God is truth, God is love.

Religion is often not in this state. Human beings are typically in a state of chaos usually from the miscommunication or conception of written words from over 2000 years ago. The differences between Judaism and the Muslim religion are very minute. They both trace their roots back to Abraham. You wouldn't know this would you? To me this is amazing. Both are my brothers and sisters. I love both of them. They are neither right nor wrong. They just are, they exist and I love both of them.

If, ultimately, God is love then how can the concept of fighting exist? Most wars are driven from the ego and have a strong basis in absolutes formed by our religious convictions. This is all from the mind not the intuitive self. Stop judging; connect to the love that is everywhere. It really is simple. Don't you think?'

'Intuitively it sounds very simple; however, speaking from a personal nature, it is very difficult to give up your belief system, so this seems impossible.'

'Then don't give up your belief system. Believe in a green skinned, eight foot Godzilla as your God. I do not care. Just do not judge me or anyone else, live from a state of integrity and come from a place of truth, a place of love; accept and love all living beings and be curious about the world. This is all I care about.' I said.

'This makes sense, tell me more about the contradictions you had with the traditional religious model.'

'OK. There are plenty. When you begin to look at the Bible or any other religious text, you see the foundation of many myths, the foundation of a story that was needed to explain something.'

'For example?'

'Noah's Ark comes to mind. Think of it; you live in an area that is devastated by a flood – think of our modern day Hurricane Katrina – and you need to make sense of this. How could this happen to us? How could so many people die? Especially if you want people to follow your model, your belief system (hear the ego). Stay with me here, as I will probably state some things you will not want to hear. I come from a business background, and spent plenty of time in marketing various products. When I look at organized religion I see a very well executed marketing plan.'

'Oh, I have to hear this. Please explain,' you said sitting up.

'OK. Look at a particular religion as a product. With any product you want the most customers as possible, right?'

'Sure, makes sense.'

'OK. So if I am marketing, say, Christianity, I want the most people following my product and I want them very committed. In other words, I do not want them jumping ship to another product, or religion in this case. This makes perfect sense. So, let's go back to the time of Jesus (by the way, you can use this same method to look at Judaism or any other religion). The people were oppressed; there were classes of people, slaves; the Romans were taking over, and from an outward, superficial standpoint life was miserable. Now with Christianity there was a message that said a 'poor' person had the same spiritual rights as a rich person. The message from Jesus was simple yet very effective; it gave people hope. His words to this day are beautiful; however, looking at history he was one of many 'preaching' a different way. At his death, he had very few followers, and in essence the message was dead. The earliest messages from his followers didn't appear until at least thirty-three years after his death, and many believe it was much longer than this. Think of it; at the end of today I would guess you could remember a good portion of our discussion. After a week, you would probably paraphrase a good percentage. We are talking at least thirty-three years later. Writing was not pervasive in this timeframe, so inevitably the message would have changed. Now, fast forward two hundred or so years after this and the Romans are in trouble. Their empire is about to crumble. Lots of reasons, corruption, too big to manage, pick a reason; it became very evident that they needed a message to appeal to the masses to control, or put them in line back under the Roman 'cloak'. Christianity became the vehicle to do this. Christianity became the center of the Roman Empire over night as dictated by the Emperor Constantine. Although it didn't save the empire, it created a huge business and religion of choice across the Roman Empire. If you don't believe religion is a business, then I encourage you to read your history. Be curious about the roots of your faith with an open mind. Remember the destructive passions are everywhere and very persistent. Do not be surprised; follow the money; follow the power; it is always the case. So, now, back to my marketing exercise; I need the most committed people as possible for my product, right?'

'OK... Go on.'

'So, I immediately tell them that anyone who is not a Christian is condemned to this fire pit called Hell that you adequately described earlier from your Sunday school days. Anyone outside of this Christian model is out, condemned for eternity; everyone else 'with our message' gets this magical place called Heaven. Kind of gets your attention out of the gate doesn't it? Next, I need to build the masses. I need to ensure that my product has more followers than any other as we need to 'fight' or 'control' to keep our business intact, or alive, right? So, the next thing I say is, NO BIRTH CONTROL. 'God says he does not believe in birth control'. Have you ever asked yourself intuitively why this exists?'

'No. I just took it as fact, a rule passed on by God.'

'Yes, by the same white-bearded God, sitting at the throne that we have been discussing. I just intuitively cannot get onboard this model of an angry God, basically filled with EGO, 'How dare you do this to me?' who believes you should just keep having children no matter your economic means, or place in life. It wasn't until the mid to late 1960s that birth control was legal in America. It just doesn't make intuitive sense. What makes more intuitive sense is to say, I need as many followers as possible so let's enact 'God's message' and – wow – look at our contingent grow. Look at the Church of Latter Day Saints; the norm was for a man to have multiple wives to multiply with children. The masses always rule, whether this is a controlling interest in politics, or especially when you inflict war and violence to 'wipe out those that oppose'. This is a simple rule of warfare, or controlling other cultures – the masses rule. In the book *Guns, Germs, and Steel* Jared Diamond depicts this as one of the reasons behind the rise of the Northern European cultures as they were farming communities and could have more children, versus a hunter gatherer society who could not have a new child until the previous child could keep up and walk with the tribe, roughly at age four. The farming communities didn't have this restriction.

Back to my marketing plan, I put in place rules that say the church is the absolute, and all thoughts or decisions come from the church. In other words, no more thinking for yourself, we will do this for you. This is right out of the example we gave earlier from the book 1984. Just put an 'It is God's will' in front of anything and you are on your way. I can hear the Ministry of Truth and thought crimes in this message. I can remember being at a village in France where I read a plaque in remembrance of all those who died at the hands of the Christians who came over from Italy and massacred all of the people 'in the name of God'. The Church had sanctioned them to do whatever they needed to do to spread their word, their beliefs. We could talk for days about these examples. Don't think intuitively; just do as you are told.

Next, from a business standpoint, you destroy the competition, right? This is a natural next step in business. The church did this systematically from burning 'witches', killing off the Pagans (who, by the way, were simple people, very in tune with the earth and nature. Now they have been marketed as the Devil), the Spanish Inquisition with the 'heretics'. I could go on.

Finally, I need to put a message around Jesus that he cannot be mortal. He needs to be a living 'God', if you will, and thus cannot have any typical, mortal man qualities. So, his birth was constructed as immaculate. His relationship with Mary Magdalene was dramatically changed as this would hurt the 'son of God' message. The church converted her image as that of a prostitute and basically, systematically demeaned her from this point forward. In marketing my product, this product needs a clean, absolute message. Jesus as a mortal man, with relationships and possible children, or a normal death and burial doesn't sell. He needs to rise from the grave. Recently, there was a special about the possibility of finding the grave of Jesus and his family, and the possibilities that this 'rising from the grave' three days later had been used many times in ancient Judaism philosophy. This is a very difficult proposition to prove; however, this information was discredited before it even came out as the Ministry of Truth did a good job of ensuring that people did not ask questions, and just follow the church's message, the message from the Bible. There are many spiritual people in India, Masters if you will, who have families and normal lives but they are very connected to the Divine. If Jesus was one of these individuals, does it lessen the message? Not to me, his words as transcribed have great beauty. Does this make sense?' I asked taking a deep breath.

'Wow! I am not sure I can comment on these thoughts around Jesus. With respect to the Inquisition and control, the church is in a very different place now.'

'Is it? The examples might be different, but the control and fear is still being used. The root of both of our Protestant backgrounds comes from King Henry the VIII wanting to divorce his wife and realizing the church had more power than the King of England. How dare people believe the church has more power than the King?

Today's examples come from other forms of control, such as women, or homosexuals. Do you know women still cannot lead a church in the Catholic religion? Why? Because they supposedly came from the rib of man and thus are not his equal. Of course this is not explicitly stated; however, it is today's reality. It truly makes me sad. Homosexuals in the early 21st century are the new oppressed race in America. Apparently God said this was wrong in the Bible, even though two people might come from a place of truth, a place of love, have no control over their sexual preference, yet they are oppressed. I personally might not understand how homosexuals can be attracted to the same sex;

however, guess what? They don't understand how you and I can be attracted to the opposite sex. How can a person filled with love and truth be ostracized? As long as one person is not harming another person, why judge someone based on who they intimately love? The church is on a mission today toward homosexuals. They are today's heretics. Even Buddhists do not support homosexuals. Wow! When Buddhists are not backing you, you have reached the bottom. I feel saddened. Take away the labels, the roles, the gender, and at the core of the soul you have vibrant energy that is the essence of love. How could I possibly judge or ostracize anyone? In this, only love is the way.

How about the enforcement of Catholic priests in not marrying or being celibate? This is just not natural. This is not nature. The scandals about the altar boys and the Catholic priests might well end their reign over time. As a business man, this business is in need of a turnaround.'

'Wow! I can see you have put a lot of thought into this.'

'It may seem that I am picking just on the Catholic religion but I could take examples from Muslim, Protestants and other religions or faiths. From our standpoint in the Protestant religion, just the name of Jerry Falwell rings hypocrisy, or in this case, messages of fear that are far from truth and love. Listen to his words: 'Christians, like slaves and soldiers, ask no questions'. Or, how about this: 'AIDS is not just God's punishment for homosexuals; it is God's punishment for the society that tolerates homosexuals'. This does not come from a man that is in a place of truth, or a place of love. Mohammad consolidated a bunch of nomadic tribes to unite the Arabs under the Koran as Muslims. There is great beauty in a lot of the messages in the Koran; however, because Mohammad united these people under the 'sword', this message and action is still used today. Many Muslims still use this train of thought and the 'sword' toward those who do not believe in life or Allah (God) in the same way – 'You are either with me or against me'.

To me this violence stems directly from these religious texts. Using the Old Testament, or the Koran, again, you have a God, or Allah, that is – number one – a male and – number two – very angry; do not cross him. How dare you eat from that tree? I will turn you into salt, or I will flood you if you don't obey. This message flows into the cultures that follow these religions. The mistreatment of other human beings, women, children and animals is a direct reflection of this message. This is the ego that states *my way or the highway*, or *you are either with me or against me* if your belief system is different to mine. This is presumptuous. This is the same message that comes from the Bible directly from God. If you betray me, or disobey, I will punish you. Again, you are either on my team or you are in Hell. This is the difference we discussed earlier between the Western and Eastern mind and the separation going back to the Greeks to have this omnipresent God that dictated his will upon the universe and living beings.

If you go back and look at the history of different religions and how the messages were changed and then implemented you will understand exactly what I am saying. All of them were manipulated in some way or another to benefit the individual religion or entity, or in my mind the corporation that is the church. Let me pick a very innocent looking religion from the outside, Buddhism. Siddhārtha Gautama, the Buddha, was a man that went within himself through meditation to find truth, to find awareness, to find love and connection to all beings. If you look at the history of Buddhism, you will find tremendous time passed after his death, over 600 years and individual ideas were put forth on the meaning of his messages. Rituals were added to bring more of a following, more of a 'follow' message, versus a personal quest within you. Now offerings of food and the burning of incense is made to Buddha. If you go back and look at the history you will see this very clearly. This makes me sad because the bulk of the message from Buddhism is beautiful; it concerns love and finding this within yourself. It is not about offering oranges and burning incense to the previous vessel or body of Buddha. The energy of Buddha still exists and is connected to the divine source. His previous physical body is meaningless. However, Buddhism in general is filled with beauty and a path to clear the mind of attachments and end suffering. In this there is truth.

At first it is very disconcerting looking beneath the surface level messages in organized religion; however, once you open your mind, you understand this is just the ego in man driving toward more power, greed, more of everything. Now when I look at this, life in its essence is very simple. Very far from the truth, or from love, but at the core, very simple and easy to see the manipulation and fear that is being used. This is sad because in nearly every faith there is beauty, there is a foundation of love. However, the *Ministry of Truth* has manipulated the message into that of control, that of fear, that of guilt to follow the path. It does not benefit the church to be an independent thinker. It is too hard to market. As a business person, having a common demographic is much easier to market. Does this make sense?'

'I guess so. I guess I am curious, but very cautious right now. I don't know what to believe.'

'Good answer. I encourage you to go investigate for yourself. Just keep an open mind, as long as you see a different color other than black or white, you will find your own answers,' I said. 'As I mentioned, the church or religion is not all bad. The church is often very charitable and giving to the local community. It is a place of community, a place to interact with the neighborhood. The church is typically very family-centered. Not all people who follow a religion or church are close minded. I know plenty of people who come from an open, place of love that are involved in the church. I have gratitude for these people. However, if you take a macro view of religion as a whole, I see fear driving a controlling message that inflicts our culture at the deepest levels. This is what saddens me.'

'So, what ultimately do you believe?' you asked.

'Ahh… yes, the difficult question, let me start with what I do not believe in. I do not believe in any message that does not come from a place of truth or of love. Thus, I do not believe in anything that uses fear, guilt, or any other forms of control or oppression or the destructive passions. I do not or cannot believe in a God or creator, or the source of energy that comes from a place that is full of judgment, ego, control and fear. I believe we are all connected, that we are all vibrant, energy and ultimately the same. I believe I am just as connected to a tree or animal as I am to you, or a child in the heart of Africa. We are all brothers and sisters. We are all love. I believe we are all this drop of water waiting to go home and connect to the same energy or, in this case, a spiritual ocean. In this we have a piece of God within us, so in essence we are all the sons and daughters of God. We all have this capacity; it is within all of us. To sum it up, I guess I believe in truth or love. I guess my church is love, TEAM LOVE, or TEAM TRUTH. This is a hard message to explain as it is very personal. I choose to live my life as an example of this love and attract this energy back. I understand I will alienate and anger people with my message. This is their choice. I cannot control them. In the end, I still love them; I do not judge them for their beliefs. I am attached to nothing yet love everything; this is the way I choose to live. Does this help?'

'I am beginning to understand. The message is just very different than I have been told.'

'Then begin to listen to yourself; listen to your heart; fill yourself with love; come from a place of truth filled with integrity; be curious; ask questions, and find your own answers. This is all you can do.'

Chapter 11

Reflections on Truth

'This is a lot to take in,' you said.

'I understand. These are my thoughts, down my rabbit hole. Your curiosity will bring your own intuitive thoughts. Continue to be centered and in a state of truth and live from your heart full of forgiveness, compassion and gratitude. This is the blueprint. Attach to nothing and love everything. The most important thing is not to judge yourself; just be the best person you can be everyday filled with positive energy, curiosity, and gratitude for life. Love will pour out of you, and you will begin to smile all the time. How can it not? Life is beautiful,' I said smiling.

'I am just so conflicted inside right now. I have trouble imagining this moment.'

I let this comment find its place, and echo around the near empty coffee shop. There was only one other customer in the coffee shop engrossed in his computer. The barista was doing the same in the back of the room.

'Your mind is still trying to control.' I said. 'I understand. Just remember Bruce Lee; take it in slowly, mull over it, meditate on it, over and over again, until your mind is clear and you reach the point of not thinking about it. It will come. You will reach a point of 'empty mind' or 'childlike' state. You will feel your spirit free and open. You will begin to do things without worrying about judgment from others. This may be going down the slide with your kids, or beginning to learn to play the guitar, or taking surfing lessons; you will feel free like a child. Your heart will sing with gratitude and love. You will attract beautiful people in your life. You will have quality conversations and 'moments in truth' all of the time. You will take trips for no reason what so ever, and understand there is no destination, just the journey. You will learn the concept that being lost is not possible. How can you be lost? You are exactly where you are supposed to be, filled with curiosity and love and seeing beauty in everything. You will feel like a kid again as each moment will feel new, fresh, alive. You will understand your purpose in life, your passions, and the muses that let your creativity flow. People will begin to wonder and possibly even be angry at you because of your happiness. Strangers will sit next to you for no reason and open up to you as they have never opened up before about their lives. They will not understand why, they will just do this. You will listen without judgment and you will feel gratitude for the moment and positive energy and love will flow out of you. They will see this. They will trust you; they will feel connected to you. You will be an inspiration to those that come into contact with you. You will be this light to your children and you will inspire them to be better people just by your actions and thoughts alone. What do you think?'

'I would like all of this. I would feel very fulfilled if this was to be,' you said.

'Then, let it be.'

'Well, this is easier said than done,' you said looking around the room.

'Either we do or we do not; this is your choice. Let me ask you a question; what is holding you back from taking this journey?'

'I don't know. I guess I am scared. I am afraid of judgment from others for one. I am afraid they will laugh at me. I am afraid my spouse will not accept me. I guess looking at this I am filled with fear. I am filled with thoughts that I will be alone and not accepted.'

'I appreciate your honesty. These are deep feelings that you just shared. This was a very honest moment from you; I am so grateful that you were brave enough to share. I understand. Please do not feel alone; I felt the same way as you. I am going to be up front with you, this is an isolated path. It is very different to the path the rest of the people living in the Matrix are following in life. You will have trouble connecting to those outside of a path of truth. This may be hard to understand now, but you will begin to value priorities differently to other people. They will put priorities on things like new curtains, or how big their house is. You will understand that having real conversations with these people will be very difficult. You will feel like a stranger. You will turn off the TV as it doesn't offer any value to you. Yes, I understand what you are afraid of, I truly do. I have felt alone on this path many, many times; however, I wouldn't trade this journey for anything. This journey is real. This journey is coming from a place of truth, a place of love. I would rather have fewer 'real' relationships than have many superficial relationships. I would rather view the world as a complete organism, rather than having my identity in the 280 Million or so people in the United States versus over 6 Billion across the globe. I would rather view a tree, and a cow as my brother and sister. I would rather view myself as the wind dipping and rising across the Universe.

This journey is scary. Joseph Campbell calls this 'The Hero's Journey', where the hero feels there is something missing in life and they either accept the call to adventure or not. This is an adventure. Life is a journey. You will cry. You will find emotions inside of you that only you can deal with. This journey is about finding yourself, stripping away these layers and becoming the real 'you'. You are beautiful. You are vibrant. You are love. Do not expect fear and ego to go away easily; they are constantly by your side. All you can do is become aware of them and not let them control you. You are much stronger than them. When your spirit is in control of your mind, you have unlimited power and creativity. I shudder and smile to think of the possibilities. The potential we as human beings have within ourselves is truly remarkable. Driven by truth, we could fill this world with love.

It would be magical to see this. You are worried about laughter. Let them laugh. I love a quote from the Tao Te Ching concerning this laughter:

'When the superior man hears of the Tao,
He immediately begins to embody it.
When an average man hears of the Tao,
He half believes it, half doubts it.
When a foolish man hears of the Tao,
He laughs out loud.
If he didn't laugh,
It wouldn't be the Tao.' (Mitchell, 1988)

Let them laugh, right?' I said with a shrug.

'Again, I think, in practice, it is much easier said than done.'

'I understand. However, I cannot help you. You will either do, or you will do not. At some point in your life you will understand, the only opinion that ultimately matters is your own. This is an exercise in understanding who 'you' really are. Once you understand this, then these fears concerning judgment and laughter will dissipate. This is OK. I understand. We all go through this phase, and, again, in full disclosure, some cannot get beyond this point. The external pressures are too great. The world sucks them back in. This is OK too. I still love these people. I have sadness for the potential that was lost, but I understand. The world beats everyone up. As you get older, you realize this more and more. Some choose to reflect on this and find a way to absolve themselves from it in a spiritual way, some wrap themselves in drugs and alcohol, some in power, or greed, and many are led by their ego. Again, I do not judge, I am just observing. I do not judge you for having these fears. In fact, I am glad you have them. I believe this is natural.'

'Well, I find it hard to believe my being scared as a natural feeling. I feel stuck, confused, out of place. My mind is cluttered, and very busy. Do you know what I am saying?' you said in full defeat.

'Of course, do you think your mind is going to give up control this easily? It has been programmed for a very long time to be in control. It is the three year old that has never been given guidance, and then you show up with a new discipline plan. Do you think this is going to go over well in the beginning? Of course not, get ready for a lot of disruption from the little green Hulk. It is very powerful. Just have a positive attitude, perseverance, and most of all, patience. I cannot tell you how long it will take for your spirit to gain control over your mind; however, I can tell you that it is a daily battle. Sooner or later, like dealing with a wild colt, 'you' will gain control. It will happen. You will get frustrated. You will want to give up. You will make mistakes. This is all natural and completely understandable. Nothing worthwhile in life is easy. In my opinion, this is the most worthwhile thing in life, so of course it will be extremely difficult. The end product is well worth the effort. Those around you will agree as well. Thoughts?'

'I understand... I just feel out of place. I don't even know where to start.'

I took a break here, refreshed our tea with more hot water and took a seat again to address your question.

'Start with you.' I said. 'Start with trying to understand who you really are. You cannot love another until you love yourself. Start a love affair with yourself. Take 'you' on dates, by yourself. Dedicate one or two hours a week to take yourself on a date that inspires your creativity. Cleanse your mind and your body. I cannot tell you where to start as we all start from a different place and find some of these harder than others. Start today with forgiveness. Start today with a gratitude journal. Start with compassion.

'Look at these words in the Tao Te Ching concerning compassion:

'Compassion is the finest weapon and best defense.
If you would establish harmony,
Compassion must surround you like a fortress.
Therefore,
A good soldier does not inspire fear;
A good fighter does not display aggression;
A good conqueror does not engage in battle;
A good leader does not exercise authority.
This is the value of unimportance;
This is how to win the cooperation of others;
This to how to build the same harmony that is in nature.'[30]

To be in harmony we must have compassion, and gratitude. We must be in balance like the Yin and the Yang. To love we must have forgiveness. These are requirements. It is impossible to love another, or to love everything until you love everything about yourself, until you are that continuous '10'. Start with you. Start today. Be the best possible person you can be everyday, filled with positive energy and love. Strip away all of those layers and find the 'you' inside. Just be,' I said with a sigh.

'I guess in a way I am scared. I am not sure I really know who I am, or at least I don't have a full grasp on WHO I am. I am not sure what I will find.'

'Of course you are scared. Of course you do not know who you are. The journey is to find this out. This fear is the veil that the world is living under; this is the world of the Matrix. The journey is to find the inner truth and break out from the ordinary and find balance in the Universe. Again, using the Tao Te Ching, Lao Tzu talks about the ordinary man indifferent to the master or the sage:

'*The ordinary man seeks to make himself*
the centre of his universe;
the universe of the sage is at his centre.
He loves the world, and thus remains unmoved
by things with which others are concerned.
He acts with humility, is neither moved nor moving,
and can therefore be trusted in caring for all things.'[31]

You see, this book was written thousands of years ago. Do not be afraid of what you will find inside, as you are beautiful. You are filled with love. Just find it, and live in the present at all times. This is life.'

'I understand. I understand this is not out of the ordinary. I am motivated but still feel stuck. I know I keep saying this but I guess I am just overwhelmed right now.'

'If I were you, I would be overwhelmed as well. This is a lot of information to take in over a few weeks. You came to me with a simple question about happiness and here we are, weeks later, still talking about it. Right now you need to just absorb, just take it in, and most importantly after this absorption, find your own way. Be curious, research things, ask questions, find the real you. This can only come from within you. So, right now, this message is coming across as from 'me'. This probably feels uncomfortable. This is a good thing. This means the intuition within you is questioning things; it is not settled until you come to terms with this message yourself. This is not a cookie cutter experience; all I can do is express my journey, express a blueprint and for you to explore. You are experiencing a battle between your mind trying to stay in control and the inner 'you', led by your intuition. This battle will not stop. However, over time, you can control it and feel extremely peaceful in who you really are inside. The vibrant, beautiful 'you' will come out, full of love and at peace. Does this make sense?' I asked.

'Yes, this eases my mind somewhat. Thank you. I feel I will

want, that I will need to talk to you again, and again. I do not want to impose on you.'

'I would do anything for you. Although I hardly know you, I love you. I will always be here for you. I will try and help in any way possible. It helps to have a person you can ask questions or just listen as you are going through this journey. Like it or not, we are connected as siblings on this journey. We are one. I am here for you. I have tremendous gratitude that you are here right now, that you are curious, that you want to move toward truth. I love you for this. I will always have positive thoughts for you and anytime you need me, I will be present with you.'

'So, what's next?' you asked with a heavy sigh.

'You live in truth. You live with integrity. You love everything. Be the best that you can be at all times. Whenever I feel out of place in how I should be feeling I remember a trip I took to Jamaica. I watched two men communicate with each other and as they were to leave, rather than just a goodbye or a hug, they clenched one fist to their chest, looked each other in the eyes and just said 'truth' (or perhaps it was 'truth m'an' in their Jamaican accent), followed by a deep, meaningful hug. It was a beautiful moment. Basically, they are saying to each other, live in truth, live in love. Reggae music reflects a lot of this. Bob Marley's song, *No Woman, No Cry*, could very possibly be the greatest song I have ever listened too. In times of strife I remember the chorus 'everything's gonna be all right... everything's gonna be all right.' Look at the lyrics to his song *One Love*:

'One Love, One Heart
Let's get together and feel all right
As it was in the beginning (One Love)
So shall it be in the end (One Heart)
Give thanks and praise to the Lord and I will feel all right.'

Or, how about his song *Redemption Song*? Look at these lyrics as I think they apply very well on our journey of truth:

> *'Emancipate yourselves from mental slavery;*
> *None but ourselves can free our minds.*
> *Have no fear for atomic energy,*
> *Cause none of them can stop the time.*
> *How long shall they kill our prophets,*
> *While we stand aside and look? Ooh!*
> *Some say it's just a part of it:*
> *We've got to fulfill de book.'*

I find it nearly impossible to be in a bad mood listening to his music. There is so much love. His lyrics from Redemption Song are very compelling; *'emancipate yourself from mental slavery'*-this is getting control of the mind. *'None but ourselves can free our minds'*- a beautiful reminder that we alone are in control of this journey. *'We've got to fulfill de book'*-this is just living, just being, living with our Karma. There is nothing we can do about it, don't worry, just be, and just love. What wonderful music.

Another song that captures my thoughts if I feel I am getting off track in feeling gratitude is the song by Alanis Morissette called *Thank you*. Listen to these words; you have to smile when you hear them:

> *'How about me not blaming you for everything?*
> *How about me enjoying the moment for once?*
> *How about how good it feels to finally forgive you?*
> *How about grieving it all one at a time?*
> *Thank you India.*
> *Thank you terror.*
> *Thank you disillusionment.*
> *Thank you frailty.*
> *Thank you consequence.*
> *Thank you, thank you silence.'*

This is such a wonderful song that fills my heart with gratitude. I am so grateful for this song.'

'I guess music helps you get to a place of feeling versus thinking. Is this a fair statement?' You said.

'Yes, I believe you have stated the obvious. To me, music changes the mood in a room; it comes from the same energy that we are trying to tune into so of course there is beauty in music. Music is poetry with a vibration. I use music to put me into a positive, loving vibe. Find your muse, find the creativity and love within yourself. Live in this moment and truth at all times.

Listen, I know you are scared. I believe in you. I love you. Live for the present moment at all times. There is no yesterday as you did the best that you could do at that moment, and tomorrow has not arrived yet. Do not miss out on RIGHT NOW. The word in Hinduism for the evil lord, or their devil if you will, is KAL. They also use this same word to mean tomorrow. Do you understand the significance of this? Thinking of tomorrow is death; it is evil. Live right now; give your full energy to right NOW, this MOMENT. Be fluid, be soft not hard. I have a friend who says 'be green', or 'stay green'. This means be alive, not rigid. Be curious, be filled with forgiveness, be filled with gratitude, be filled with love, and be filled with truth. There is a passage in the Tao Te Ching that summarizes the teachings:

> 'I have just three things to teach,
> simplicity, patience, compassion.
> These three are your greatest treasures.
> Simple in actions and in thoughts,
> you return to the source of being.
> Patient with both friends and enemies,
> you accord with the way things are.
> Compassionate toward yourself,
> you reconcile all beings in the world.' (Mitchell, 1988)

Whether you take this journey or not, I will love you either way.

Buddha summarizes this journey well in his words:

'No one saves us but ourselves. No one can and no one may. We ourselves must walk the path.'

I stood and gave you a big hug, looked you deeply in the eyes and then hugged you again. 'I wrote you a letter last night followed by a Native American prayer. Take this home and read it. My blessings are with you.'

'Thank you,' you said, walking out of the coffee shop and into a diminishing sun.

I sat and smiled at peace in my unlimited possibilities.

A Letter to You

You are truth
You are love
You are integrity
You are everything
You are me
I am you
You are vibrant and full of positive energy
You are intuitive and from the heart
You are forgiveness
You are compassion
You are gratitude
You are beautiful
You are curious
You are inspiration
You are alive
You are soft, and yielding
You are grace
You are nothing
and

I LOVE YOU

Native American Prayer

Oh, Great Spirit
Whose voice I hear in the winds,
And whose breath gives life to all the world,
hear me, I am small and weak,
I need your strength and wisdom.
Let me walk in beauty and make my eyes ever behold
the red and purple sunset.
Make my hands respect the things you have
made and my ears sharp to hear your voice.
Make me wise so that I may understand the things
you have taught my people.
Let me learn the lessons you have
hidden in every leaf and rock.
I seek strength, not to be greater than my brother,
but to fight my greatest enemy – myself.
Make me always ready to come to you
with clean hands and straight eyes.
So when life fades, as the fading sunset,
my Spirit may come to you without shame.[32]

Acknowledgments

To my girls, Morgan and Julienne Craig, my blessings in this world, I love and will always love you. You both are a gift to me. I hope that through this book you can better understand your father.

To my cousin, Diane Weber, you have such a beautiful spirit. Thank you for always being present with me. You are loved.

To my spiritual brother, Matthew Jones; we are on this journey together my friend. I am very grateful to have such a friend.

To my parents, in my most dire need, you have always supported me.

To my Sedona family, Shama Smith, Kirsten Edin, and Matthew Fuller; I have tremendous gratitude that I have met you.

To my agent Devra Jacobs, I am forever grateful you believed in me and my message. I will never forget this.

To Dan Millman, thank you for challenging me to be better. I will always remember this lesson.

To Jack Johnson, Ben Harper, Eddie Veddar, Bob Marley, Alexi Murdoch, Glen Hansard and Marketa Irglova; your music filled my spirit, and inspired me while writing this book, for this I have tremendous gratitude for all of you.

To Ravenheart Coffee shop in Sedona; your energy filled my spirit as I wrote this book, my blessings to you.

To Jon and the staff at Café Ladro in Kirkland, your warmth and sincerity blessed me during challenging times.

Bibliography

Butler, S. (1935). War is a Racket. New York: Round Table Press Inc.

Easwaran, E. (1978). Meditation: An Eight-Point Program. Petaluma: Nilgiri Press.

Frankl, V. E. (1959). Man's Search For Meaning. Boston: Beacon Press.

Johnson, J. (1939). The Path of the Masters. Punjab, India: Radha Soami Satsang Beas.

Mitchell, S. (1988). Tao Te Ching. New York: HarperCollins.

Robbins, J. (1987). Diet for a New America. Tiburon, CA: HJ Kramer with New World Library.

Ruiz, D. M. (1997). The Four Agreements: A Practical Guide to Personal Freedom (A Toltec Wisdom Book). San Rafael: Amber-Allen Publishing.

Saotome, M. (1986). Aikido and the Harmony of Nature. Boston: Shambhala Publications, Inc.

Notes

1   Stan Rosenthal translation http://www.vl-site.org/taoism/
      ttcstan3.html
2   Chief Seattle Speech, Seattle 1851
3   Schrauf, Robert W. and Julia Sanchez (2004). 'The prepon-
      derance of negative emotion words across generations and
      across cultures.' Journal of Multilingual and Multicultural
      Development, 25(2-3), 266-284.
4   Huston AC, Donnersteine, Fairchild H, et al, Pig World,
      Small Screen. The Role of TV in American Society, NE:
      University of Nebraska Press 1992.
5   http://www.psychologymatters.org/mediaviolence.html
6   Matthew 18:21-22 (New International Version of Bible)
7   Source: USDA, National Agricultural Statistics Service
8   http://www.stopanimaltests.com/animalTesting101.asp
9   http://www.hsus.org/furfree/cruel_reality/the_cruel
      _reality_of _fur.html
10   http://planetaryrenewal.org/ipr/vegetarian.html
11   Livestock's Long Shadow: environmental issues and options,
      Food and Agriculture Organization of the United Nations,
      Rome 2006, Authors: Henning Steinfeld, Pierre Gerber, Tom
      Wassenaar, Vincent Castel, Mauricio Rosales, Cees de Haan
12   http://www.farmsanctuary.org/issues/factoryfarming
      /environment/cultivating.html
13   http://www.peta2.com/college/pdf/enviroNew72.pdf
14   http://www.farmsanctuary.org/issues/factory
      farming/environment/cultivating.html
15   WorldWatch Institute, 'Fire Up the Grill for a Mouthwatering
      Red, White, and Green July 4th,', 2 Jul. 2003.
16   Motavalli from http://www.goveg.com/environmentpol-
      lution.asp
17   http://www.farmsanctuary.org/issues/factoryfarming/

environment/cultivating.html

[18] CNN, 'Study: Only 10 Percent of Big Ocean Fish Remain,' CNN Online, 14 May 2003.

[19] Earth Talk, 'The Environmental Beef With Meat,' The Bay Weekly, 6 Jan. 2005.

[20] Smithsonian Institution, 'Smithsonian Researchers Show Amazonian Deforestation Accelerating,' Science Daily Online, 15 Jan. 2002.

[21] Danielle Knight, 'Researchers Highlight Overgrazing,' Terra Viva.

[22] Gold and Porritt., John Robbins, p. 298.

[23] Mark Gold and Jonathon Porritt, 'The Global Benefits of Eating Less Meat,' 2004, p. 22.

[24] Mark Gold and Jonathon Porritt, 'The Global Benefits of Eating Less Meat,' 2004, p. 22.

[25] Motavalli

[26] Ann Mangels, Virginia Messina, and Vesanto Melina, 'Position of the American Dietetic Association and Dietitians of Canada: Vegetarian Diets,' Journal of the American

[27] Physicians Committee for Responsible Medicine with Amy Lanou, Healthy Eating for Life for Children, New York: John Wiley and Sons, 2002, p. 49.

[28] Robbins, J. (1987). Diet for a New America. Tiburon, CA: HJ Kramer with New World Library.

[29] SPEECH BY SEATTLE AT THE TREATY OF 1854

[30] GNL's Not Lao Version 2.07, Copyright 1992, 1993, 1994, 1995 Peter A. Merel

[31] Stan Rosenthal translation http://www.vlsite.org/taoism/ttcstan3.html

[32] Translated by Lakota Sioux Chief Yellow Lark in 1887, published in Native American Prayers-by the Episcopal Church.

BOOKS

O is a symbol of the world, of oneness and unity. In different cultures it also means the "eye," symbolizing knowledge and insight. We aim to publish books that are accessible, constructive and that challenge accepted opinion, both that of academia and the "moral majority."

Our books are available in all good English language bookstores worldwide. If you don't see the book on the shelves ask the bookstore to order it for you, quoting the ISBN number and title. Alternatively you can order online (all major online retail sites carry our titles) or contact the distributor in the relevant country, listed on the copyright page.

See our website www.o-books.net for a full list of over 500 titles, growing by 100 a year.

And tune in to myspiritradio.com for our book review radio show, hosted by June-Elleni Laine, where you can listen to the authors discussing their books.

MySpiritRadio